Subin Nijhawan

Multilingual Content and Language Integrated Learning (CLIL) in the Social Sciences

A Design-based Action Research Approach to Teaching 21st Century Challenges with a Focus on Translanguaging and Emotions in Learning

AF085579

NOTA BENE—
BILINGUALISM AND INTERCULTURAL DIALOG

1   *Bernd Klewitz*
       Content and Language Integrated Learning (CLIL):
       A Methodology of Bilingual Teaching
       ISBN 978-3-8382-1513-6

2   *Jasmin Peskoller*
       The Multicultural Classroom: Learning from Australian
       First Nations Perspectives
       ISBN 978-3-8382-1587-7

3   *Bernd Klewitz*
       Bilingual Unterrichten – CLIL Fachdidaktik
       Content and Language Integrated Learning
       ISBN 978-3-8382-1512-9

4   *Subin Nijhawan*
       Multilingual Content and Language Integrated Learning
       (CLIL) in the Social Sciences
       A Design-based Action Research Approach to Teaching
       21st Century Challenges with a Focus on Translanguaging and
       Emotions in Learning
       ISBN 978-3-8382-1715-4

Editor:
Dr. habil. Bernd Klewitz—Lecturer, Marburg

Advisory Board:
Prof. Ingrid Zeller—Northwestern University Chicago
Marie Schaper—Angelaschule Osnabrück
Jasmin Peskoller—Universität Innsbruck
Hamish McKenzie—MA, National Trust for Scotland
Ana Djordjevic—Kole Rašić Belgrad
Prof. Leo Schelbert—University of Illinois

Subin Nijhawan

MULTILINGUAL CONTENT AND LANGUAGE INTEGRATED LEARNING (CLIL) IN THE SOCIAL SCIENCES

A Design-based Action Research Approach to Teaching 21st Century Challenges with a Focus on Translanguaging and Emotions in Learning

Bibliografische Information der Deutschen Nationalbibliothek
Die Deutsche Nationalbibliothek verzeichnet diese Publikation in der Deutschen Nationalbibliografie; detaillierte bibliografische Daten sind im Internet über http://dnb.d-nb.de abrufbar.

Bibliographic information published by the Deutsche Nationalbibliothek
Die Deutsche Nationalbibliothek lists this publication in the Deutsche Nationalbibliografie; detailed bibliographic data are available in the Internet at http://dnb.d-nb.de.

Covergrafik: © copyright 2022 by Susanne Asheuer

Copyright D.30

ISBN-13: 978-3-8382-1715-4
© *ibidem*-Verlag, Stuttgart 2022
Alle Rechte vorbehalten

Das Werk einschließlich aller seiner Teile ist urheberrechtlich geschützt. Jede Verwertung außerhalb der engen Grenzen des Urheberrechtsgesetzes ist ohne Zustimmung des Verlages unzulässig und strafbar. Dies gilt insbesondere für Vervielfältigungen, Übersetzungen, Mikroverfilmungen und elektronische Speicherformen sowie die Einspeicherung und Verarbeitung in elektronischen Systemen.

All rights reserved. No part of this publication may be reproduced, stored in or introduced into a retrieval system, or transmitted, in any form, or by any means (electronical, mechanical, photocopying, recording or otherwise) without the prior written permission of the publisher. Any person who does any unauthorized act in relation to this publication may be liable to criminal prosecution and civil claims for damages.

Printed in the EU

A Preliminary Remark about Text Conventions of the Single Chapters

This monograph was composed on the basis of a fully revised paper-based dissertation, consisting of a binding text, three journal articles and one book chapter. Chapters III-VI, each of them single articles, were reproduced in accordance with the conventions of the respective publisher. Thus, there are inconsistencies with e.g., title capitalization, because the publishers provided different style sheets. Furthermore, footnote numbering was started anew each chapter, to mirror the original source. In line with the monographic format, the book contains only one single bibliography, in accordance with the conventions of the American Psychological Association ("APA 6th"). The same style sheet was used within the binding text.

Abstract

This monograph contributes to research in content and language integrated learning (CLIL). Amidst the absence of any educational standards as well as other research deficits, *Chapter II* sketches a conceptual framework with a competence model for multilingual CLIL classes in the social sciences. It develops a line of argument for the promotion of global discourse competence for democratic participation within a transnational civil society. The subsequent four chapters, comprising one conceptual, one methodological and two empirical contributions, look at different aspects of the conceptual framework.

Chapter III defends the developed competence model and further specifies its idea of thought in proposing the construction of multilingual 'cosmopolitan classroom glocalities' for the genesis of 21st century skills. The example of #*climonomics*, a multilingual EU parliamentary debate about climate change, illustrates its practical realization within school education and exemplifies the contribution to education for sustainable development (ESD) and the value of democratic and participatory learning arrangements.

Chapter IV introduces design-based action research (DBAR), the method used in *Chapters V & VI*. DBAR is a hybrid of action and design-based research and is thereby ideally suited for bridging the gap of theory and practice in educational research. Chapter IV argues for closer cooperation between academics and practitioners, along with pragmatic stakeholder participation by involving students and teachers into research, in a quest for inductively making practical knowledge scientific.

Chapter V, more language-biased, draws on the notion of translanguaging and presents the concept of 'trans-foreign-languaging' as a multilingual approach to CLIL with first language (L1) use. During six weeks DBAR, a comprehensive CLIL teaching model with judicious and principled L1 use was designed together with the study group. The model offers affordance-based and differentiated methods for different learner types. Its genesis is reconstructed by a thick description of the natural classroom dynamics.

Chapter VI, rather subject-based, asks about the influence of such bilingual language use on emotions, in particular on the formation of political judgments. It suggests different ways to measure emotions during various natural classroom settings. The chapter concludes that CLIL with L1 use has the potential to engender a perfect equilibrium of emotional and rational learning, integrating emotions into learning and valuing its positive contribution towards appropriate and multilayered political judgments.

The concluding *Chapter VII* binds the previous chapters together and discusses the results. Criteria for the generalization of the results are assessed, and limits demarcated. It highlights the contribution to CLIL research and looks into the future, suggesting further direct classroom interventions, also with the goal to prepare the research field for larger undertakings.

Keywords: *CLIL, content and language integrated learning, bilingualism, multilingualism, translanguaging, social sciences, emotions, DBR, design-based research, design-based action research, globalization, ESD, education for sustainable development, climate change, 21st century skills, sustainability*

Zusammenfassung

Die vorliegende Monografie widmet sich dem Themenbereich des *Content and Language Integrated Learning* (CLIL). Aufgrund nichtverfügbarer Bildungsstandards und weiterer Forschungsdefizite skizziert *Chapter II* einen Orientierungsrahmen mitsamt eines Kompetenzmodells für CLIL in den Sozialwissenschaften. In erster Linie wird die Förderung globaler Diskurskompetenz mit dem Ziel einer demokratischen Teilhabe innerhalb einer transnationalen Zivilgesellschaft geltend gemacht. Der folgenden vier Kapitel, in der Reihenfolge der Beiträge konzeptionell, methodisch und zweimal empirisch, behandeln verschiedene Aspekte des Orientierungsrahmens.

Chapter III gestaltet das Kompetenzmodell weiter aus. Die Erschaffung mehrsprachiger ‚kosmopolitischer *classroom glocalities*', so wird argumentiert, fördere die Genese von *21st century skills*. Anhand des Beispiels von #*climonomics*, einer mehrsprachigen EU-Parlamentsdebatte zum Klimawandel, wird die praktische Umsetzung des Konzepts exemplifiziert und der Beitrag für eine Bildung für nachhaltige Entwicklung (BNE) im Sinne demokratischer und partizipativer Unterrichtskonzepte aufgezeigt.

Nachfolgendes *Chapter IV* führt in *design-based action research* (DBAR) als angewandte Forschungsmethode innerhalb *Chapter V & VI* ein. DBAR, ein Hybrid aus Aktions- und designbasierter Forschung, eignet sich besonders, um eine Brücke zwischen didaktischer Forschung und schulischer Praxis zu erschaffen. Eine stärkere Verzahnung durch eine pragmatische Inklusion aller Akteur*innen, d.h. Lernende und Lehrende, im Rahmen von Forschungsvorhaben wird vorgeschlagen, um praktisches Wissen induktiv zu verwissenschaftlichen.

Das eher sprachdidaktische *Chapter V* stellt auf Grundlage des Konzepts des *Translanguagings* einen Ansatz des *trans-foreign-languagings* zum mehrsprachigen Lernen innerhalb CLIL vor. Als Ergebnis einer sechswöchigen DBAR entstand ein umfassendes CLIL-Unterrichtsmodel mit systematischem und planvollem Einsatz der Erstsprache (L1), welches gemeinsam mit der

Forschungsgruppe konzipiert wurde. Es beinhaltet affordanzbasierte und differenzierte Methoden für verschiedene Lerntypen. Dessen Entstehung wird durch eine dichte Beschreibung der natürlichen Unterrichtsprozesse rekonstruiert.

Chapter VI mit sachfachdidaktischem Schwerpunkt untersucht den Einfluss von bilingualem Unterricht auf Emotionen, und insbesondere auf die Fällung politischer Urteile. Verschiedene Verfahren, welche Emotionen während des regulären Unterrichtsgeschehens messen, werden präsentiert. Die Evidenz lässt vermuten, dass CLIL mit L1 möglicherweise ein perfektes Gleichgewicht von emotionalen und rationalen Lernprozessen fördert. Damit wird die herausragende Rolle von Emotionen während des Lehrens und Lernens und hinsichtlich der Genese eines angemessenen und mehrschichtigen politischen Urteils gewürdigt.

Die Schlussdiskussion in *Chapter VII* verbindet alle Ergebnisse der vorherigen Kapitel. Fragen der Generalisierung bzw. der Reichweite der Ergebnisse werden diskutiert. Der Beitrag zu CLIL-basierter Forschung wird herausgehoben sowie ein Blick in die Zukunft vorgenommen. Insbesondere wird ein Plädoyer für weitere direkte Interventionen in natürliche Lernumgebungen formuliert, auch mit dem Ziel das Feld für breitangelegtere Forschungsvorhaben vorzubereiten.

Schlagwörter: *CLIL, bilingualer Unterricht, Mehrsprachigkeit, Translanguaging, Sozialwissenschaften, Emotionen, designbasierte Forschung, designbasierte Aktionsforschung, BNE, Bildung für nachhaltige Entwicklung, Globalisierung, Klimawandel, 21st Century Skills, Nachhaltigkeit*

To my parents…

…for all their love, affection and support and everything else that cannot be expressed by simple words…

Contents

Abbreviations i
Preliminary Remarks: Structure of this Monograph iii
Acknowledgements ix

Chapters

I. Introduction and Motivation 1
II. CLIL: a Door Opener to Globalization 15

Paper 1

III. The Construction of Cosmopolitan Glocalities in Secondary Classrooms through Content and Language Integrated Learning (CLIL) in the Social Sciences 75

Paper 2

IV. Bridging the Gap between Theory and Practice with Design-based Action Research 113

Paper 3

V. Translanguaging… or trans-foreign-languaging? A comprehensive CLIL teaching model with judicious and principled L1 use 137

Paper 4

VI. Finding the 'perfect equilibrium of emotional and rational learning' in content and language integrated learning (CLIL) in the social sciences 199

VII. Discussion, Conclusion and Outlook 227

Bibliography 247

NB: The capitalization of chapter names reads inconsistent, because it was kept on purpose in accord with each of the journals' conventions they were published in.

Abbreviations

AR	Action research
BICS	Basic interpersonal communication skills
CALP	Cognitive academic language skills
CLIL	Content and language integrated learning
DBAR	Design-based action research
DBR	Design-based research
DESI	*Deutsch Englisch Schülerleistungen International* (Assessment of Student Achievements in German and English as a Foreign Language)
DGFF	*Deutsche Gesellschaft für Fremdsprachenforschung* (German Association for Foreign Language Research)
EEC	European Economic Community
EMILE	*Enseignement d'une Matière par l'intégration d'une Langue Erangère* (French counterpart of CLIL)
ESD	Education for sustainable development
EU	European Union
FFF	Fridays for Future
FL	Foreign language
GERM	Global Education Reform Movement
GND	Green New Deal
IQB	*Institut zur Qualitätsentwicklung im Bildungswesen* (Institute for Educational Quality Improvement)
KMK	*Kultusministerkonferenz* (The Standing Conference of the Ministers of Education and Cultural Affairs in Germany)
L1[1]	First language (the most dominant language of an individual)
L2	The target language in SL or FL teaching
LAC	Language across the curriculum

---

[1] Within the single *Chapters III-VI*, L1 is at occasions used for German as official school language, in order to distinguish it from L2 English as the target language during bilingual teaching. I am fully aware that several students might have different L1. Remarks are made accordingly within the respective chapters.

LIKE	Bedeutung der Erst- und Zweitsprache bei Lernern der Fremdsprache Englisch für die kooperative Bearbeitung textbasierter Lernaufgaben
Lx/LX	Any other language beyond L1 an individual possesses competences in
MBM	Mode-based model
MCALL	Multilingual computer assisted language learning
MuViT	Fostering multiliteracy through multilingual talking books
OECD	Organization for Economic Co-operation and Development
OPAC	University online public access catalog
OPOL	One parent one language
PBM	Phase-based model
PISA	Program for International Student Assessment
QDA	Qualitative data analysis
RBM	Role-based model
RD	Research desiderata
RQ	Research questions
S4F	Scientists for Future
SL	Second language
SOAS	School of Oriental and African Studies
TR	Teacher researcher
Trans-FL	Trans-foreign-languaging
UDHR	Universal Declaration of Human Rights
UK	United Kingdom
UN	United Nations
UNESCO	The United Nations Educational, Scientific and Cultural Organization

Preliminary Remarks: Structure of this Monograph

This monograph is the result of a thoroughly revised paper-based dissertation that was compiled and written for fulfilling the requirements of the *Regulations for obtaining the academic degree of Doctor of Philosophy (Dr. phil.) at the Johann Wolfgang Goethe University Frankfurt am Main*. It affiliates to my work within the *PolECulE* project of Goethe University Frankfurt, a joint undertaking of the Didactic Departments of English and Social Sciences (see the Introduction of *Chapter I*). I was deputed into that project with 50% of my regular teaching obligation as teacher at an ancient language grammar school in the State of Hesse for the subjects English and Politics & Economics. I mainly teach in the school's content and language integrated learning (CLIL) program in Politics & Economics (a detailed description of the program is available in *Chapter V*). As the spokesperson *(Fachsprecher)* of the program, I also hold responsibility for its evaluation and further development.

In total, this monograph consists of four separate papers *(Chapters III-VI*, in the following referred to by their respective chapter numbers), defining its very core. Furthermore, the binding text of the extended outline, comprising a more narrative introduction in *Chapter I*, a literature review (along with the delineation of research deficits) in *Chapter II* and a final discussion in *Chapter VII*, constitutes an integral part of the dissertation requirements. This overall structure mirrors the outline of a monographic dissertation.

The assembly of the paper-based part of *Chapters III-VI*, respectively, is as follows:

(1) a conceptual publication *(Chapter III)*

> **The Construction of Cosmopolitan Glocalities in Secondary Classrooms through Content and Language Integrated Learning (CLIL) in the Social Sciences**

(2) a methodological article *(Chapter IV)*

> **Bridging the Gap between Theory and Practice with Design-based Action Research**

(3) and two empirical contributions *(Chapters V & VI, respectively)*

> a) **Translanguaging... or 'trans-foreign-languaging'? A comprehensive CLIL teaching model with judicious and principled L1 use**
>
> b) **Finding the 'perfect equilibrium of emotional and rational learning' in content and language integrated learning (CLIL) in the social sciences**

Those contributions are all tied together by *Chapter II*, leading into the overall topic matter and delineating research deficits and desiderata, and by *Chapter VII*, discussing the results and providing an outlook.

To provide assistance to readers in constructing their expectations towards the submitted work at hand, going more into detail seems appropriate at this instance, in order to display the academic contribution and achievement of this monograph to the field of CLIL classes with a particular focus on the Social Sciences (specific subject name: Politics & Economics[1]). The introductory body of *Chapter I* delineates my very personal motivation of pursuing the overall project at first. It closely relates to me as a person and my work as a CLIL teacher in Politics & Economics, and the endeavor to bridge the gap between theory and school practice as a teacher researcher (TR). *Chapter IV* justifies the overall methodological approach, resulting in the empirical contributions of *Chapters V* and *VI*. Thus, to pinpoint beforehand, the writing style in *Chapter I* and parts of *Chapter V*, respectively, will be indeed very personal and

---

[1] The binding text speaks of *Politics & Economics*, for directly establishing the link to my research location. Within the following chapters, *Social Sciences* has been mostly used, in order to create a link towards the global debate.

narrative. At times it is very challenging, for involving the readers from the perspective of a TR, communicating that science can be made out of very personal contributions and thus should value the magnitude of practical knowledge.

Chapter II gives an overview about the research fields of this monograph. First, it approaches to review the CLIL experience of Europe and Germany, thereafter taking a subject focus on CLIL in Politics & Economics. This is followed by multilingual approaches to CLIL with mainly first language (L1) use. The chapter ends with research desiderata, addressed by the consecutive *Chapters III-VI*.

The conceptual account of *Chapter III*, the first published paper, presents the merits of CLIL in the subject Politics & Economics for promoting global discourse competence and engendering 21st century skills as panacea towards global challenges. Why does cosmopolitanism, synchronically rendering classrooms into *glocalities*, matter? What role does a bi- and multilingual approach with L1 use play for unfolding and evolving the full potential of CLIL in Politics & Economics? *Chapter III* already illustrates the established framework with a practical example for filling it with real meaning. *#climonomics*, a multilingual European Union parliamentary debate about climate change with about 200 students from all over Germany, intends to demonstrate that even highly idealized and romanticized theories can really work in practice.[2]

Chapter IV consists of a contribution to methods for school research, introducing design-based action research as my investigatory tool in a 10th grade CLIL classroom in Germany. Mainly, it adds to the mosaic of academic research and argues for stakeholder participation with the goal to construct a science of practical knowledge within pragmatic research designs. Here, one of the two reviewers had suggested to include an empirical example from past research. I followed that recommendation in including my lesson

---

[2] Information about *#climonomics*, including a promotional video, the comprehensive media portfolio and the digital conference reader, can be accessed here: http://polecule.com/2019/11/05/climonomics-solief-unsere-mehrsprachige-eu-klimakonferenz-fuer-schuelerinnen-25-10-2019/. The digital reader was published in 2021 in a revised version (Nijhawan, Elsner, & Engartner, 2021a).

series from my teacher training thesis *(2. Staatsexamensarbeit)* about how *The Simpsons* can contribute to bilingual teaching in Politics & Economics (Nijhawan, 2013). It exemplifies the application of the method that has thereafter been used with the empirical research *(Chapters V & VI).*

The latter two chapters present the empirical research in line with the research aims and the research method of the preceding chapters. It is worth mentioning that climate change serves as exemplary *leitmotif* for global 21st century challenges, same as already with *Chapter III*. This approach underlines the conceptual argument of *Chapter III* about the transformative power of classroom *glocalities*. *Chapter V* has a clear language bias, challenging the notion of immersion within CLIL and seeking a multilingual approach with L1 use instead. It defines the very core of six weeks intense fieldwork in one of my CLIL classes in school. The ultimate goal was to develop a comprehensive CLIL teaching model with judicious and principled L1 use, amidst the repeatedly formulated need over the last decade to develop pedagogies *how* to integrate L1 into everyday teaching. In this context, the chapter explores the merits of translanguaging. Thereafter, looking beyond second language (SL) learning, it adapts the concept into a framework of trans-foreign-languaging (Trans-FL), enabling CLIL as multilingual approach for foreign language (FL) learning with L1 as an integral part. In the fashion of a thick description with mixed methods during the DRAR, the genesis of the comprehensive CLIL teaching model with judicious and principled L1 will be presented. A key characteristic is the stakeholder development of that model within the natural learning environment of the students, along with an affordance-based and differentiated approach.

Chapter VI, the second empirical contribution and final paper, looks at subject-based issues of CLIL. Till now, subject-based questions have only been marginally researched within CLIL, because it is mostly commissioned by language departments of universities, which logically focus more on a set of general as well as more language-specific issues. Here, from the side of Social Science didactics, the question in how far L1 integration into CLIL (as proposed in the preceding *Chapter V*) influences emotional and rational learning, ultimately causing different outcomes on political judgments, defines the center of gravity. In particular, the genesis of what I call a 'perfect equilibrium of emotional and rational learning', constitutes a focal point of the theoretical framework as a milestone towards more global justice and solidarity. This publication serves as an example of what could provocatively be called a 'by-product', constructed from surplus data of the research. During the field research, I noted that students' behavior in L1 appears different, more emotional, as compared to regular immersion we had used to practice before. Thus, the surveyed data was closely examined, in order to frame the argument accordingly, as the chapter elucidates. A developed coding scheme to analyze written texts whether arguments are either emotional or rational, and inflicted by rather self-interest or rather altruism, is applied on bilingual exams.

The discussion of *Chapter VII*, the last part of the binding-text, finally ties all results into one entity, showing the contribution to the field of research with the submitted scientific work, stating questions that deserve further investigation, and providing an outlook for potential further research in the field. Also, questions about the validity of the findings as well as generalization issues are asked on a more general level. The chapter ends with an outlook.

Every single paper of *Chapters III-VI* as such constitutes a closed entity, written as a single work product (mostly within the common structure introduction/problem – state of research/literature review – research question(s) – research method – data – discussion). Three papers *(Chapters III, IV & VI)* that have already been printed and published are an *exact* reproduction of the published version, also including journal-specific conventions. Only the figure and table numbering has been adapted to match the layout of this monograph, each chapter starting from new, also with the footnotes. *Chapter V* was published as the *author submitted manuscript*. It significantly differs from the *author accepted manuscript* that has been published recently. Each chapter's title page is more detailed about the status of the respective paper.

Consequently, it is also but understood that there are inconsistencies in e.g., capitalization and a few other conventions, because the journals have their own policies. Moreover, certain theoretical and conceptual topics will be recurring throughout. The latter especially refers to the competence model that first appears in *Chapter II* already and has been introduced again in *Chapters III & VI*, respectively. Also, in a number of instances, papers had already been cross-referenced, again elucidating how they are interrelated to each other within my work of the *PolECulE* project, although they indeed cover a wide topic area. Topics not covered in the papers but requiring deeper attention will be dealt with in *Chapter II*. Reference to the single chapters will be taken whenever needed, to point towards the most salient results of the research and prepare the ground for the final discussion.

The monograph will now start with the acknowledgements, and thereafter lead into the topic, mainly from my perspective. Both parts explain why a more narrative style was adopted there.

Acknowledgements
(...about saying THANK YOU!)

"I have no special talents. I am only passionately curious." – *Albert Einstein*

The motivation to remain engaged in this long-term project could have never been sustained without the intellectual exchanges, inspiration, help, support, friendship, love and affection from those many people who accompanied me for almost five years—people simply giving me a good time. How can one, for such a long time, endure the workload, stress, if not only for curiosity and *passion* for the topic? Everything here is about passion. And, inferring from Einstein, to be passionately curious, I would say, is a talent itself, because passion and the attached emotions transform to positive energy in motivation—if not dedication and humility—in the end, I would argue. To break it into one formula: *it's all about passion*.

A doctorate—a strong character test, very much clear to anyone who has been through this process—is mainly the result not only of individual research, but of myriad debates and discussions, serving as a source of inspiration. This includes people from within the field with an emic perspective (ideally 'better than you'), and people with other perspectives, offering the etic point of view. This multifaceted interpersonal contact was decisive for the heartbeat within this period, outspokenly enriching for my academic and personal development. Hence, many have become an integral part of this project, fully deserving to be eternized there.

Writing these acknowledgements, typically at the end of a project, helps to time travel back to the beginning of the project, once a singular idea, and retaking the emotional journey from this retrospective with an inner and outer smile. The order I name everyone here does not indicate any ranking, except the very first and the last ones. Obviously, let me start with Goethe University and my supervisor. Throughout, I have had a professional and very passionate relationship with **Daniela Elsner**. Not only did Daniela lead me the way back to academia, but also became a close friend within the long and intense time, a period we planned and carried out many projects pragmatically. I learned that not being better necessarily matters but being different, ultimately making the difference you want to see in this world! I could continue with the laudation forever here...! The relationship to my second supervisor has become very affectionate as well. **Tim Engartner** throughout was a person who offered me a special place in the Institute of Political Science. Our relationship can be characterized as that of two close friends, with similar philosophies, ideas, dreams and visions.

Back to university, I had deep intellectual exchanges with many interesting personalities. These include **Judith Bündgens-Kosten, Matthias Eichhorn, Michael Gehrig, Mona Hasenzahl, Annika Janßen, Christine Junghans, Yvonne Karacic, Alexandra Kemmerer, Almut Küppers, Carina and Jan-Erik Leonardt, Viviane Lohe, Marc Meller, Helena McKenzie, Matthias Munsch, Heike Niesen, Lotte Schmerbach, Frank Schulze-Engler, Maria Skejic, Simon Spengler, Mariella Veneziano-Osterrath** and **Britta Viebrock**. And, of course, I made countless contacts beyond Goethe University Frankfurt during the academic journey who inspired and influenced my work. Thanks to **Miriam de Boer, Tilman Grammes, Celeste Neelen, Lorraine Nencel** and **Anke Wegner**. The Scientists for Future Regional Group Frankfurt offered me a safe space for mutually deliberating on my climate-related projects with relevance to this monograph. I am particularly grateful to **Norbert Dichter, Jürgen Eiselt, Angela Helbling, Bettina Knülle, Julia Krohmer, Thomas Seifert, Brigitte Suchanek** and **Georg Sebastian Völker**.

My school was very supportive throughout, making the doctorate possible at all. Special thanks to **Thomas Mausbach, Gerhard Köhler, Uwe Paulsen, Birgit Vollrath** from the school management. Many colleagues demonstrated their support, namely **Beatrix Blell, Jan Czudai, Fatma Karaca, Anja Klobetanz, Heinz-Georg Ortmanns, Tomek Pawletko, Hendrik Raab, Jessica Rother** and **Aljoscha Schütte**. From the students' side, my special gratitude belongs to **Jonas Singer, Vincent Börsch-Supan** and **Charlotte Wittich**. My teacher trainers **Christian Doiwa** and **Waltraud Kallenbach**, of course, deserve special mention. Furthermore, I am grateful to the Ministry for Education in Hesse **(Hessisches**

Kultusministerium) for issuing the permit without bureaucratic hassle, allowing me to proceed with the dissertation project. Special thanks to **Ulrike Naumann** for the important input I received from her side.

The following friends each have a special role within in this work—be it 'old friends' from childhood, SOAS or anywhere else… be it my daily life within my Frankfurt 'hood'… or from any other occasion, yet always very personal. Describing each individual's role would indeed fill the volume of another book, and everyone individually knows, so I just keep it short and alphabetically: **Procolino Antacido, Vivek Boray, Jochen Brähmig, Julian Culp, Franziska Dübgen, Enrico Dunkel, Vijay Eagala, Georgios Evangelou, Detlev von Graeve, Stefan Hantel** *aka* **Shantel, Michael Hauer, Anna Henrichs, Binu Joseph, Petra Klaus, Pedo Knopp, Marie Lall, Markus Lücker, Projit and Monjita Mukharji, Andy Nelson, Karin Rahts, Ezra Rashkow, Kristina Roepstorff, Itesh Sachdev, Katja Schmela, Kathrin Schmitt, Gunnar Schneider, Tim Schuster, Anne & Jan Schwarz, Nitin Sinha, Christoph & Ayesha Sprung, Alexander Theiss, Karim Touati, Jean and Sylvia Trouillet, Antje Witte** and **Marcel Zeitinger.**

And now, last but definitely not the least, I will turn to the smallest unit, namely my family. Thanks to the support and motivating words throughout from my sister, **Shobna Nijhawan,** my brother-in-law, **Michael Nijhawan,** and **Mayur,** all living in Toronto, Canada, where I also completed parts of my work. But 'back to Germany': **Sharmila** and **Shashank,** or **Chhammo** and **Bola,** first living with me, now in Kronberg, have made our existence much livelier. Everyday some very strange, new and exciting story! They have wonderful company with **my parents Veena & Subash Nijhawan.** And the world *wonderful* says everything, this affection, and love. No wonder the PhD is dedicated to them, keeping in mind how we all had to struggle to become what we are in a *'foreign country'*…

Chapter I

…about the teacher researcher and his motivation….

Introduction

"Non, rien de rien, Non, je ne regrette rien, Ni le bien qu'on m'a fait, Ni le mal, Tout ça m'est bien égal" (Édith Piaf, 1956)

The 'warning' that this introductory part with the **motivation for this monograph will be written very *narratively and emotionally*,** indeed very challenging in its genuine writing style, has already been expressed. This includes a swift transition to the *first person I*, meaning to amplify the deliberately personal notch of the overall work. The motivation is strongly related to me having acted as teacher researcher (TR). Thus, the following part will contain elements of my curriculum vitae, for elucidating the project's approach and idea, and my personal role within. It should help to partly enter my perspective as TR, also for the interpretation of the results along with their *caveat*. Balancing emic and etic points of views will become instrumental, as both constitute important parts of the mixed methods mosaic, here biased towards qualitative inquiry (Richards, 2003). To already announce at this point, there will be a sudden back transition of the writing style to a more academic and rational version, in parts with a persuasive language use when presenting this project's significance for content and language integrated learning (CLIL) research as well as the research desiderata (RD) in *Chapter II*.

I am using the word 'warning' once again, already in this second paragraph—yet for another reason. What I will present in the following is science, based on research and facts. As one will univocally discover, I love science! On the one side, my work deals with multilingual education. But on the other side, in a twist of a subject turn, **the selected *leitmotif* going through all chapters of this monograph is *climate change***. Ever since I grew up, I have been very concerned about the state of the environment and wanted to pursue a sustainable lifestyle, promoting the transition towards a society with an economy fostering active degrowth. Establishing the nexus of multilingualism with sustainably is among the core of this work, as climate change is real, and the human footprint immane. This is what science tells us, and immediate climate action is required. For that reason, I joined the Scientists for Future (S4F), supporting the cause of Fridays for Future (FFF), a *glocal* network of engaged young people with the quest for a sustainable society.

I am fully aware that this might be an unusual way for delineating the motivation for a monograph, but similarly believe that choosing this more personal notch highlights the overall project aptly and underscores the importance of TRs' initiatives in the field of didactics overall, attempting to consolidate theory and practice, ultimately increasing the impact of the research. In a field like teaching, with emotions defining one of the cornerstones of teacher-student interaction (see also *Chapter VI* on CLIL and emotions), there is no harm in defying the odds and taking a higher risk at challenge. As a matter of fact, I felt very encouraged to proceed as suggested after a conversation with a leading Professor of Didactics of Romance Studies during my visit to the 28th Congress of the German Association for Foreign Language Research (*Deutsche Gesellschaft für Fremdsprachenforschung* — DGFF). The acclaimed researcher, personally rather disappointed with recent doctoral research in the designated area, strongly delivered his expectations towards coming PhD students to not desperately abide *"to the rules of the game"* but rather take risks and challenges as border walkers and rejuvenate the field, especially referring to freshly new and innovative methodological pathways. Only rebels, he literally (!) and firmly argued, lead to desired and needed progress and change.

About the Teacher-Researcher: Relevance of Previous Experience for the Research Project

The motivation for this research project is closely related to my professional experience as a teacher at a public secondary school with a focus on ancient and new languages, whereby I mainly teach in the school's CLIL program in Politics & Economics. The research presented was planned organically, pragmatically and stakeholder-centered during the curricular section of environmental economics. This underlines the quest to inductively develop subjective views optimistic about my prospects within the academic world, having a holistic view of me as a person.

Although I liked the idea — and even felt extremely flattered — I first decided to do my 21-month teacher training, to secure the teaching degree (security and freedom, or both?). Thereafter, I immediately received an offer from another school with a compulsory one-year CLIL program in Politics & Economics. Again, delaying the option of a PhD, I did not wish to surrender the opportunity, because the principal eagerly convinced me of the professional vision I could pursue, which was closely juxtaposed with my personal vision. And as a matter of fact, I quickly developed admiration and passion for teaching CLIL classes in Politics & Economics, because they deal with global challenges and opportunities of the 21st century, among that global climate education defining the center of gravity. Amidst the absence of any formal training for CLIL, not to speak about the non-availability of material or a long list of rules in an otherwise overregulated field, my classes mainly had an 'experimental trial-and-error' outline. This as a matter of fact matches my personal philosophy, as someone who rather likes to make own rules instead of obeying the same, thus perpetually challenging existing boundaries. In my CLIL classes at school, I was my own researcher in a liberal and hardly regulated space, with a curriculum only defining keywords as topic areas. Therefore, I had almost all the freedom to proceed as I believed it was correct. On the positive side, I also witnessed students' behavior to be completely different as compared to 'classical classes' in either English or Politics & Economics. It was nice to deviate from regular, more formal arrangements — often in a 'teaching-to-the-test-fashion' — and pursue rather experimental and thus creative teaching, with problem-oriented and cooperative settings. Furthermore, my reputation of a person acting in 'English-only' with all the students, also out of class time and during any other communication, causing spectacular reactions and a lot of applause also by parents feeling privileged, needed to be preserved, I concluded.

The first two years of bilingual teaching in the school's CLIL program were driven by overt passion and happiness, resulting in a new form of intrinsic motivation, because I believed I had finally found what I had been looking for. During this time, many questions from my nature or talent of being 'passionately curious' had developed, keeping me busy throughout during reflection and re-planning, and honestly for long nights. These questions were both on the language and subject side. In a more colloquial tone, not yet in the fashion of formal academic research questions (RQs), the most seminal questions I had were:

Language:

- Why is it actually called *bi̱lingualer Sachfachunterricht* at all, although immersion is a common practice? So, what role should the official school language German play, and *how* can it be incorporated systematically into lessons? Or, on a more banal level: *how* do you actually teach *bi̱*lingually?
- Why, as I could note at certain instances, do students all of a sudden struggle to even have informal conversations in German about topics taught during immersion? Often, they would refer to the terminology in English, the target language (L2) and in most cases also a foreign language (FL), almost rendering anglicisms 'cool' during a naturally-feeling language mesh-up. *How* can *real bi̱lingual education* possibly be an answer to this problem, without compromising on FL learning?
- As the CLIL program was meant for all students, and not solely designed for a comparatively homogeneous elite easier to teach: *how* can weaker students as well as students having different resources, be promoted and enjoy the benefits of the unique pedagogy? *How* to include them on eye level into regular classroom processes?

Subject:

- What potential do CLIL lessons in Politics & Economics, with its globalization-related curriculum, have to prepare students for their future in a transnational civil society, realizing the role of English in our globalized world?

- Why is a CLIL approach for subject education in Politics & Economics with English as L2 so important, realizing our 21st century challenges?
- Can CLIL promote cosmopolitanism from below, along with empathy, global justice and solidarity within such a framework?
- Does the FL use influence students' decisions, owing to the merits of FL didactics with its potential for perspective changes, empathy, etc.?
- Can a CLIL approach, as it appeared to me, actually be a precursor for education for sustainable development (ESD), first and foremost for combatting climate change?

Mainly, the *how* within the questions dominates, and amplifies the personal and rather explorative and action research (AR)-based approach with its focus on practical pedagogies. This is quite diametrically opposed to the recent growth of large-scale quantitative undertakings (Aljets, 2014). In general, I took the time to address such questions and to perpetually set small research aims during planning the lessons. My ambition consisted of developing subjective theories, but solely for improving my own classes in the fashion of a reflective practitioner (Schön, 1983) — so just for me and myself. Often, this included student surveys (using e.g., Moodle) and classroom feedback. The degree of reflectivity evident from students' responses deeply impressed me. I was stunned what input students were able to give on such meta- and on subject questions, in their own language, insinuating original and reflective ideas. I learned that students were able to participate in all of such debates, without prejudice, often very emotional and ardent yet reflective and passionate, hence more genuine than adults in most instances.

But I missed the space of discourse to systematize and disseminate my impressions and create theoretical approaches from my knowledge and the small empiricism, something 'grander', also recognizing that every learning group and every context is distinct in the end. It happened, that after two years, finally, a professor I had remained in touch with after university in Frankfurt (thereafter becoming the supervisor of my dissertation) called me a late Friday afternoon. We met outside for a wine, and I learned about her plan to establish the *PolECulE* project. She formulated the need for experienced personnel with practical teaching and management experience — and the skills to systematize and theorize such experience for making them scientific, and in turn back-transfer didactic research to school. I talked to my principal who himself was enthusiastic about the overall idea and the positive prospects for the school of being part of such a novel initiative. I applied for the 50% deputed position and was later successful during the competitive job interview. Indeed, I could not wait to start to bring in my experience from school for the success of the ambitious and important project, and, *inter alia,* to look at the aforementioned questions also from an academic point of view (see *Chapter II*), with relevant departmental support. As a matter of fact, it was just the spirit and passion I have described here that constituted my motivation and interest for this research project.

From now on, my job was defined to inductively contribute to theory development in academia, in close conjunction with my remaining 50% teaching obligation at school. In other words, a part of the terms defined to use my classroom as research field and thus contribute to theory-generation of CLIL didactics in Politics & Economics. *Quid pro quo,* the school at first would receive innovative teaching concepts and material for the further development of its CLIL program. For me, it was important that, during my work with *PolECulE,* I would continue teaching at school and yet again occupy an *in-between space,* in order to consolidate academic didactic research with school practice, embodied within me as future TR. I wanted to contribute to *real change* with *theories that work in practice* yet stay *down to earth* — all in line with the philosophy of the *PolECulE* project.

PolECulE: Consolidating Theory with School Practice

The *PolECule* project of Goethe University Frankfurt, a joint undertaking of the didactic departments of English and Social Sciences, was founded as an initiative for contributing to research and development in CLIL in the Social Sciences. The hitherto absence of educational standards for CLIL—neither general nor subject specific for Politics & Economics—defined the starting point for developing a conceptual framework with an integrated competence model. This includes the capturing any of its language and subject-specific bilingual surplus. The ending of *Chapter II* presents the competence model and its conceptual idea of thought.

In a nutshell, the philosophy of the project can be described to raise awareness for a cosmopolitan outlook on our global 21st century challenges, *inter alia,* climate change and poverty & inequality. Such 21st century challenges are always political, economic and cultural (e.g., climate change, the *leitmotif* of three of the four chapters). In line with the philosophy of problem-based learning (Barrows, 1996) and its close nexus to 21st century skills (Trilling & Fadel, 2009), *PoleCulE* designed concepts and material for the promotion of students' skills for the analysis of facts and their later participation in a global culture of debates in English and beyond. This approach means to make everyone recognize that there are many different points of views and pathways to work towards abating 21st century challenges. In the end, this is constitutional for agency within a democratic and transnational civil society, supporting approaches towards ESD within the framework of global justice and solidarity. The need to rejuvenate democracy in the 21st century has become apparent especially within the last years, mainly in a quest to counter recent trends in populism, renationalization and chauvinism, threatening global peace and sustainability as a whole.

For this first phase of *PolECulE*, not only theoretical thoughts in general, but in particular the experience from practice was highly relevant for the development of the full-fledged conceptual framework (published in Elsner et al., 2019, along with methodological advice and a teaching example). The second phase of the project was scheduled to directly intervene into classrooms, using material and teaching methods that had been developed in line with the conceptual framework. After developing an agenda—*parallel at university and in school*—the research was carried out. I fused AR and design-based research (DBR) into design-based action research (DBAR), amplifying the need for collaborative research between theory and practice, in the end personified in me as TR *(see above and Chapter IV)*. *Figure 1* sketches the proceedings of the *PolECulE* project.

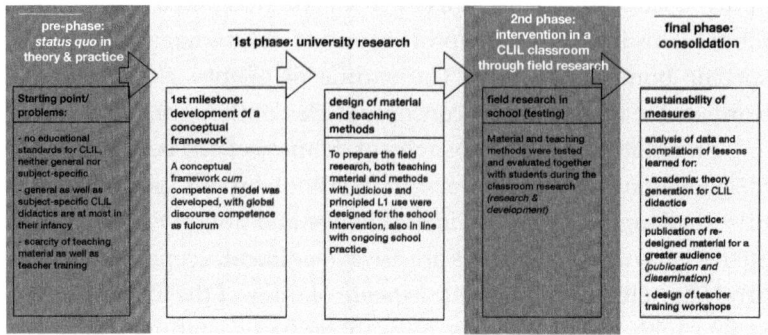

Figure 1 illustrates the proceeding of the *PolECulE* project.

Thanks to *PolECulE,* I had the opportunity to address the aforementioned questions, *inter alia,* also from an academic point of view, in context of international CLIL research. The stakeholder research, led by me as TR together with my students, meant to contribute to the further development of CLIL teaching. I collected data and generated new theories. In a nutshell, the work can be called 'making a science of practical knowledge from teaching at school'. Not only was I able to present my work at conferences and other occasions, but also I could fruitfully exchange with other scholars. I was able to make my research, coming from my regular teaching obligation, available to a wider audience through publications (both academic as well as for school practice) and through teacher training workshops. In other words, I presented scientific findings from teaching practice in a consolidation effort of these two *de facto* two often very distinct fields. The main results will be presented in *Chapters III-VI*, and discussed in *Chapter VII*, where I will unambiguously expound the contribution to science and CLIL research.

Looking back, I cannot be more grateful for this opportunity to have been part of the *PolECulE* team. To sum up the journey: it was a very personal and maybe also in parts unusual journey, which I believe has strongly influenced my working ethics during researching and writing, so my overall intrinsic motivation. I want to clearly state that the research project was a very emotional endeavor, driven by passion, as this introduction hopefully elucidated. This is, at least in my case, equally relevant for teaching, researching, and at every other instance, in the end to make science a human endeavor as well. This journey, with the temporary halt to submit this research project, has made me what I am now, while I tend to chant the famous words of Edith Piaff: *"je ne regrette rien"*. So everything made sense in the end, maybe it was *Karma*. And I can already say: more will come...

Now, the next chapter has the announced back swift to a more rational writing style. My motivation, mainly coming from personal interests during the practice of teaching, was meant to not only solve 'my problems', but, since joining *PolECulE*, was now embedded within a larger context in CLIL theory and research. Hence I was motivated to follow the rules of the game of science, although I must admit it was not always easy for me as not only a pragmatic border walker but rather the typical border crosser. The next chapter, after presenting the genesis of CLIL in Europe and its practice in Germany, mainly looks at two different fields of research, namely CLIL in Politics & Economics and CLIL and multilingualism. I will thereafter conclude the chapter with academic RD, ultimately leading to the paper-based section. It will not be difficult to realize that the RDs and the formal RQs of the single papers have a close proximity to the questions addressed at the beginning of the chapter, again showing that teaching and research may define two sides of a coin, nevertheless on the same coin.

Chapter II

...about global challenges and opportunities of the 21st century...

Very singular parts of this chapter were reproduced verbatim from the following publication:

Nijhawan, S. (2019). Designing teachers' action research: CLIL and the functional use of the L1 in Politics, Economics & Culture. In A. Kreft & M. Hasenzahl (Eds.), *Aktuelle Tendenzen in der Fremdsprachendidaktik* (Vol. 64, pp. 147-163). Berlin: Peter Lang.

CLIL: a Door Opener to Globalization

> [...] CLIL developed as an innovative form of education in response to the demands and expectations of the modern age. Input from different academic fields has contributed to the recognition of this approach to educational practice. In an age characterized by 'quick fix' solutions, however, which may or may not lead to any form of sustainable outcomes, it is important to contextualise CLIL historically. CLIL is not merely a convenient response to the challenges posed by rapid globalization; rather, it is a solution which is timely, which is in harmony with broader social perspectives, and which has proved effective. (Coyle et al., 2010, p. 5)

After more than 15 years of CLIL in Europe, the authors paint a very optimistic picture about the success and transformation of CLIL as a modern educational practice in the 21st century. Mainly, they praise its transdisciplinary outline as well as its problem-solving nature. CLIL as a concept was first coined by Marsh (1994, no page) as *"situations where subjects, or parts of subjects, are taught through a foreign language with dual-focussed aims, namely the learning of content, and the simultaneous learning of a foreign language"*. Forerunners were various indigenous concepts of bilingual education within Europe and beyond, now subsumed under CLIL as umbrella term, proclaiming it as a genuinely European approach to promote multilingualism within a linguistically diverse region.

This chapter will proceed as follows. At first, the genesis of CLIL in Europe will be presented. Since the empirical fieldwork of this monograph was located in Germany, the next part will introduce Germany's CLIL experience for accordingly contextualizing the empirical *Chapters V & VI*. This includes both administrative as well as academic accounts, often diverging in their understanding of CLIL. After focusing on cultural education and language diversity, which *per se* are closely juxtaposed, most recent results of CLIL research in Germany for both language and subject competences, respectively, will be analyzed, to attain an idea about the current status of the research field.

It will become obvious several times that *de facto* CLIL is mainly seen as a new approach to FL learning. But there is much more behind, as this and the following chapters show. A strong argument will be made for CLIL in Politics & Economics[1] as a congenial subject to prepare learners for their agency in a global community. And this, from a conceptual basis, also includes students' first language (L1) use. The overall train of thought will be exemplified throughout by climate change as *leitmotif* in the subsequent chapters of this monograph. Surprisingly, research in subject-based CLIL, both related to that subject as well as to more general issues, is hardly visible, whereas L1 use and multilingualism *per se* is a bigger research field, albeit hardly within CLIL. Therefore, an attempt to borrow latest insights from FL teaching will be made.

Finally, the chapter will end in presenting the achievements of the *PolECulE* project of Goethe University Frankfurt. The conceptual framework with an integrated competence model should be seen as a proposition for a subject-based CLIL didactics in Politics & Economics. Of course, such conceptual work demarks areas deserving further scrutiny and intervention. Hence, the section closes with RDs, the segue into Chapters *III-VI*.

Taking the Fast Track: CLIL Becomes Mainstream in Europe

On the political level, language policy in Europe, a region with multiple official languages, has been on the political agenda throughout, long before the foundation of the European Union (EU). Immediately after establishing the European Economic Community (EEC) with the *Treaty of Rome* in 1957, *EEC Council Regulation 1/1958*

---

[1] In Germany, education is administered independently by each of the 16 federal states. When talking about Politics & Economics, similar reference is taken to subjects like Social Studies, Social Sciences, Civics, or any subject encompassing a blend of, *inter alia*, political, economic and cultural content. The *Länder* were thus far not able to find a uniform name for social science education, ultimately resulting in this cacophony. And, of course, the divergence is even bigger on the European or global level. In the remainder of this chapter, I will refer to *Politics & Economics*, the official subject designation in the State of Hesse. It should, however, be mentioned that some of the presented articles of *Chapter III-VI* instead speak of Social Sciences, in an endeavor to join the global discourse.

declared all national languages of the member states official working languages. Until the EU was founded, many of the member states had already designed bilingual language education policies. Accordingly, they had already gained first-hand experience with bilingual education *per se*.

Such initiatives, often AR driven, delivered inestimable knowledge, experience and theory for the formal adoption, development and professionalization of CLIL within the EU. The *language across the curriculum* (LAC) movement in the United Kingdom (UK) in the 1960s constitutes a prominent vanguard how alternatives to traditional FL instruction had been implemented in early times. Breaking up subject boundaries and enabling a more communicative language learning beyond 'traditional FL education' were some of the main goals on the agenda of a few British educators in secondary schools (Burns, 2013; May, 1997). LAC's general idea was later adopted by many other educationalists within the EU. It is designated to be, more or less, a direct antecessor of today's CLIL approaches (Hanesová, 2015).

The momentum to create CLIL as common European policy approach can be directly related to the foundation of the EU, which today comprises 24 official languages within the member states. The *Treaty on the European Union*, signed in Maastricht and entering into force in 1993, recognizes language diversity and defines the EU officially as a multilingual region. To add, *The Treaty on the Functioning of the European Union* requires the member states to actively promote plurilingualism[2] among its citizens through language education, as finally communicated in the *White Paper of the European Commission* in 1995.[3] Consequently, the target to promote their

---

[2] According to Beacco and Byram (2007, p. 8), multilingualism as a more *collective* concept refers to *"the presence in a geographical area, large or small, of more than one 'variety of language'"*, whereas plurilingualism as *individual* concept means *"the repertoire of varieties of language which many individuals use [...]; it includes the language variety referred to as 'mother tongue' or 'first language' and any number of other languages or varieties."*

[3] *White Papers* are meant to communicate decisions of the EU Commission, and thus constitute a firm policy stand.

citizens' proficiency in two additional EU languages beyond L1 was set.[4] These landmark decisions Marsh (2012, part I) calls *"both political and educational"*, in the retrospective clearly designated the early roadmap for language learning through CLIL for Europe's future.

The first-hand experience that had grown organically from below inevitably had an impact on language education policy as a direct answer towards meeting natural demands on local, regional or national levels. Mostly, this is especially related to borderlands, or to countries that *de jure* are multilingual (Marsh, 2002) with recognized regional or even more than one official national languages. To provide an example: as a country merged between two *de facto* world powers, Luxembourg has a long tradition of subject classes in German as second language (SL) and FL as well as English as FL, respectively (Hanesová, 2015). Overall, due to diverging local and national circumstances and difference in curricular provisions, today myriad forms of CLIL programs exist throughout the EU, each with their unique DNA. This also includes the detailed outline of programs, ranging from singular modules to full immersion. To track the overall development, a very detailed and decade by decade overview since the 1950s, even before CLIL had been inaugurated, was compiled by Marsh (2002), or more recently also by Hurajová (2015).

It took until 2006 when Eurydice, an agency acting on behalf of the European Commission, took a major consolidation effort and published a comprehensive status report on CLIL within the EU member states. The legal EU definition of CLIL henceforward covered *"all types of provision in which a second language (a foreign, regional or minority language and/or another official state language) is used to teach certain subjects in the curriculum other than languages lessons themselves" (Eurydice, 2006, p. 8)*. CLIL was formally adopted by the European Commission as an educational policy recommendation for promoting plurilingualism among EU citizens (for a thorough analysis of EU documents with reference to CLIL and its role to

---

[4] See https://europa.eu/european-union/about-eu/eu-languages_en with an updated overview about official languages in the EU and set targets to promote plurilingualism among its citizens.

promote plurilingualism, see for instance Deutsch, 2013). The French counterpart *Enseignement d'une Matière par l'intégration d'une Langue Erangère (EMILE)* is also often being used. This means that EU references often speak about CLIL/EMILE, at the same time giving it a multilingual notch.

Details about the multiplicity of CLIL models in Europe are included within the report, with nearly every official European language being taught within some CLIL program. With modern globalization in its rapid nature and the (almost) uncontested rise of English as the global *lingua franca*, English now has become the dominant language for CLIL classes within the EU member states (Cenoz, Genesee, & Gorter, 2013). CLIL can range from singular modules to full immersion over a longer time span, although Genesee (1987, p. 172), out of the Canadian experience, calls immersion and bilingual education *"natural enemies"*. Legally, this means — for once to define extreme points — that a course with only a limited time in a SL or FL, just greater than 0%, can fall as much under CLIL as a fully immersive course with the SL or FL as sole language of instruction. To sum up from the report, CLIL captures a diverse range of models within Europe, with most of the EU official languages, although mostly English, as L2.

In the meanwhile, academia had also been caught within European consolidation efforts and started to take a partly different approach towards CLIL. The center of gravity for substantiating its pedagogical meaning was set, and, in line with Genesee (1987), the scope especially towards immersion was delimited. CLIL goes beyond L2 as sole language of instruction, defining L1 as integral part of the methodology. Lasagabaster and Sierra (2010), in their comparison, go deeper and display both similarities but mainly differences of CLIL and immersion. As a new and sharp contrast to Eurydice, they point out that L2 in CLIL is normally a FL, and not a surrounding SL, a position accepted by many European scholars thereafter (Dalton-Puffer & Smit, 2013). Importantly, also the role of content was upgraded with the induction of CLIL (e.g., Dalton-Puffer & Smit, 2013; Marsh, 2002). The promotion of cognitive academic language proficiency (CALP, see Cummins, 1979, 1981), enabling students to take part in subject-related discourses in more than one language, has crystallized as a seminal outcome. This is opposed to solely earmarking rudimentary language expressions labeled as basic interpersonal language skills (BICS) for mastering 'to get along with daily businesses'. Due to the promising results of promoting FL competence and multilingualism *per se*, Merino and Lasagabaster (2015, p. 11) conclude in their longitudinal study within the Basque country that *"CLIL can be a useful approach to boost multilingualism in schools"*.

Upgrading the role of content and regarding upon CLIL as a pedagogy with benefits beyond language learning, lead to a significant transformation of the main cornerstones of its original idea of thought. Coyle et al. (2010, p. 41) developed the *"4Cs framework"* as an ideal type of CLIL lessons, highlighting the emergence of a bilingual surplus in establishing a nexus to modern globalization *(Figure 1)*. It includes *"content (subject matter), communication (language learning and using), cognition (learning and thinking processes) and culture (developing intercultural understanding and global citizenship"*. Mainly, one can infer the swift away from seeing CLIL only as a serious competitor for traditional language teaching, and rather acknowledging its methodology as a solution in the sense of meaning-making and problem-solving in a globalized world, as this chapter's introductory statement by the same authors already elucidated. The 4Cs framework has not only been used ever since as a roadmap for CLIL in the coming decade but fueled the discussion about the general aims of and further development of CLIL accordingly.

Figure 1 shows the 4c framework by Coyle, Hood, and Marsh (2010, p. 41).

Finally, the *"bilingual advantage"*, as Marsh, Díaz-Pérez, Frigols Martín, Langé, and Pavón Vázquez (2020) point out in a very recent publication, is highly relevant for this overall approach. The authors succinctly compile findings of interdisciplinary CLIL-related research from the last decades, including the positive effect of bilingualism on mind & brain. They advertise the innovative methodology of CLIL as solution-based approach to present global 21st century challenges. The latter idea will reappear within this chapter multiple times, also realizing the role CLIL in Politics & Economics can play as a pedagogical response to modern globalization. Now, the focus shifts to the German context, in order to contextualize the subsequent chapters within the national discourse.[5]

Bilingualer Sachfachunterricht: Germany's CLIL

CLIL in Germany has its original idea of thought in language and culture learning as a roadmap towards peace education. CLIL lessons, hitherto officially called *bilingualer Sachfachunterricht* (or *"Bili"* in a colloquially abbreviated form),[6] were introduced in the 1970s in French as a part of post-Second World War reconciliation efforts with the Western neighbor in the wake of the *Élysée Treaty* of 1963 (Märsch, 2007). The founding idea was the bicultural character for learning more about history and people of the target culture. Mainly, lessons took place in history and were directed towards promoting peace and stability within Europe. Following the promising early-time pioneer experience in schools where CLIL had been taught rather pragmatically, a small number of state education boards included provisions for CLIL classes from the 1980s onwards. In accordance with the general trend in the wake of modern globalization since end of the Cold War, English as the almost uncontested global *lingua franca* gradually became the dominant

---

[5] Actually, one should speak of CLIL in the plural form CLILs, because despite all European consolidation and harmonization efforts, educational policies still remain a national affair. Many indigenous forms and national policy provisions of bi- and multilingual education in the EU member states have been running ahead of CLIL.

[6] Eurydice suggests *bilingualer Sachfachunterricht* as official German translation of CLIL (Eurydice, 2006, p. 64). The literal meaning actually is slightly different, because there is no *bilingual* connotation encapsulated in CLIL itself.

language for CLIL classes in German schools. Breidbach and Viebrock (2012, p. 5) call the 1990s in the retrospective *"the heyday of the implementation of English-speaking CLIL programmes"* in Germany.

CLIL in German Schools: the *Status Quo*

Ever since the promising pioneering experience in the German-French context, CLIL has been becoming a more common phenomenon in German schools. Breidbach (2013), after almost two decades of CLIL in Europe, underlines its erratic growth in Germany, following European unity and the adoption of CLIL as policy approach for the promotion of multilingualism. Looking at the administrative side, according to the *The Standing Conference of the Ministers of Education and Cultural Affairs* (KMK, 2013), three different organizational models of CLIL exist in schools: (1) full bilingual schools or schools with established bilingual branches; (2) bilingual classes with the FL at least for one year, and (3) singular bilingual models with shorter sequences.

The absence of official statistics constitutes an obstacle to delineating a clear-cut *status quo* of CLIL in Germany. A scattered overview has only been surveyed twice by the KMK, the last time in 2013. However, there is no official statistical section providing numbers about how many of about 36,000 schools in Germany offer CLIL. A rough estimate has been calculated by Wolff (2017), reproduced in *Table 1*. It echoes the problem about the nondisclosure of numbers by the administration.

Table 1 lists the number of schools with CLIL in Germany (according to Wolff, 2017; in total about 36,000 schools are registered in Germany).

School type / CLIL model	(1) and (2)	(3)
primary schools	287 (including 113 private schools)	unknown
secondary schools	1,500	140(+)
vocational schools	120(+)	60(+)

Roughly 6% of all schools in Germany have some CLIL option as the data indicates. Looking at secondary schools, the proportion there is much higher and can be estimated to 25%-30% (Statista, 2021).⁷

According to the KMK (2013), the full canon of subjects in German schools is represented within these numbers, although the official statistics do not include any information about their detailed quantitative representation. Krechel (2013) writes that CLIL is mostly held side-by-side with FL classes, with an addition or change of subjects. Geography, Biology, History and Politics, according to him, are the most common subjects. Furthermore, he points out the remarkable growth of singular CLIL modules within regular lessons, because small units can be flexibly integrated into the regular curriculum without major bureaucratic hurdles.

As no information on the subject representation of CLIL was available in other secondary sources, information was sought directly from the administration, but limited to *Gymnasiums* of the State of Hesse where the empirical research of *Chapters V & VI* was located. Yet the research turned out to be very complicated. The most reliable data also indicating subject representation was only available from a minor interpellation of the political opposition in 2014 towards the State Ministry for Education.⁸ It is worth mentioning that the data does not differentiate whether it comes from a full bilingual school or just from singular modules, so whether such classes include a few lessons within a year or are held continuously. Thus, *Table 2* only includes the simple quantitative representation

---

[7] This statistics of Wolff (2017) lists 3,124 *Gymnasien* (secondary grammar schools with in general stronger students than average) and 3,234 other secondary schools (integrative and cooperative comprehensive schools) in Germany for the year of 2013. This totals 6,358 secondary schools. If we take this as baseline, about 27% of all schools have some CLIL provision. In accordance with statistical error tolerance, we can carefully infer an estimate of 25%-30%.

[8] See Degen, Barth, and Yüksel (2014). It needs to be said that the data does not appear as fully consistent and thus has a *caveat*, because during 2014, the year of the source, the school reform of cutting secondary schooling from nine to eight years *("G9 nach G8")*, by now again repealed, was in due progress. A cross check revealed that some schools were double listed with G8 and G9 and counted twice. Hence, the data was compiled to best knowledge.

of subject-based CLIL, limited to 186 Gymnasiums (Hessisches Statistisches Landesamt, 2020).

Table 2 shows the subject representation of CLIL in *Gymnasiums* in the State of Hesse. As a considerable number of those schools offers CLIL in multiple subjects (no matter if singular modules fully established branches within bilingual schools), the total sum of CLIL classes in the table, of course, is higher than 45.

Language / subject	History	Geography	Biology	Politics & Economics	Chemistry	Math	Physics	Ethics, Religion or Philosophy	Music	Physical Education
English	27	14	13	11	3	1	1	3	1	1
French	4	-	-	5	-	-	-	-	-	-
Italian	1	1	-	-	-	1	1	-	-	-

In total, 45 *Gymnasiums* with CLIL were identified, a share of around 24%, and thus comparable with the federal representation of *Table 1*. Mainly, in line with Krechel (2013), the biggest representation can be found with History, Geography, Biology and Politics & Economics with English as L2, respectively. Surprisingly, CLIL in Politics & Economics in English is only ranked 4th, not even close to the establishment of CLIL in History in English, and even after Geography (although hardly taught in school at all anymore) and Biology as a life science.

The tedious research of the numbers for at least providing some overview on the *status quo* of CLIL in schools, insinuates the obstacles for its induction and development across the country. It can be carefully claimed that such subject representation within the State of Hesse can be, with a reasonable error margin, extrapolated to the Federal level, although education in Germany is governed independently by the Federal States (*Länder*). As a matter of fact, a formal federal strategy has to date never been outlined, because the KMK cannot issue official directives and decrees but only recommendations to the *Länder*. Notwithstanding, after more than three decades of *bilingualer Sachfachunterricht* in Germany, the KMK officially acknowledged the success of CLIL in Germany and explicitly recommended an active expansion (KMK, 2006). According to the KMK, CLIL classes in Germany are defined as subject lessons with the majority of the content taught in a FL, taking the same broad approach as Eurydice.

Their status report update seven years later further amplifies earlier recommendations (KMK, 2013). The given appraisal of Germany's CLIL experience happened in close reference to the large-scale *Deutsch Englisch Schülerleistungen International* (DESI — Assessment of Student Achievements in German and English as a FL, in the following referred to as *"DESI study"*), which will be dealt with more in extent while investigating competence development in CLIL during a later part of this chapter. The KMK highlights that certain competence areas of students in 9th grade CLIL classes are on average comparable with 11th grade students of non-CLIL contexts. Furthermore, motivation towards English as a subject has significantly increased because the language is applied in context and filled with meaning, fully in line with the communicative turn in modern language teaching, instead of primarily focusing on grammar and form. Finally, the KMK repudiates worries about a negative impact on subject learning. Teachers and students concluded in surveys that the increase in active participation as well as the application of new and innovative didactical concepts and teaching methods, triggering deeper cognitive processes, result in more sustainable learning experiences.

Although the genuine evaluation of the KMK rather includes a cheerleading tone about Germany's CLIL experience, the report once again failed to substantially define any clear-cut roadmap about the *how*. No federal strategies have thus far been outlined on how to implement CLIL across Germany for various types of students and in teacher training. There are no recommendations on how programs should be structured, not to speak about any comprehensive or subject-based CLIL didactics, respectively. The idea what CLIL means in detail has not been explicitly incorporated into the report. Taking a closer look helps to identify official aims and didactical principles, providing more information about *bilingualer Sachfachunterricht* as the German interpretation of CLIL.

Aims and Didactical Principles of CLIL in Germany

The Administrative Side

Aims and didactical principles have so far only been vaguely defined by the KMK (2013, pp. 7-8). The main proclaimed aim is the equipollent subject discourse competence in L2 and L1, implicating the bilingual surplus out of administrative eyes. Elements of both subject and language didactics compose the didactical principles of CLIL, underscoring its interdisciplinary nature. But unambiguously, the report points out the primacy of the subject in terms of assessment, designating the FL as mere vehicle, in line with the modern *"message before accuracy"* principle. The paradox is, however, that assessment is required to be in L2, putting the FL again indirectly into the foreground.

Different subject traditions, according to the KMK, are the reason why no comprehensive CLIL didactics yet exists. Single subject didactics, in turn, are defined as desiderata within the report. A missed opportunity indeed for the general and subject development of CLIL was the failure to define educational standards for CLIL classes in the wake of the paradigm shift from input- to competence-based education. Basically, again to provide the example of the State of Hesse, the new core curricula for the canon of subjects do nowhere include any singular and exclusive document defining general aims for CLIL lessons. To escalate this account, looking at the subject side paints a similar picture: CLIL is only marginally mentioned within the curricula of the single subjects. To provide the example of the core curriculum for Politics & Economics: one small section just states that CLIL classes are permitted in accordance with the same aims and subject competences of monolingual L1 classes (Hessisches Kultusministerium, 2016, pp. 20-21), without indicating any merits from tailored CLIL didactics in that subject. A-level *(Abitur)* exams, however, are explicitly possible in CLIL classes with the same standards as with L1 lessons. But major courses *(Leistungskurse)* cannot be elected. In other words, the recommended subject-specific particularities for CLIL lessons by the KMK, indicating subject specific bilingual surpluses, have to date not been specified.

CLIL Research in Germany

Preponderant support for the further development of CLIL in 'no man's land', having grown organically and bottom-up from the grassroots, has always been coming from academia. Debates about aims and didactical principles of CLIL were launched accordingly in a gradual attempt to theorize and professionalize CLIL after its perceived success. Theory generation as the first step to create an academic research field, for being able to understand the novel dynamics of this new and, as a matter of fact, revolutionary style of teaching, became necessary.

Taking about theory generation, Doff (2010), in the introduction to her edited volume, looks back at CLIL research of the past and concludes that the German CLIL discourse has been transforming tremendously during the preceding decade. Not only has CLIL become a major field of inquiry of FL learning, but also a *"theoretical turn"* (Doff, 2010, p. 12) can be discerned. Here, mainly the work of Breidbach (2007) is paramount. More than 30 years of *bilingualer Sachfachunterricht* within a more experimental space prompted his first effort to contribute towards to a comprehensive and reflexive didactic for CLIL lessons. His book contains a large set of insights from the past three decades of CLIL in Germany. Structured like an encyclopedia, a succinct overview is given not only about the state of the German discourse, but also on controversies having evolved from the myriad areas affected by CLIL (e.g., culture, education in general etc.). A proposition for clear-cut CLIL didactics, not to speak about any roadmap for its further development, however, is not given. Rather, the main achievement is the location of CLIL within important general educational debates as well as the theoretical preparation of CLIL for further development of general and subject-specific didactics.

Describing CLIL as a research field and categorizing the growing number of studies into larger subfields helps to extract more succinct didactical principles that had developed. Looking back at more than four decades of CLIL in Germany, Diehr and Rumlich (2021) divide aims of CLIL, juxtaposed with its didactical principles, into four main areas: (1) cultural education, (2) language diversity, (3) subject learning and (4) language learning. The following part will be structured accordingly to map today's overall field of investigation and to elucidate didactical principles of CLIL in Germany. The focus will be set on the latter three fields, because they are most relevant for *Chapters III-VI*, while cultural education, closely related to language *per se*, rather plays an auxiliary role. Cultural education, however, as the main foundational idea of thought, is an apt introductory starting point to understand the transformation of CLIL practice and research over the years.

Cultural Education: CLIL's Historical Starting Point in Germany

Coming from the French bicultural tradition, cultural education was used to define CLIL in earlier times and has ever since been decisive for CLIL practice in schools and academia's early discourse. Hallet's (1998, p. 119) bilingual triangle was one of the first and most seminal attempts to model the aims of early German CLIL in general, highlighting the bilingual surplus beyond equipollent language proficiency in two languages *(see Figure 2)*. Borrowing from intercultural FL didactics, he highlights the cultural dimension during learning the subject's content matter in a FL. Importantly, he pinpoints towards globalization and intercommunity. The bilingual triangle inevitably had the strongest impact on early policy planning as well as on teacher education and has been included in many official briefings by ministries or educational institutions. Hallet's work, as it can be argued, launched efforts for inductive theory generation to emerge CLIL's full potential also in other areas beyond culture, particularly related to the natural proximity to language learning.

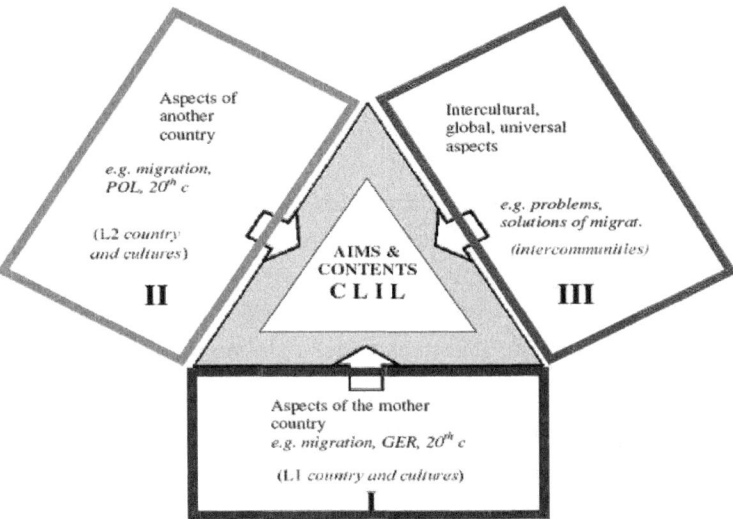

Figure 2 shows Hallet's (1998, p. 119) bilingual triangle (translated version provided by Javorčíková & Zelenková, 2019, p. 29).

For understanding how cultural education had initially influenced the 'first wave of CLIL in Germany', and how research has successively transformed into further fields of investigation, attention should be given to the edited volume of Bach and Niemeier (2010), which in the retrospect has gained the status of a classical compendium. Initially published in 2000, the 5th edition was released only ten years later. It also includes a comprehensive bibliography of research on CLIL during Germany in the period of 1996-2010 (Breidbach, Lütge, Osterhage, & Prüfer, 2010), mapping the research landscape in Germany. In the introduction to the volume, Bach (2010) delineates the historical and contemporary state of CLIL practice and research in Germany. Most importantly, in the wake of European unity, he highlights young people's quest to live in and shape a multilingual and multicultural society, and to achieve multilingual and multicultural competences accordingly during their schooling. According to him, CLIL with its interdisciplinary nature and its innovative methodological framework can be designated to be the panacea for developing multicultural competences, in accordance with the given bilingual triangle.

The cultural approach, having shaped CLIL classrooms from its onset, is closely juxtaposed with multilingual didactics and the promotion of language diversity *per se*, as he argues. This includes not only other FLs as target language, but also a growing array of students' diverging L1s (of course including the school language German), recognizing the manifestation of multilingualism worldwide and the active promotion of language diversity within the European society. Accordingly, the next part of the literature review focuses on CLIL and multilingualism as a proxy for upgrading the original bicultural approach to a more global, if not cosmopolitan level. Very contemporary developments coming from the broad field of multilingualism in education, mainly from contexts outside Germany, will be presented at first, as they had an inevitable impact on the local German landscape. It is an attempt to open the black box of one of the most controversial methodological controversies, namely the question about the role of L1 during CLIL classes. A short description of the relevance for research in general will be followed by the application within Germany mainly within the last decade.

Challenging Immersion in Recognition of the Multilingual Speaker: Language Diversity with CLIL

Close to the middle of the last decade, May (2014) and Conteh and Meier (2014) independently published each an edited volume with a stunning similarity in the book title: both titles contained *"The multilingual turn"*. With multilingual turn, a general trend in language education is described in a nutshell, namely paying tribute to the intensified appearance of multilingualism in the world, as a more common practice, more or less also as a way of life. Importantly, and as consequence of this new trend, Meier (2017, p. 132), recapturing the legacy of both publications, sees the *"need to break down boundaries between language education for so-called 'minority' and 'majority' language populations [...]"*. Such developments are concomitant with the worldwide decay of monolingualism, nowadays gradually defining an exception, especially but not exclusively with younger generations. The essays in the volume mainly include different scenarios of multilingualism from around the globe, in the daily life as well as in pedagogical settings.

To amplify the magnitude of the multilingual turn, at first a recent proposition of Dewaele (2017) will be considered. He points out that in linguistic studies dealing with multilingualism, often the concept of the native *vs.* the non-native speaker is being used. Following Cook's (1999, 2001) earlier suggestion on recognizing multicompetences, academic work about language education nowadays mostly uses the abbreviated version of L1 *vs.* L2. The L1 symbolizes the native language, whereby L2 composes the less dominant language, either a SL or FL. Dewaele (2017), in turn, first praising Cook for his groundbreaking work, reacts to the exponential increase in multilingualism ever since, the recognition of the multilingual turn and the synchronic decease of monolingualism. This also applies to countries with *de jure* only one official language (e.g., Germany,[9] France, USA). In short, he suggests, amidst the multilingual reality of the world and different proficiency levels in traditional L1, L2, L3 ... Lx (other less dominant languages) categories, instead only to speak about L1 and Lx. L1 is the most dominant language, or the language with the highest competence level, whereas the proficiency in Lx is comparatively lower. Speakers' competences in more than two languages within one singular mental lexicon are recognized. He recommends shunning the concept of 'nativeness' accordingly, paying tribute to multicompetences of speakers in different Lxs beside L1.

The recognition of the multilingual speaker, more or less a logical consequence of the declared multilingual turn, of course had an impact on new approaches towards language education. Meier (2017, p. 152) concludes that *"more research is urgently required to inform the development of user-friendly pedagogic guidance as part of more critical, crosscurricular, context-sensitive and flexible multilingual pedagogies."* Of course, as it may come into mind immediately, this

---

[9] Even a *de jure* monolingual country like Germany has recognized minority languages in certain regions, like Danish (close to the border with Denmark) and Sorbian (in East Germany, close to the Polish borderland). They only affect about 0,2% of the population, in turn fully proficient in German.

supports any multilingual CLIL-based approach. Recognizing the plurilingual speaker as the given norm, but similarly felicitating language diversity, seems a logical and appropriate pathway. Speakers shuttling and switching between language within and across conversations, and by times even mixing languages during single sentences, have become a common phenomenon.[10] This quite recent global academic trend also had a strong impact on CLIL research in Germany, with German as dominant L1, however an increase of other L1s, as it will be shown shortly after the next section.

The Last Decade: L1 Use with Code-switching, Translanguaging, and Intercomprehension

Code-switching as such, as Cook's (2001) multicompetence-based approach teaches, builds on the existence of two separate grammars. Consolidating some of his previous and other seminal work, he defines code-switching and advocates a pedagogical classroom use as follows:

> The uniqueness of L2 use is seen in code-switching where both languages are simultaneously on-line. One language is switched to another according to speech function, rules of discourse, and syntactic properties of the sentence (Cook, 1996). Code-switching is a highly skilled activity — the 'bilingual mode' of language in which L1 and L2 are used simultaneously, rather than the 'monolingual mode' in which they are used separately (Grosjean, 1989). It forms part of normal L2 use in many L2 situations outside the classroom where both participants share two languages. Such non-compartmentalized L2 use may well be part of the external L2 goals of teaching and could form part of the classroom if not nipped in the bud. (p. 408)

Cook endeavors to import natural code-switching, in accordance with Auer's (1984, 1998) seminal description, into an integrated classroom pedagogy for FL learning. Such notion from its basic assumptions has been challenged — or further developed — recently.

---

[10] At this point, the following must be clarified. All the papers assembling the following chapters were, as common, submitted and published before writing this introduction and discussion. They still refer to the 'classical L1 and L2 distinction', instead of L1 and Lx as suggested by Dewaele (2017). To avoid confusion, L1 and L2 will be used within this present chapter as well. Future research undertakings might consider an adaption accordingly.

Allegedly, the most prominent work in contemporary contexts has been published by García (2009). She promulgated translanguaging as a concept challenging language boundaries, arguing that humans have one single mental lexicon instead of separate mental lexica in L1, L2, L3 … Lx. This means that a naturally mixed language use by multilingual speakers as a more fluid practice is common, engendering different levels of bilingual dynamism. García defines translanguaging as:

> […] the act performed by bilinguals of accessing different linguistic features or various modes of what are described as autonomous languages, in order to maximize communicative potential. It is an approach to bilingualism that is centered, not on languages as has often been the case, but on the practices of bilinguals that are readily observable in order to make sense of their multilingual worlds. (p. 140)

The dynamics translanguaging has been emitting for global research on multilingualism are enormous. At present, it seems that basically everyone is speaking about it. A more detailed discussion and practical application, in a modified form, will follow in *Chapter V*,[11] also discussing recent work on CLIL and translanguaging from non-German contexts. At this place, the literature review will be limited to its application within the German context.

Finally, to elucidate the dynamics of new approaches to multilingual education, short reference to intercomprehension, with beginning relevance also for FL teaching in English, will be taken. Intercomprehension is defined as *"a form of communication in which each person uses his or her own language and understands that of the other"* (Doyé, 2005, p. 7). It originates from comparative didactics of Romanic languages, recognizing similarities in vocabulary and grammar. Entering this term in any university online public access catalog (OPAC) of any library will bring up a significant number with reference to that linguistic field. Importantly, the EU strongly

---

[11] There, also its merits and shortcomings for contexts with L2 as FL, as opposed to García's SL context, is discussed. Sequences of fieldwork in a German classroom are reconstructed by a thick description (Geertz, 1973), with the endeavor of making the concept applicable for FL teaching.

recommends intercomprehension as a language learning methodology, because it is also directed at preserving language diversity (Dzik, 2020). Due to its general methodological outline as well as students' multilingual ability to meaning making while comparing and contrasting their languages of proficiency, it does not come as a surprise that studies dealing with FL teaching beyond the Romanic canon are beginning to gradually use its methods and merits for their respective field. However, the focus of *Chapters III-VI* was not set on intercomprehehsion but solely on translanguaging and code-switching. Thus, intercomprehension only finds marginal mention in this chapter, for demonstrating how permeable and dynamic the field of multilingualism in FL teaching has become as a whole. A directed focus on intercomprehension would define an interesting future project, also in conjunction with translanguaging. The next part focuses on the question whether L1 use should become a didactical principle in German CLIL classrooms, to recognize the dynamics of the multilingual turn also in Germany and to emerge any possible bilingual surplus from the abovementioned novel concepts and approaches to multilingual education.

L1 Use as Didactical Principle?

The question about the bilingual surplus leads to another and very general issue yet unresolved deserving mention at first. A strong bias towards regarding CLIL as a modern approach towards FL learning, with a tendency of *"additive late partial immersion"* (Breidbach & Viebrock, 2012, p. 6) has been prevailing in teaching practice. As a matter of fact, most CLIL courses in Germany are *de facto* taught monolingually, with L2 declared as the primary working language (Diehr, 2012; Frisch, 2016). No didactical guidelines *how* L1 should be integrated have thus far been provided. Once again turning to the administrative side, the KMK (2013, p. 8) does not provide any official regulation and only recommends L1 German solely for mediating terminology and vocabulary, albeit without any more succinct pedagogical rule. Indeed, reluctance to declare L1 as an official didactical principle can be discerned, because L1's role mainly for scaffolding purposes is noted. On the opposite side, an equipollent language proficiency is a declared target. Not only does this stand in sharp contrast with the altered conceptualization of CLIL by Dalton-Puffer and Smit (2013) and Lasagabaster and Sierra (2010), distinguishing CLIL from immersion. But also, Diehr (2012) argues that CLIL classes taught in L2 do not automatically ensure an equivalent language proficiency in L1 and L2, as empirical evidence does not exist yet. And lastly, L1 German might be a scaffold for some students. Realizing that L1 can also be a language other than German for many students, there is a lot of work necessary to recognize the multilingual reality in present-day classrooms. *Chapter III* is much more detailed here, while *Chapter V* goes even beyond the scaffolding function and presents teaching methods incorporating L1 for other purposes as well, also for stronger student types.

It should not come as a surprise that, regardless of the multilingual turn, *"the role and function of L1 is subject to fierce debate"* (Frisch, 2016, p. 85), although genealogically the original name *bilingualer Sachfachunterricht* already implies bilingualism to be an inherent part of the approach. Defining L1 use as didactical principle is a controversial statement, because L1 use resembles a debate on fundamental principles in CLIL and FL teaching *per se*. Originally from FL teaching, one of the most classical accounts comes from Butzkamm (1973) with his idea of *"enlightened monolingualism [aufgeklärte Einsprachigkeit]"*. CLIL as an inherent multilingual pedagogy, in his eyes, serves as the apt space to render his initial position into reality. He (with Caldwell, 2009) juxtaposed the overall paradigm shift to more communicative-oriented teaching, i.e., more focus on message than on form, with identifying CLIL as an opportunity and expressing a plea for a real bilingual approach with L1 use. Among others, in a recent publication, he puts recommendations towards cooperative working forward, like the sandwich technique and mother tongue mirroring (Butzkamm & Lynch, 2018), yet only very vaguely.

Vollmer (2006) goes even further. His suggestion to foster LAC (reminding of the initial British experience), even includes languages beyond German across the full canon of subjects, to promote overall language learning and language sensitivity within a multilingual framework. Directly for CLIL, he demonstrates efforts to consolidate the merits of both immersion and multilingualism, arguing for the promotion of subject-based discourse competences. He reasons his position with the achievements of immersion in the last decades but joins the idea to proceed with multilingualism as a resource, in line with Bach (2010), who, as it was shown at the beginning of this section, sees CLIL as a harbinger of multilingual didactics towards the promotion of language diversity within Europe. In more detail, Vollmer recommends diverse language islands as a possible scaffold in the form of judicious and principled L1 use. Finally, he calls for much more research within this broad field of study (Vollmer, 2010).

On a conceptual basis, Diehr (2016) modelled a mental lexicon, in accordance with most recent studies about bilingualism, serving as a valuable tool for planning interventions into bilingual classrooms with the goal of increasing bilingual dynamism and improving dual language proficiency. Mainly she distinguishes between BICS and CALP, all stored within one single mental lexicon comprising several language memories. However, learning subject concepts in L2 does not necessarily have to be followed by an equal development in L1, as similar language equivalences are rather the exception than the rule (see also Diehr & Rumlich, 2021). This model questions García's (2009) abovementioned model that does not explicitly distinguish between different languages. On the contrary, it declares natural translanguaging in FL environments as rather uncommon. Explicit language work and goals with clear language and discourse policies during CLIL classes are recommended, as already demanded earlier by Dalton-Puffer (2007) in her study with 14 Austrian CLIL classrooms over a period of 40 lessons. A compromise would be calling for a pre-step supporting students in the initial mastering of language thresholds, before translanguaging practices become easier, if not natural, making them a daily norm in German CLIL classrooms. Diehr's (2016) model serves as an appropriate starting point for investigating and developing teaching methods towards enabling multilingual CLIL in German classrooms, e.g., applied by Scholl and Schmelter (2021) to conceptually develop mediation tasks for CLIL lessons in History. Mediation *per se* is, as to say, more than translation but not as much as translanguaging. It is an interesting tool to develop and gradually increase bilingual dynamism, realizing separate language systems within the frame of one bilingual mental lexicon, also considering cultural particularities on the metalevel.

This overall debate will be contextualized more in detail within a global context in *Chapter V*, because multilingual education *per se* is a result of globalization. The migration and movement of people, as a matter of fact, has always been one of the most popular fields of research and investigation. The long and short of it is that L1 use can yet not be defined as an official didactical principle, because practice paints a different picture, and administrative recommendations are too vague. Against this background, the end of this chapter will formulate more comprehensive RDs. Moreover, since L1 of students does not necessarily have to equal the school language German, the momentum of the controversy is propelled by new dynamics in classrooms, often with multiple L1s. *Chapter III & V* consider this development.

Now, as next step for attaining a more nuanced idea about Germany's CLIL experience, studies dealing with language and subject competence development will be examined. They also reveal more about what needs to be done for the further development of CLIL, both with a subject focus as well as more in general, recognizing its holistic nature. The primary focus is directed towards evaluative large-scale studies, whereby smaller studies with direct reference to subsequent chapters will find mention.

Competence Development in CLIL

As it was shown, official EU accounts state that CLIL is mainly seen as an approach to promote plurilingualism among EU citizens. At the same time, the primacy of the subject, upgrading the subject curricula's contents, has crystalized as well. Thus, one can appraise that CLIL has 'a subject focus with a language bias'. On the one side, it is possible to flip that coin between content and language competences. But on the other side, the bottom line is that the same coin is still being held in the hand. The overall cheerleading tone of CLIL and its language learning prospects, juxtaposed with its potential as an answer towards our 21st century challenges, resembles a romance story. Can one kill two birds with one stone with equal subject and language competences development?

The question what unifies CLIL lessons across all subjects, also explaining the overall worldwide success of bilingual education, remains an important field of inquiry. With CLIL, mainly the question of scaffolding, *"the temporary assistance by which a teacher helps a learner know how to do something that the learner will later be able to complete a similar task alone"* (Gibbons, 2015, p. 16), has throughout been placed at the center of attention, keeping in mind that the main working language is L2 as FL. Thürmann (2010), appreciating the more reformist and student-centered approach of CLIL for efficient learning, demands a distinctive bilingual method with integrated scaffolding for students' learning success. Mainly, his suggestions focus on equipping students with learner autonomy and tailored learning environments, providing affordances and promoting learner strategies to develop study skills. Among those, the role of visualizations, linguistic support and code-switching are listed. Similarly, and thus directly supporting the paradigm of defining L1 as didactic principle for CLIL classes, Wolff (2009) adds discourse strategies of teachers and students within a social interaction classroom framework as desired feature, as commonly applied in modern communicative FL classrooms. Importantly, he pleas, in accordance with the philosophy of CLIL, to see subject and content as one integrated concept during teaching and to initiate more diversified, sophisticated and autonomous learning environments, enabling students to process the content in a FL. Earlier, he had identified CLIL's distinguished potential for language sensitive classes, since language as a whole occupies a pivotal function (Wolff, 2003). This is a further argument for Diehr's (2016) model of the mental lexicon and her corresponding urge to plan classroom interventions with the goal to develop and evaluate bilingual teaching methods. The given accounts illustrate how CLIL unites reformist initiatives to focus on student-centered learning, as opposed to more traditional modes of classroom instruction. In the later proceeding of this chapter, the relevance of these overall principles for subject didactics of CLIL in Politics & Economics should become obvious.

Two central questions deserve deeper attention: (1) how do language and (2) subject competences develop through CLIL? Evidence from research so far looks, to frame it positively, quite promising. The focus is set, where possible, on bigger investigations, with a few exceptions. Apart from the widely noticed DESI study, two of the documents used as catalogues for identifying relevant studies were the literature reviews by Ohlberger and Wegner (2018) as well as by Breidbach and Viebrock (2012).

Language Competence

In the aftermath of Germany's *"PISA shock"* in 2000 (Grek, 2009, p. 30), the DESI study surveyed the competence development of almost N=11,000 9th graders in German and English in the schoolyear 2003-2004. DESI was composed of a triangulated test design, including pre/post-competence testing, interviews and videography analysis. The students who took part at DESI were spread nationwide across 219 schools. 40 schools had a CLIL program that was investigated with separate categories by DESI. Representativeness is claimed due to the overall complex design, also controlling third variables like social background data. DESI concluded that CLIL students have stronger competences in both English and German as compared to students from regular classes. Their advantage in listening can be attributed to be two years ahead of the monolingual comparison group. Further advantages in specified sub-competences (e.g., reading, grammar and writing) could be discerned as well, underlining the arguments for an expansion of CLIL in Germany (Klieme et al., 2006).[12]

The DEZIBEL study was located in a school with an optional branch of CLIL in English. It comprises a comparative setting of N=180 students at the age of 16. Zydatiß (2007) investigated both language and subject competence development. Data was triangulated with different tests as well as questionnaires, individual and

---

[12] DESI's results can be interpreted as a proxy for an improvement in language awareness. They were later confirmed by Fehling (2008) who was able to provide statistical evidence for such increase among CLIL students in her study across three *Gymnasiums* in the state of Hesse.

group interviews. Zydatiß was able to present statistically significant evidence that CLIL students' language competence is far more progressed than that of the monolingual control group. DEZIBEL also surveyed the development of subject competences which will be discussed the next section.

The results of DEZIBEL were by no means singular. During comparisons studies among federal states in Germany under the auspices of the *Institute for Educational Quality Improvement (IQB)*, Köller, Leucht, and Pant (2012) compared n=346 lower secondary CLIL students with n=9,251 non-CLIL students in terms of their reading and listening comprehension skills. Like with the DESI study, background and other third variables were controlled. Students from the CLIL cohort significantly achieved higher scores than their non-CLIL counterparts, confirming DESI and DEZIBEL.[13]

Similar as DEZIBEL, the COMBIH study of Dallinger, Jonkmann, Hollm, and Fiege (2016) looked at both language and content. The authors divided three groups of N=1,806 8th grade students: a CLIL-group (n=703), non-CLIL students of the same school (n=659) and students of a non-CLIL school (n=444). Mainly, a standardized pre/post-test at the beginning and the end of the school year was used. The results are not as positive as those of DESI and DEZIBEL, but at least confirm the advantage in listening comprehension, whereas with the C-Test results of all groups, the CLIL group has a marginal, statistically yet insignificant advantages.

---

[13] The results from both large-scale investigations are in accordance Heine (2010), a comparative study of 10th grade CLIL students in English and Geography (n=13) with non-CLIL students (n=7). She concludes that using L2 positively affects learning and understanding the subject matter, as cognitive processing and the genesis of knowledge structures was observed to be intensified. Admittedly, Heine's (2010) sample is relatively small, compared to the other studies presented thus far. However, it deserves mention, not only because the study is highly relevant in the given context, but also because it shows that single case initiatives generate inestimable detail knowledge and can later be adjoined by large-scale and more evaluative undertakings for, *inter alia*, validation and generalization purposes.

Students' subjective beliefs, self-concepts as well as their available personal resources in many cases have an effect on the development of both language and subject competences, however only shown by a handful of studies in the German CLIL discourse. For delineating the affective dimension, and this includes, *inter alia,* motivation, emotions etc., the three following studies are directly related to *Chapter III* onwards. As result of a smaller, AR-based initiative with single case studies, Abendroth-Timmer (2007) concludes that singular and timely-limited CLIL modules in English, French and Spanish mostly have a positive effect on students' language learning motivation and thus also on overall learning outcomes, both language and subject-based. This explicitly also includes students who are not necessarily smart language learners but more motivated by the content, according to their own self-assessment (see also Breidbach & Viebrock, 2012). The author clearly recommends the induction of such CLIL modules within an overall multilingual framework, also to consider different L1s as students' inherent resources. Her findings are of particular interest in the sense that they roughly define different student types and affordances, with diverging needs and resources as basis for expanding CLIL's success beyond a privileged elite. This point has a particular relevance for *Chapter V*.

Whereas the most recent COMBIH study paints a slightly different picture, the appraisal of Germany's CLIL experience is quite promising. This can be carefully explained with a CLIL-related *"creaming effect"* (Küppers & Trautmann, 2013; Rumlich, 2016), for which empirical evidence was given. After a two-year large-scale undertaking of N=1,000 students from 6th to 8th grade, Rumlich (2016) concludes that many of the felicitating findings of earlier CLIL research might have been biased by preselection of students, also partly explaining the 'hype about CLIL'. Although positive effects of CLIL on language competences seem to be likely, they can strongly vary in context, whereby Rumlich concludes that many other factors beyond CLIL's role as a modern and innovative pedagogy need to be taken into consideration as well. This includes, *inter alia,* sociodemographic factors like family background. But also, as Abendroth-Timmer (2007) had earlier shown with her comparatively smaller initiative, factors like students self-concept, juxtaposed with motivational and other affective factors, need to be considered. Rumlich's results were later in principle confirmed by Fleckenstein, Preusler, and Möller (2021) with N=617 students at the dual-immersion State European School Berlin, controlled with a representative sample of N=2,672 students from schools without CLIL. The authors of the study provide statistical evidence that the *"basking in reflected glory-effect,"* highlighting the positive self-concept and motivation of CLIL students, has a significant influence on the mostly positive development of language competence concluded by most studies. However, the authors also point out, just as Rumlich (2016), that it remains unclear whether the general success of CLIL can be attributed to the preselection of students with a positive self-concept, often related to higher social status, or the quality of each particular CLIL program. Thus, it needs to be appraised that the full truth about language competence development yet remains concealed. In other words, this calls for further, mainly large-scale investigation into as many different programs and contexts as possible, for assembling the mosaic of CLIL in Germany into one entity while isolating as many correlating third variables as possible. But on the positive side, as also the COMBIH study was able to conclude, no negative effect of CLIL on FL competences was ever detected, mitigating concerns about possible negative subject outcomes of CLIL.

Subject Competence

Subject competence evaluation of CLIL did not deserve as much attention as language-related issues, as CLIL research still mainly remains a field of language departments. DEZIBEL and COMBIH as two comparatively large studies also dealt with subject-related questions. Both studies, in short, conclude that students of CLIL programs do not encounter any disadvantage in their subject competence development as compared to monolingually taught students. In other words, no negative effect was detected, countering popular criticism of mainly subject-based didactics that the language threshold is an obstacle for subject learning *per se* (see the edited book of Bosenius, Donnerstag, & Rohde, 2007, looking at

CLIL from the side of subject didactics, where such general claims have been neutrally described). These two studies were, to my knowledge, the only large-scale undertakings of subject-based CLIL in Germany.

Other early studies have a remarkable representation from life and natural sciences, mostly very contextual and on single case basis with smaller samples. The general absence of large-scale undertakings can be again explained with the language bias in CLIL research, located within language and not within subject departments of universities. For more comprehensive subject-based accounts, researchers would need the relevant subject knowledge and its didactic principles on top, which is less required with CLIL research related to language issues only. Subject-related issues are thus mainly left to the initiative of researchers with interest and knowledge in real content and subject integration, in accordance with CLIL's original philosophy. In this vein, Wolff (2009) explicitly sets such research as goal for the future.

Two studies, delineating two diametrically opposite outcomes, will be introduced as exemplary for a number of other studies that followed similar contextual patterns. Bonnet (2004), in a micro analysis of one CLIL 10th grade in chemistry and one control group of non-CLIL students, comes to a similar result like DEZIBEL and COMBIH, concluding that the CALP of both groups is quite similar. For biology, Osterhage (2009), using test items of the program for international student assessment (PISA) from the natural science section with a comparatively large population of nine 9th grades from three different schools for his study, has even more optimistic results. He found out that CLIL students are far better achievers than non-CLIL students. However, he admits that third variables could not be isolated and controlled, questioning whether these results can be generalized at all or only apply to the context setting.

Such scarce accounts, all very contextualized, paint the picture for any representative evidence for subject competences in CLIL. As an appraisal, so far at least no study has shown any adverse effect of CLIL on subject competences, mitigating concerns that classes in a FL impair subject learning *per se*. Heine (2013) offers a very promising outlook, reasoning deeper concentration and cognitive processes of classes in an FL.[14] But it remains unknown whether the creaming effect could also apply to these selected examples. This should motivate research on didactical principles and methods in accordance with the *how* question as first step, as also highlighted with language competences in the previous section. Making CLIL available to a broader student population with new and innovative teaching methods, and thereafter evaluating them as well as investigating CLIL with a larger set of comparison groups, could lead to further overall improvements.

What remains remarkable, however, is that none of the large-scale includes any subject focus on Politics & Economics. Therefore, the next part will now try to find the needle in the German haystack, with first delineating arguments why this underrepresentation of this globalization-related subject should find more consideration by research and practice.

CLIL in Politics & Economics

The introduction to this chapter revealed CLIL's strong nexus to globalization. Globalization-related content *per se* characterizes the curriculum of Politics & Economics as subject, amplifying the special role of a CLIL approach, especially with English, the global *lingua franca* of the 21st century, as L2. On the one side, a proper use of English by individuals often relates to personal success within a globally interconnected and market-led business world. On the other side, to look beyond the challenge of individualism, ESD can be located within this subject, making it even more relevant for learners and their future 21st century challenges. Climate change and sustainability, poverty & inequality or living together in unity and diversity serve as examples for debates with a global dimension. Yet by the world population, they are mainly negotiated locally, often more informally in—both official and unofficial—surrounding languages. A multilingual approach to ESD and persisting 21st century challenges and opportunities, without any doubt,

---

[14] See also *supra fn.* 13 of this chapter.

recognizes and acknowledges language diversity. G*local*ization (Robertson, 1990; Robertson, 1995), also in education, is the buzzword to feed this idea conceptually. The theoretical framework of *Chapter III* mainly focuses on this topic.

CLIL's potential in Politics & Economics with English as L2 as a door opener to globalization, in a world strongly interacting through global mobility, and increasingly in the digital space, hardly needs further explanation. In an encyclopedia, I illustrated this train of thought more in detail (Nijhawan, 2020a). Furthermore, *Chapter III* with its conceptual account argues for the transformative power of cosmopolitan classroom *glocalities* with a multilingual approach to CLIL in Politics & Economics. It also looks at L1 beyond the official school language German, because an increasing number of students has other home languages, leading to an increase of different L1 in classrooms. Therefore, that chapter swifts from bi- to 'real multilingualism', meaning the inclusion of more than two languages in CLIL.

Subject didactics juxtaposed with results of general CLIL and non-CLIL research, respectively, delivers many interesting arguments for the realization of subject competence aims by the means of multilingual CLIL. Some of them deserve special attention.

Didactical Arguments for CLIL in Politics & Economics

Multiperspectivity

Using a FL during learning processes facilitates perspective changes. The FL, a mirror of history and culture, helps to compare own L1 perspectives with new perspectives (Albrecht & Böing, 2010; Leisen, 2015). This is further amplified by English as language of globalization, also relating to Hallet's (1998) idea of intercommunity as well as to Coyle et al. (2010) with their 4Cs framework. Looking further, English au pair with a multilingual language use promotes cosmopolitanism with its roots in *unity in diversity*. The access to a wider variety of teaching material, and especially online sources, broadens the horizon and transforms the world into a microcosm. Again, *Chapter III* will be more specific here.

Breaking News and Originality

Globalization with its nexus to Politics & Economics is a fast-moving day-to-day business. Many seminal articles and other sources directed towards a global audience are published in English. The access to multilingual pool of material from other regions even expands this general reach and should be seamlessly made accessible to students. Didactically pre-structured material from genuine sources thus often supersedes the value of textbooks that may be outdated (see for example Gaster, 1990; Rösler & Schart, 2016; Teixeira, 2018). The value of digital sources, like videos available in the internet, for FL learning with a strong subject focus has been strongly advocated for teaching practice (Thaler, 2008). This enables solutions and political judgments beyond and independent of regional, cultural and language boundaries, as harbinger of cosmopolitan education. In turn, access to genuine sources can prevent to fall into the fake news trap in a mainly digital world of (dis)information (Bundeszentrale für politische Bildung, 2020).

Study and Problem-solving Skills

The section on CLIL's didactical principles highlighted the importance of study skills and learner autonomy. The surplus in cognitive and thus deep-working processes supports the genesis of well-structured sustainable working and problem-solving strategies. From a neuroscientific perspective, the deeper level of cognitive processing is a valid explanation (Böttger, 2016). This explicitly also includes—against popular claims and perceptions—weaker students (Steinlen & Piske, 2016). Schwab, Keßler, and Hollm (2014) were able to demonstrate at the example of one modern secondary school *(Hauptschule)* that also non-intellectually gifted learners can enjoy CLIL's distinguished benefits as much as the traditionally elite student population in the past. CLIL prepares students not only for their future careers, but also for *"democratic and decisive processes of society and culture in their future"* (Hallet, 2007, p. 97; my translation). The juncture of content and language and their real integration into one holistic concept, facilitated by CLIL's general language sensitive approach, au pair with the aforementioned focus on learner autonomy and method variation (Wolff, 2003, 2009), thus seamlessly concurs with general subject didactics of Politics & Economics as well. The central pillars comprise better general education, problem-solving skills, and cross-cultural discourse competence (Bonnet, Breidbach, & Hallet, 2013, p. 180). In the end, it is concordant with the proposed *Education for Democratic Citizenship and Human Rights* of the Council of Europe (2010) as well as with ESD.

Empathy

FL lessons facilitate perspective changes (Kramsch, 1993, 1998) and thus have a positive effect on empathy. Sociology argues that empathy requires positive emotions (Davis, 2006). Engartner and Nijhawan (2019) highlighted why emotions in the subject Politics & Economics are instrumental for successful learning outcomes, as opposed to popular beliefs of rationality in the form of *homo economicus* as nostrum. For ESD, sustainability didactics and cosmopolitanism, emotions are an inestimable resource (Flam & King, 2005; Korte, 2015; Skutnabb-Kangas, Phillipson, & Mohanty, 2009; Stein-Smith, 2016). An example is climate change, hardly felt immediately by local students in the global north, being geographically far away from hazardous areas mainly in the global south. Rather often, the quotidian disastrous news in the world still composes a remote phenomenon for many students. In turn, links across and knowledge about the world are brought along more often, providing inestimable classroom resources. This also includes multilingual sources with various L1 beyond the school language German, pedagogically and systematically embedded through bilingual education. *Chapter VI* will highlight in how far multilingual education and the interplay of emotions and rationality, caused by an alternated L1/L2 use, can provide as a didactical panacea for ESD.

Against the given arguments why Politics & Economics comes close to a natural subject area for CLIL, two issues remain remarkable: at first, the representation of CLIL classes in Politics & Economics is quite modest, as the earlier provided numbers of the State of Hesse suggest. Furthermore, CLIL research with that subject focus is hardly visible. Before designing any conceptual account for

CLIL in Politics & Economics, the next section deals with the few studies in that area.

Locating CLIL Research in Politics & Economics

Reviewing academic contributions to CLIL with a subject focus in Politics & Economics has proven to be a complicated task. Ohlberger and Wegner's (2018) catalogue, not including any single reference to CLIL in Politics & Economics, insinuates the given deficit. Earlier, Breidbach et al. (2010) assembled a comprehensive bibliography of research in all kinds of different CLIL areas since 1996. Section 3.4 (pp. 256-259) contains all surveyed work that had been published with L2 English, combined from the subjects History and Politics (without Economics[15]). In total, 30 publications are listed. Out of these, 29 are from history, the remaining from Politics (Ditze, 2007, with a teaching example about the classics of philosophy). A similar overview for History and Politics, without particular reference to L2 English, is part of the bibliography's general section (pp. 216-219). In total, 20 publications are listed. Also here, only three publications are from Politics, none of them empirical. They appear rather modest as compared to 17 publications from CLIL in History. The lack of research in CLIL in Politics & Economics is striking against the delineated merits of this subject given in the preceding section.

A comprehensive literature review of CLIL in Germany by Breidbach and Viebrock (2012), mapping the German CLIL discourse mainly within the preceding decade, helps to partly unlock the black box. Generally speaking, they point out that CLIL as research field has diversified in the course of years, with an ongoing trend, but also point out the aforementioned language bias. They group their review into five categories. Among those, *"Classroom discourse, subject-specific knowledge and cognitive 'peculiarities' of CLIL learning"* show the required subject focus.

It can already be noted that subject-specific studies only contain a minority of CLIL investigations within the overall review,

---

[15] Economics as separate or combined category does not find mention at all within the bibliography.

mainly showing categories of general, language and culture-related CLIL research. On the positive side, the first comprehensive study of CLIL in Politics & Economics, namely Wegner's[16] (2011) *"micro-analysis of one Grade seven and one Grade nine CLIL class in Politics (in a German Realschule)"*, finds ample space within their subject-review section. From triangulated data consisting of observations, interviews and group discussions with students and teachers (exact number of the students in the two learning groups unknown; 8 teachers), she concludes by naming a vast deficit, namely the absence of *"viable classroom practice"*, as Breidbach and Viebrock (2012, p. 11) summarize in a nutshell. It deserves to look closer at this study, as the overall outline and the findings have a direct reference to all following chapters.

Wegner (2011) echoes the nonavailability of interdisciplinary and empirical studies of CLIL in Politics & Economics. At first, she establishes a very clear and nuanced framework of Politics & Economics as subject with global relevance, linked to CLIL in English as global *lingua franca*. Thereafter, she defends the explorative framework of her single case study in a thitherto uninvestigated area. Her criticism towards common research in CLIL states that everyday practices and learning processes are not being reconstructed for understanding natural dynamics in classrooms, a symptom of a lack of interest in further developing education *per se*. Highlighting the merits of CLIL in Politics & Economics, she reasons the close nexus of political education with CLIL classes in English in an age of globalization, with the potential for global democracy and world citizenship. Fully in line with the 4Cs framework by Coyle et al. (2010), her theoretical justification builds upon the ability to take part in discourses for developing political maturity, to ultimately take action in a transnational world society as individuals with fluid identities. The center of gravity of her study are the students as main stakeholders. Their participatory role during the research defines the core of her data, helping readers to reconstruct quotidian discourses and dynamics in CLIL-centered classes, also

---

[16] It should be noted that Wegner (2011) is not the same author as with Ohlberger and Wegner (2018).

exploring in deep the didactical side of CLIL in Politics & Economics. In a nutshell, she pleas for putting students' perspectives into the center of attention. Democratic arrangements in CLIL classes in Politics & Economics and beyond, in the sense of a pedagogical double-decker, provide for democratic and cosmopolitan education. She calls for further explorative and participatory investigations, especially with reference to defining learning processes and making the perspectives of learners visible. Although Wegner's study is contextualized in an environment with weaker students, a medium degree of generality is likely due to the rich and triangulated data.

Surprisingly, Wegner's contribution from 2011 constitutes the only empirical investigation dealing with subject prospects of Politics & Economics in CLIL, till date never followed by similar research ventures. Thus, research still resides in its infancy as she had already concluded in 2011. One can witness that most CLIL research is still mainly related to language. Even studies with a subject focus rather deal with language acquisition or practical teaching examples. So far, speaking of available main pillars of CLIL didactics for Politics & Economics is very remote, similar as with other CLIL subjects.

Lastly, one very recent publication deserves mention, although it is not a classical study but mainly directed towards meeting practitioners' resonating demands for 'ready-to-teach' concepts. Klewitz (2019) published his book *"Bilingualer Sachfachunterricht in Politik & Wirtschaft"*.[17] It is a positive example to use more recent research in multilingualism for sketching a CLIL didactics in Politics & Economics. His main goal is the incorporation of such up-to-date approaches into practical teaching material. The motivation, same as with Wegner (2011), is to balance subject and

---

[17] His more comprehensive CLIL didactics, with a focus on the social sciences (Klewitz, 2021), has been published very recently. It will be interesting to combine any pathways from his work with that of *Chapter III-VI* of this monograph.

language, respectively, in line with CLIL's original idea of thought, namely the amalgam of subject and language.[18]

This section contained quite a desperate attempt to compose a literature review of CLIL in Politics & Economics. As nothing significantly has changed since Wegner's (2011) study, the next section focuses on the conceptual and empirical work required, respectively.

Catching up with the Global Community: Much Work to Do in Germany

The title of this section already suggests that a lot of work is waiting for those scholars who earmark to use some of the comparatively new concepts for the integration of multilingualism into CLIL classrooms. Thus, to narrow this part of the literature review, sources from the last decade find mention at first, because, as shown above, translanguaging found global attention mainly during that time. Intercomprehension, in turn, has been mainly applied within Romanic languages, to my knowledge without consideration during CLIL teaching so far.

Deutsch (2016), after an analysis of official EU policy briefings, provides evidence that CLIL is officially recommended as a roadmap for the promotion of multilingualism. The empirical part of her study investigates whether this policy recommendation has already left traces in school practice. Her study with triangulated data, consisting of interviews with n=21 teachers and n=75 students with CLIL in History L2 French, challenges theory with reality. The EU approach is not seen affirmatively by the stakeholders themselves. On the contrary, CLIL classes are mainly taught immersive in the FL, confirming the analysis about CLIL in Germany from the

---

[18] Noteworthy is his very close cross-reference to the work of the *PolE-CulE* project he uses to build his arguments. I met the author at one of *PolECulE*'s teacher training sessions I led myself. In a longer personal conversation after the session and thereafter, we discussed many of the issues I had presented, which he correspondingly also referenced in his book. *PolECulE*'s approach which had already received brief mention in the introduction of *Chapter I*, will be delineated more in detail at the end of this chapter.

beginning of this chapter. Any reference to L1 is often perceived as disturbing practice for the declared goal of L2 learning, she concludes, which means that multilingual approaches do not constitute the reality of CLIL practice. Intercomprehension, despite the EU recommendation, is not practiced at all, as the *status quo* from her sample suggests. Overall, without tailored multilingual pedagogies, as she concludes on a more general level, the EU Commission's goals and objectives to promote multilingualism in Europe are nearly out of reach. This point needs memorization for the remainder of the chapter.

Apart from Deutsch's contribution, the research with a direct nexus of CLIL and the three afore listed multilingual methods in Germany provided unsuccessful. Combining CLIL with code-switching, translanguaging and intercomprehension in various academic metasearch engines yielded nil results. A desperate attempt to nevertheless find relevant sources prompted to search for such concepts in traditional FL teaching. A comprehensive bibliography of the DGFF for the years 2014-2019 was retrieved (Informationszentrum für Fremdsprachenforschung der Philipps-Universität Marburg, 2019). However, one needs to note that the focus area was limited to digitalization, in line with the annual congress topic of 2019. Noteworthy, after closer investigation, it can be inferred that the threshold for being classified as a relevant source for the congress topic was very low. Indeed, 'something digital', instead of a comprehensive digital pedagogy, sufficed to be qualified for the designated criteria. To give examples, the requirement was met when sources were available online or digitalized, when students were simply sitting in front of a computer, or simply using videos. So, unsurprisingly, in total the bibliography comprises 266 pages, also including short abstracts. Arguably, it contains a high degree of representation of current issues in FL teaching, realizing the ongoing digitalization hype even before the Corona pandemics. It provided as insightful to attain an overview about the broad and dynamic field of FL teaching, because such a comprehensive up-to-date assembly of sources was not available elsewhere.

The bibliography contains index words covering a broad array of relevant topics. Two simple procedures were used for retrieving a mirror of the state of the field: (1) looking for relevant keywords in the index, and (2) a full text search to find out whether these words nevertheless find mention with auxiliary importance in the abstracts beyond the indexing. The full text search mainly indicated appearances beyond. *Table 3* shows the results of the research. Double appearances have only been counted within the first column.

Table 3 contains the results of a keyword and full text search of relevant keywords in Breidbach et al. (2010).

Keyword (*in original German*; if two are given as with the first, they were listed as separate categories)	# of studies listed in the index	# of studies having the word included in title or abstract (*optional extra*)
Bilingualer Sachfachunterricht (bilingual education) and CLIL	7	1
Mehrsprachigkeit (multilingualism)	21	-
Mehrsprachigkeitsdidaktik (multilingual education)	3	-
Code-switching	4	-
Translanguaging	- (*not indexed at all*)	1
Interkomprehensation (intercomprehension)	2	-

As anticipated, no intersection of CLIL (or *bilingualer Sachfachunterricht*) with any of the index categories below could be found, which implies that CLIL and multilingualism are still seen as quite distinct. Especially the representation of the last three categories remains on a very low level. Surprisingly, translanguaging as concept, despite the international hype, has not been chosen as index category at all.

However, the edited book of Bündgens-Kosten and Elsner (2018b) has a significant match with, *inter alia*, three of the categories, namely code-switching, intercomprehension and multilingualism. But, as already indicated with the quantitative representation in *Table 3*, there is no reference to CLIL. The volume as such contains several accounts dealing with code-switching and intercomprehension but not translanguaging, as the titles of the essays already indicate. As alternatives from direct CLIL contexts could not be retrieved, the reference to studies in FL teaching nevertheless serves the purpose for mapping the overall research field of multilingualism.

The editors' introduction on multilingual computer assisted language learning (MCALL) sketches the research field and the use of multilingual methods in general (Bündgens-Kosten & Elsner, 2018a). They argue for pedagogical L1 use mainly beyond a simple fallback option (e.g., time-saving or disciplinary action), in order to enable real multilingual language teaching as a norm. Dedicating a closer look on the essays delivers interesting insights into multilingualism in German FL teaching contexts.

Most interesting at first is the editors' own article on awareness of multilingual resources (Elsner & Bündgens-Kosten, 2018, with receptive code-switching already given in the title). The authors explain the complexity to integrate concepts for the promotion of plurilingualism within German schools, although such reaction would be desired, following the increase of students with different L1 and thus of language diversity in classrooms. The *"Fostering multiliteracy through multilingual talking books"* (MuViT) project at Goethe University Frankfurt under the leadership of Elsner, funded by the European Commission during the period of 2011-2014, was the first attempt to react towards this need. The authors declare the proximity of their approach with the pedagogical idea of translanguaging by García and Sylvan (2011). Concluding, they explicitly recommend content integration into language learning for supporting natural translanguaging by multilingual learners. In MuViT, this was facilitated by integrating five different languages (German, English, Russian, Spanish and Turkish) into multimodal, digital storybooks. As opposed to regular classroom environments, students are actively offered the initiation of receptive code-switching with the stories in any of the named languages. Thus, an exposition to their L1 from home as well as the official school language German, here the SL, is possible. The approach also caters students' affordances, develops meta-awareness of languages and supports to enter, from code-switching as a starting point, into both pedagogical and natural translanguaging practices, respectively. Intercomprehension through comparing languages is promoted as well.

In 2013, the *"Bedeutung der Erst- und Zweitsprache bei Lernern der Fremdsprache Englisch für die kooperative Bearbeitung textbasierter Lernaufgaben"* (LIKE) project, using the MuViT application within FL environments, was launched under the same project leadership. One of the conclusions is the assumption of the authors that *"a maximum of affordances of multilingual language use has a positive impact on pupils' learning processes in English"* (Elsner & Bündgens-Kosten, 2018, p. 67). This means that multilingual students apply individual strategies during both SL and FL learning. This includes not only code-switching but very likely also translanguaging and intercomprehension, because these three concepts cannot always be easily discerned. Cutting it to the chase, preexisting linguistic knowledge cater the students with resources for positive learning outcomes, their conclusion reads.

As translanguaging in German academia *per se* seems to be an exception, the attention will be directed towards Lohe (2018), who wrote a monograph within the MuViT project, examining this very approach in more detail. She found out that young multilingual learners equipped with affordances are indeed able to engage in natural translanguaging strategies. Most importantly, she developed the concept of translanguage awareness, and recommends substituting the well-known concept of language awareness as consequence of the new multilingual settings in schools today. She defines as following:

> Language awareness of multilingual individuals [including those of learners with very basic and rudimentary competences], possessing knowledge and awareness in language and languages, and are able to interconnect and increase their knowledge, and furthermore are equipped with the ability to use such knowledge in a varied and dynamic way in different situations (Lohe, 2017, p. 199). (Lohe, 2018, p. 288; my translation, approved by the author)

She concludes that even very basic and rudimentary language skills of students in other languages suffice for being able to enter translanguaging strategies. This finding is seminal, because it insinuates that clear-cut pedagogies can facilitate translanguaging also for FL learning in CLIL contexts after passing a certain language threshold. Looking ahead at this point, *Chapter V* discusses this question in extent, and will suggest adapting the concept of translanguaging to Trans-FL.

As the empirical work with translanguaging in *Chapter V* constitutes one of the main focuses of this monograph, the search was extended to non-FL teaching contexts dealing with education in general. Very recently, Schastak (2020) published his book on peer interaction in an elementary school with bilingually raised German-Turkish students. While this study does not come from a direct CLIL or FL teaching context *per se* but rather deals with a cohort of bilingually raised children and their natural translanguaging practices in elementary school, it nevertheless has some interesting findings. From his mixed-method study with an analysis of peer-learning arrangements, he concludes with reference to code-switching and translanguaging that teachers should design tasks in accordance with the theory of translanguaging as well as with empirical literature to natural bilingualism in educational contexts. On a rudimental basis, he recommends certain multilingual methods, like sequenced code-switching as well as language comparisons within such set of tasks. Finally, he concludes that comparative metalinguistic reflection and bilingual analysis of the content leads to higher cognitive processing and thus to a progressed degree of elaboration.

Schastak (2020) recommends integrating L1 into tasks and teaching practices. However, his recommendations are not very detailed. Thus, amidst this deficit, a direct intervention into natural learning environments for investigating possible translanguaging strategies with L1 use becomes necessary, in order to design possible pedagogies and tasks. Moreover, his research cannot be applied to FL contexts. He himself admits that bilingual pedagogies would be difficult to integrate with *"limited and suboptimal resources of regular schools"* (originally: *"[…] begrenzten und suboptimalen Ressourcen der Regelschule […]"*; p. 415, my translation). Moreover, he highlights the role of cooperative learning arrangements as well as of teacher training in this context. Intercomprehension as a method of

FL learning does not find single mention within his entire book. This does not surprise, because the outset of his study is very contextual, which, it needs to be mentioned clearly, limits the application of his study. Many of his findings beyond translanguaging nevertheless have the potential for generalization, as his field work has a robust theoretical underpinning, same as with his data analysis and discussion. It would exceed the scope to mention all of it at this place.

Lastly, the very recently published handbook of multilingualism and education (originally *Handbuch Mehrsprachigkeit und Bildung*, edited by Gogolin, Hansen, McMonagle, & Rauch, 2020) includes interesting insights into the current state of multilingual teaching in German schools. The 373 pages volume consists of 55 different contributions, subdivided in seven thematic chapters. Such volumes normally also mirror important areas of contemporary academic discourses. *Table 4* shows the results of a full text search about how many of the 55 articles use certain terms with the same terms as with the DGFF bibliography (obviously without multilingualism, as that is what the book is about).

Table 4 contains the results of a keyword and full text search of relevant keywords in Gogolin et al. (2020).

Search term	# of studies retrieved
Bilingualer Sachfachunterricht (bilingual education)	3 (two intersections with CLIL)
CLIL	3 (see above)
Code-switching	13
Translanguaging	7
Interkomprehensation (intercomprehension)	3

It can be discerned that some concepts have been applied more often lately, but still considerably little. Almost 25% of the articles refer to code-switching. Again, intercomprehension has only been used three times, including by Bündgens-Kosten (2020), one of the authors of the MCALL article above, writing about the achievement of the project. Translanguaging appears in seven articles, but mostly marginally with the classical reference to García, and nothing noteworthy beyond. As a noticeable exception, there is one short article explicitly focusing on translanguaging, presented henceforward.

Gantefort (2020) reviews how translanguaging can be used within multilingual contexts in German classrooms. Reasoning the theory in line with its origins, he clarifies that languages in schools should not be separated but facilitate the emergence of learners' full linguistic repertoire, very similar to the LAC idea. Furthermore he states that any language use should develop naturally without any artificial infliction, to provide ample room for a natural negotiation of meaning among students. His account in general mirrors the state of translanguaging in German schools. Research in this area is completely in its beginnings.

First of all, it becomes obvious that students' L1 as potential resource has so far not sufficiently been explored. More importantly, however, as the short analysis of his article quite explicitly shows, translanguaging again only refers to its more natural form in SL contexts, with students already being equipped with a considerable repertoire in the relevant languages. What can be inferred once again is that no one has actually clear-cut methodological advice *how* to implement translanguaging effectively into classrooms, not to speak about making it available for FL teaching environments. And for FL teaching, as Gantefort's (2020) short survey shows, one would need a significantly adapted and altered concept. To reiterate, *Chapter V* presents Trans-FL as developed concept, to make the merits of translanguaging as a distinctive approach also available for FL learning, offering a possible remedy for this deficit.

The review will be closed here. With reference to CLIL and multilingualism, the accounts available are at most modest. The field of FL learning and multilingualism has interesting approaches that serve as inspiration for the development of multilingual approaches with L1 use in CLIL. This means that a lot of conceptual work will be required at first, before developing clear-cut multilingual methods for intervention into CLIL, as the research deficits of the last part will elucidate. Before, a turn to the work of the *PolE-CulE* project within the reviewed research fields will be presented.

What Conceptual Work Has Already Been Done?

Within the *PolECule* project of Goethe University Frankfurt, a conceptual framework for CLIL classes in Politics & Economics was developed amidst its absence from the administrative side (printed in Elsner et al., 2019, reasoning the idea of thought and exemplified at a teaching example for its implementation).[19] With Hallet's (1998, p. 119) bilingual triangle as a starting point, the original bicultural approach from the history of CLIL in Germany was amended. Here, an even more global approach was taken, in line with the introductory narrative and the 4Cs framework (Coyle et al., 2010), recognizing the potential of Politics & Economics for globalization-related classes. Realizing the magnitude of our global challenges, juxtaposed with the increase in English L1 speakers mainly in post-colonial nations outside the *"inner circle"* (Kachru, 1992), the project focused on, to say it very generally, the promotion of global democracy and ESD, concomitantly embracing unity in diversity.

Overall, the triangle of Politics, Economics & Culture was put into the foreground, meaning to address many of the deficits as described in this chapter. Language, placed within the middle of the triangle, is not only seen as a mere vehicle but postulated as central for the achievement of subject competences, fully integrating it with content. Culture was added as addendum, not only to highlight that 'language is culture' and influences decisions, according to the famous Sapir-Whorf-

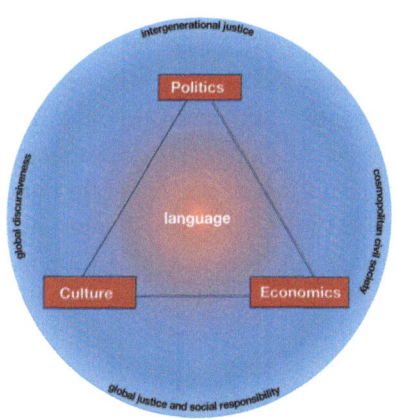

Figure 3 shows the triangle of Politics, Economics & Culture, with language in the center, and the general aims framing the model (Elsner et al., 2019, p. 9).

---

[19] A review of the conceptual framework has been published by Wohnig (2020).

Hypothesis (Whorf, 1956). But also, it was meant to reiterate the global dimension and the dynamism of change, integrating human perspectives directly into the framework and amplifying its humanist approach. Ultimately, culture foregrounds feel for language *(Sprachgefühl)* as the center of gravity within subject-based classes. The overall aim is to prepare students for participating in discourses on, *inter alia*, global justice and social responsibility within a democratic and cosmopolitan civil society, as *Figure 3* shows. The triangle's idea of thought is fully in line with Wegner's (2011) aforementioned conceptual ideas for CLIL classes in Politics & Economics as apt space for the promotion of a framework for democratic education in a global and cosmopolitan world. *Chapter III* will argue in detail why such approach, besides L2 English as global *lingua franca*, should ideally even be multilingual, with different L1s of students beyond the official school language German.[20]

Global discursiveness defines the fulcrum of the model. This train of thought has been translated into global discourse competence as the main interdisciplinary bilingual competence aim for CLIL classes in Politics & Economics, comprising L2 and L1. The combination of six competence fields in *Figure 4* includes at first the four main official competence aims from the subject Politics & Economics (i.e., analysis, judgment, agency and methodology). The two remaining competences borrowed from Modern Languages round the competence model out and define the integrated and functional use of L1 as instrumental for CLIL classes. Inter- and transcultural literacy mainly envisages the understanding of alternative perspectives, along with the ability to feel unity in diversity,

---

[20] Aims and objectives of the conceptual framework have been defined in accordance with Siege and Schreiber (2016), who initially developed the framework for global development for German schools under the auspices of the United Nations Educational, Scientific and Cultural Organization (UNESCO). In the preface, the German Minister for Economic Cooperation and Development states that *"students should acquire central competences, like the ability to enter perspective changes, to develop empathy in order to consider themselves as global citizens in one world"* (Siege & Schreiber, 2016, p. 9, my translation). In 2022, the new edition will be published, amongst others, with my authorship.

togetherness and develop empathy. Realizing the merits of intercultural and language didactics, FL and communicative competence includes the ability to communicate in L2 and L1 on an equal level. Here, the conceptual pillars for L1 use in CLIL have been set.

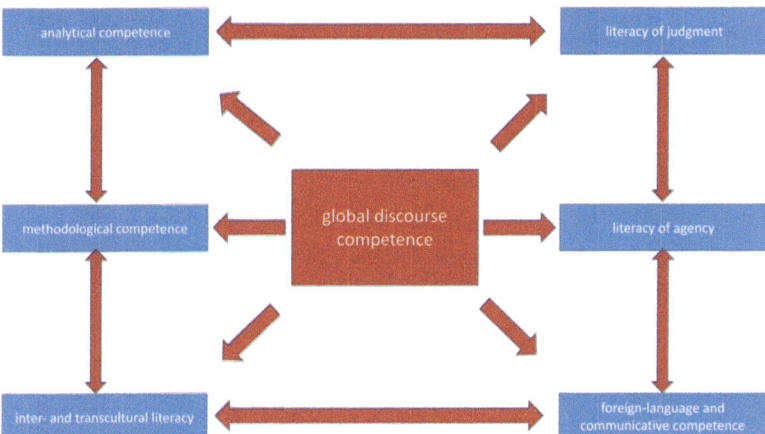

Figure 4 The competence model with the global discourse competence at the center (Elsner et al., 2019, p. 24).

The end of the chapter reveals that a major part of the intervention into my natural classroom environment dealt with developing and exploring methods for judicious and principled L1 use in CLIL in Politics & Economics, in line with new approaches to multilingualism in schools like particularly code-switching and translanguaging.

What Work Needs to Be Done Now?

So far, the content side, especially in Politics & Economics — despite its unique potential for CLIL — has not received the attention by research it actually deserves. This calls for more groundwork beyond the presented conceptual framework, also as a first milestone towards the desired subject-based CLIL didactics for Politics & Economics. As a first step, the nexus of language and globalization, one of the main characteristics defining the merits of CLIL in Politics & Economics, has been intermingled within the given conceptual framework. Here, the integrated nature of CLIL, with a fusion of content and subject, should be kept in the foreground.

Clearer pedagogical pillars about L1 use to ultimately decentralize globalization and multilingualism into classrooms need specification. Against this background, L1 use is often suggested. The foundations of the conceptual framework serve to examine teaching methods in order to engender a full CALP (Cummins, 1979, 1981) in both L2 and L1. Any guideline needs to look beyond mere repetition of the content and vocabulary lists, rather building on code-switching and translanguaging (Frisch, 2016) within an affordance-based and differentiated pedagogical framework. In a short literature review, Frisch (2016) groups dynamic bilingualism into five additional functions, namely *cognitive, communicative, time-saving, affective* and *pedagogical*. In the end, she recommends developing teaching and learning methods as well as tasks that more closely define a *systematic* and *reflected* use of L1. To turn it around and make it clearer, arbitrary L1 use, simple word lists, or vocabulary dropping, cannot be the solution (see also Diehr, 2016). In a nutshell, *how* L1 can be systematically integrated into CLIL deserves empirical investigation. Once clearer pedagogical suggestions have been designed, *if* questions can be investigated separately, with more comparative and large-scale methodologies. The outlook of the last *Chapter VII* will be more detailed here.

A functional use of L1, as I will suggest in *Chapter V*, can have further synergetic effects even beyond mere dual language proficiency, mainly for different student types. When developing conceptual and theoretical accounts as basis for classroom interventions, auxiliary questions need to be contemplated as well. It has not been explored so far whether L1 integration has any influence on teaching and learning outcomes from the subject side. *Chapter VI* looks at the affective dimension in line with the presented competence model for Politics & Economics. It investigates in how far judgments might be positively influenced by L1 integration for achieving the overarching goals of the competence model.

Transition to *Chapters III-VI*

This section finally captures many of the open issues of this and prepares for the research of the following chapters. In general, the research was planned along the lines of the competence model. Designing pathways *how* CLIL teaching in Politics & Economics can be effectively implemented into practice, realizing its potential both on the subject and language side, generally characterizes the research. To reiterate without ambiguity, *if*-questions, providing for full-fledged research initiatives investigating whether global discourse competence as main competence aim *can* be achieved with CLIL in Politics & Economics, would rather be a venture for a large research project, but only after *how*-questions will have been clarified. This would need a bigger team, more schools for comparative work, and more sophisticated tools and resources in terms of quantitative inquiry. As it became visible from the introduction in *Chapter I*, all chapters of this monograph are a result of a single research initiative by me, within my everyday natural teaching environment. An intervention with specific tools that distract regular teaching or create an artificial, lab-like environment, was not intended, but – to again repeat my purpose – the *how* question as well as involving and integrating stakeholders into design and action on eye level.

The following part presents the RDs in line with this chapter, investigated in *Chapters III–VI*, respectively. The original titles as initially published have been used as headings.[21] All chapters except *Chapter IV* (DBAR as research method) have climate change as *leitmotif*, serving as a proxy for today's 21st century challenges.

---

[21] On purpose, I will not present the detailed research questions (RQ) here but sketch the overall research deficits. RQ as such have been succinctly developed in *Chapters IV & V*, partly repetitive with the theory here, albeit on a more global level. The research aims there are described within the 'classical paper structure of journals.

RD 1 (*Chapter III*, conceptual):

The Construction of *Cosmopolitan Glocalities* in Secondary Classrooms through Content and Language Integrated Learning (CLIL) in the Social Sciences[22]

It was shown that it is not really possible to speak about an own field of research in CLIL in Politics & Economics yet. The last part of this section sketched a conceptual framework with a competence model for CLIL in Politics & Economics as response towards the given deficits, laying the groundwork for establishing a subject-based CLIL didactics. However, many questions about detailed principles of the conceptual framework still remain unanswered, and thus require more due diligence from the theoretical side. In general, this refers to questions in how far CLIL in Politics & Economics can serve as instrumental for a new literacy towards addressing our 21st challenges in our classrooms, also in line with Wegner's (2011) study, making her global and cosmopolitan approach tangible. The role of multilingualism and L1, juxtaposed with subject aims, defines the center of gravity.

Chapter III thus takes a more conceptual approach. It specifies this framework towards the construction of cosmopolitan classroom *glocalities* with a tailored CLIL pedagogy, also as a positive and resource-driven response to an increase of transculturality and hybridity in our society. It emulates the real world with different spheres of global discourses, encompassing a variety of languages. Furthermore, multilingualism is juxtaposed with cosmopolitanism from below, indigenously inherent and homegrown among many students nowadays. Importantly, *Chapter III* suggests that L1 beyond the official school language German should find consideration in CLIL teaching as well. In order to abate claims that the admittedly quixotic approach reads nicely on paper only, data from #*climonomics*, a multilingual EU parliamentary debate on combatting climate change with almost 200 students and 28 languages

---

[22] See *supra fn.* 1 of this chapter.

represented, is presented.[23] It not only demonstrates how such full-fledged multilingual concept can be the result of such sophisticated pedagogy but also provides evidence that ambitious and innovation-driven ideas really work in practice. Hence, *Chapter III* is a bit more than just conceptual, as #*climonomics* already provides insights how global discourse competence can be practically fostered with an appropriate design.

RD 2 (*Chapter IV*, methodological):

Bridging the gap between theory and practice with 'design-based action research'

Chapter IV justifies the method of the empirical classroom research in *Chapters V & VII*, respectively. Both chapters proceed with the same research method and use the same data pool from the same intervention. They have an abridged methodological description there as well, contextualizing it with the given RQs.

One more train of thought deserves explicit mention. Under 'regular circumstances', a RQ and the extended research outline determines the research method. The nature of this research initiative within the *PolECulE* project from its beginning was highly characterized by the masterplan to define new and innovative pathways, defining best practices for theory-practice cooperation, as the introduction of *Chapter I* elucidated. Intervention within my regular classroom teaching thus always constituted a desired procedure. Under such arrangement, the research method is *de facto* 'upgraded' to be au pair with the content, also explaining the appearance of DBAR in the title of this monograph. Hence, it will also be reflected within the final discussion. Especially *Chapter V* echoes many voices from academia for engaging into explorative classroom research within the given areas of CLIL and translanguaging.

---

[23] Information about #*climonomics*, including a promotional video, the comprehensive media portfolio and the digital conference reader, can be accessed here: http://polecule.com/2019/11/05/climonomics-so-lief-unsere-mehrsprachige-eu-klimakonferenz-fuer-schuelerinnen-25-10-2019/.

The research project is explorative in nature and endeavors further theory generation in two comparatively neglected areas. These include modeling CLIL in terms of an interplay of L2 with L1 *(Chapter V)* as well as the influence of such altered language use on learning outcomes in Politics & Economics with its close nexus to globalization and the resulting 21st challenges and opportunities *(Chapter VI)*. As this study desires the development and evaluation of teaching methods and teaching material in a real-life classroom context, design and action synchronically are required. In the introduction, it was shown that such hybrid practice is embodied in me as TR. The research framework is directed towards triggering and investigating learning processes in the natural classroom environment in its very core. Thus, the overall study sees itself in the traditions of AR as well as DBR. They are something like fraternal twins due to the commonalities of the approaches. *In Chapter IV*, I discussed and suggested to combine both methods within the single framework of DBAR for transforming practical knowledge and subjective theories of teaching into scientific theories that 'really work', ultimately bridging the gap between theory and practice. There, I also argue for an inclusion of DBAR into teacher training. DBAR in *Chapter IV* is exemplified with a past project about what *The Simpsons* can contribute to CLIL in Politics & Economics (Nijhawan, 2013, 2014).

The demand for such research, supporting scientific theory generation in a thitherto rather unexplored area, is in extent contextualized in *Chapter V*, establishing the link of CLIL with translanguaging. It conglomerates a significantly high and repetitive number of voices calling for such interventionalist procedure into natural learning environments in line with the given RQs there. In light of democratization of classroom environments and, in this case, for providing students with a voice within the discourse, mutual undertakings of stakeholders should serve as a best practice example for future research, in accordance with Wegner (2011), who, as it was shown, pleaded for recognizing students' perspectives as the center of gravity during CLIL classes. *Chapters V & VI* reveal more about the collaborative team structure at school and university.

RD 3 (*Chapter V*, empirical with language focus):

Translanguaging... or 'trans-foreign-languaging'? A comprehensive CLIL teaching model with judicious and principled L1 use

The literature review about multilingualism, and mainly L1 use in CLIL and beyond, revealed that there is a lot of work to be done to define practical teaching methods, paying tribute to the growth of innovative approaches. As translanguaging at present is *en vogue*, how does this refer to L2 in CLIL as FL? Thus, it must be questioned whether code-switching and translanguaging as pedagogical approaches work without significant pedagogical adaptations, because translanguaging *per se* mainly refers to natural language use with L1 and L2 as SL. In line with Frisch (2016), *Chapter V* explores a functional L1 use and clearly define phases and sequences for the systematic and reflective use of L1.

So far clear-cut methods have not been designed and tested for L1 use in CLIL. A single and universal panacea for any such definition of phases for L1 and L2 seems unlikely because the learning level of students as well as their self-concept varies. Furthermore, pointing back to Abendroth-Timmer (2007) and her classification of students either motivated by content or language, different learner types call for individual and differentiated solutions to cater manifold learning needs of a nowadays superdiverse student population. Consequently, the goal was set to develop a comprehensive CLIL teaching model with judicious and principled L1 use, providing affordances to different student types as well as differentiated pedagogies to generate different intensities of dynamic bilingualism. Translanguaging, *Chapter V* reveals, was modified to Trans-FL for facilitating FL learning. In short, translanguaging and code-switching are blended, to make L1 use a profit-driven venture, nonetheless maintaining the FL learning objective (Lasagabaster, 2013).

Also in line with *Chapter IV*, the nature of this research, juxtaposed with RD 2, suggests that an inclusion of all the stakeholders is necessary in order to answer the RQs. This, of course, includes the students' voice at its core. Scenes from a Thick Description

(Geertz, 1973) make them visible, mirroring overall classroom dynamics. As Wegner (2011) concludes for CLIL in Politics & Economics, learners' expectations should be integrated into classroom practices (see also Breidbach & Viebrock, 2012). Moreover, also in line with Wegner's (2011) opinion, the semester topic *Economics & Environment* already amplifies the need for a global cosmopolitan approach as harbinger of global citizenship and sustainable development, also supporting the given conceptual framework *cum* competence model. Thus, classes have been planned accordingly using her general framework. As it has also been indicated with RD 2, this approach is also in accordance with the overall idea of *PolECule* to transform CLIL teaching in Politics & Economics into education for democratic and cosmopolitan citizenship (see also Osler & Starkey, 2015) as well as ESD. It is not wrong to say that this chapter constitutes, more or less, the heartbeat of the research. The reason is that, on the one side, it delivers an empirical account of the conceptual work (RD 1) as well as of the research method (RD 2). Moreover, it also defines a viable procedure for exploring benefits of L1 use for the achievement subject-competences in Politics & Economics in general, as an eye-leveled byproduct, as RD 4 shows now.

RD 4 (*Chapter VI*, empirical with subject focus):

Finding the 'perfect equilibrium of emotional and rational learning' in Content and Language Integrated Learning (CLIL) in the social sciences

Academic inquiry about subject-based questions, especially with reference to Politics & Economics, is modest and plays only a marginal role within CLIL as a stratified research field at its best. As stated above, L1 use and *Chapter V* was initially, quite from the beginning, considered as the heartbeat of this monograph. But the suggestive nature of the competence model with its innovative 21st century literacy approach for ESD earmarks at actively promoting a 'better world' and sustainable future. It prompts to partly abate the language bias and synchronically take a subject focus. This ultimately unites content and language, in accordance with Wolff's

(2011) insistent demand. *Chapter VI* contributes with empirical work towards a CLIL didactics in Politics & Economics in line with the idea of thought of general didactics in Politics & Economics, juxtaposed with FL didactics. To say it short, political maturity was defined in Germany as a timeless goal in political education after the end of the Second World War. Accordingly, the demand for didactical instruments becomes obvious to promote transnational forms of democracy in a globalized world.

Recently, ESD and students' agency, realizing the dimension of our 21st century challenges, has been obtaining significant attention in Germany (and beyond). RD 1 in *Chapter III* already focused on a new literacy approach, realizing the positive role cosmopolitanism can occupy in constructed classroom *glocalities*. Furthermore, in order to seamlessly adjoin the last contribution of *Chapter VI* with the preceding *Chapter V*, the question whether L1 use in CLIL in Politics & Economics actually has any consequences for subject didactics and learning outcomes, developed. In the case of Politics & Economics, such question is most obviously related to the (arguably) main competence aim, namely the literacy of judgment as pre-step towards agency. The antithesis that an altered language use has no influence at all on subject outcomes would hypothetically be difficult to model and prove, realizing the abovementioned nexus of language, thinking and culture.

It is a well-known fact that an intellectual, academic and well-reasoned — i.e., rational — analysis of controversial political questions is inevitable for any legitimate and efficient judgment (e.g., core curriculum of the State of Hesse: Hessisches Kultusministerium, 2016). On the flipside, sociology has provided ample evidence that emotions are the main pillar for the creation of empathy (Davis, 2006), in turn necessary for global justice and solidarity. Moreover, emotions *de facto* occupy a significant part of human reality and existence, with both positive and negative characteristics. In other words, judgment and agency need both emotions and rational thinking, providing checks and balances in a setting of a controlled interplay of L2 and L1. *Chapter VI* theorizes this train of thought in detail and introduces the so-called emotional turn and its application to CLIL in Politics & Economics.

In Germany, rationality as the main criterion for an appropriate judgment, has lately been partly jettisoned, following the emotional turn as well as the accepted fact that empathy cannot engender without emotions. Language didactics itself has been promoting empathy as a positive side effect. *Chapter VI* brings the language and subject side together, fully in line with CLILs original idea of thought. Dewaele (2013) illustrated the interplay of emotions in different languages spoken by multilingual speakers. Furthermore, theory suggests that decisions and judgments are dependent on whether L1 or a FL is being used, due to feelings and morals (Hayakawa, Tannenbaum, Costa, Corey, & Keysar, 2017; Keysar, Hayakawa, & An, 2012). Binding the arguments together, a perfect equilibrium of emotional and rational decision-making appears as cornerstone for achieving the aims as defined by the conceptual framework, as *Chapter VI* will put forward. The question whether L2 and L1 use in CLIL can have any effect hereon in terms of balancing rationality and emotions, as something like a harbinger for the achievement of global discourse competence, will be investigated, offering empirical insights. *Chapter VI* is insofar also interesting from the language side, as emotions, correlated with motivational factors, not only influence subject outcomes but most likely also overall CLIL learning aims. In investigating the role of learner emotions, it partly addresses the open questions of Rumlich (2016) and Fleckenstein et al. (2021) about the attribution of the rather positive results of CLIL, independent of student types and their learning levels and abilities.

As said, one can argue that *Chapter VI* is a typical byproduct of the main research. But I would even go beyond in arguing that the significant intervention of *Chapter V* would not be complete without also looking at the subject side, keeping in mind CLIL's idea of thought and the integrative nature of the conceptual framework and the competence model. Moreover, I can announce that this part of the research has been reconceptualized as a clear-cut didactical instrument and published for further consideration in classrooms (Nijhawan, 2020c).

Summary of RD

Looking at all four RDs and the more narrative introduction in *Chapter I*, the proximity of the RDs with the questions that had engendered from my practice of teaching in the first instance becomes obvious. In short, the research beginning with *Chapter III* now starts with a deeper conceptual account of CLIL in Politics & Economics, in line with *PolECulE's* model presented above. Thereafter, in *Chapter IV*, DBAR as a new research method, embodied in me as the TR for bridging the gap between theory and practice, will be introduced, also anticipating the two empirical contributions. *Chapter V*, building on the adapted concept of Trans-FL, will develop teaching methods for judicious and principled L1 use together with the students. *Chapter VI* takes the subject turn and investigates, in a more suggestive fashion for promoting the achievement of the competence model's overarching aims, in how far multilingual CLIL can have an influence on learning outcomes in Politics & Economics. *Chapter VII* finally discusses the results of the four preceding chapters, consolidates their contribution to theory generation and ends with an outlook. All in all, this structure renders the four separate contributions into one entity.

Chapter III

...about the merits of cosmopolitanism...

The Construction of Cosmopolitan Glocalities in Secondary Classrooms through Content and Language Integrated Learning (CLIL) in the Social Sciences

Abstract

Our article argues for content and language integrated learning (CLIL) in the social sciences, as part of a new literacy towards 21st century challenges at school. At first, we will show how multilingualism is closely juxtaposed with global discourses in a worldwide network of glocalities. Thereafter, for the conceptual framework of the suggested pedagogy, we explain why cosmopolitanism must constitute an integral part thereof, accompanying the genesis of classroom glocalities. The heart of our competence model for CLIL in the social sciences fosters the promotion of global discourse competence with adolescent students. In short, this learning aim is a hybrid of subject and language learning, incorporating the merits of language didactics as well as "21st century skills". Finally, in the last step, we will present *#climonomics*, a simulation of a multilingual EU parliamentary debate about climate change and climate action for secondary students. This example intends to demonstrate how multilingualism through CLIL amplifies the magnitude of global discourses during a simulation yet realistic setting. It should provide 'food for thought' for similar initiatives in research and teaching, to encourage the facilitation of cosmopolitan visions in classroom glocalities.

Keywords: *sustainability, climate change, multilingualism, cosmopolitanism, content and language integrated learning (CLIL)*

Acknowledgements: We would like to thank the anonymous reviewers as well as the editors for the very detailed and helpful comments to improve the course of arguments in the article.

Statement about my contribution within this multi-authored paper

The first draft of the paper was prepared independently by me as lead author. Thereafter, it was commented by the other two authors and submitted. The communication within the review process and all changes and amendments were done by me, and again commented by the other two authors.

Status: **Published**

Nijhawan, S., Elsner, D., & Engartner, T. (2021). The Construction of Cosmopolitan Glocalities in Secondary Classrooms through Content and Language Integrated Learning (CLIL) in the Social Sciences. *Global Education Review, 8*(2-3), 92-115.

Listed in the bibliography as Nijhawan, Elsner, and Engartner (2021b).

'World, we have a problem...!'
About Our 21st Century Challenges

> *Greta Tintin Eleonora Ernman Thunberg,*
> *Climate Activist,* and founder of the
> Fridays For Future (FFF) Movement:
>
> *"I have learned you are never too small to make a difference."*
> [her speech at the United Conference of Parties (COP) 24 Climate Talks, Katowice, December 2018]
>
> *"Together and united, we are unstoppable."*
> [her speech at the largest climate strike in history with around 250,000 people attending globally, New York, September 2019]

After reading this article, it hopefully becomes evident why these two quotes, lucidly illustrating young people's urge for climate action, were chosen for opening this article. The young Swedish climate activist Greta Thunberg was able to attract the world's attention for one of the utmost and pressing 21st century challenges, namely the hazardous condition of the climate for our sustainable future. Owing to scientific reason, to her passion and commitment, and out of her personal concern but also for reasons of solidarity, FFF, a global movement of thousands of local groups, emerged. FFF stands for democratic activism and civil disobedience of the present younger generation to raise awareness for acting against climate change. FFF is an illustrative example for the emergence of so-called *glocalities*, a hybrid of the global and the local. Glocalities, as we will show in this article, are a space where the global and the local cannot be strictly distinguished anymore. They provide for democratic negotiation and political action, a precursor of agency. Thunberg's quotations underline her commitment, and it deserves to respectfully note the pressure a young adolescent exerted on political decision makers, along with its tremendous policy impact. We will also be closing this article with Greta Thunberg's words, as her voice is likely the most relevant and impactful in speaking to these issues.

The article will be structured as follows: we will map the vicissitude of modern globalization, and outline the nature of 21st century challenges, calling for immediate democratic action. Here, we will amplify the juncture of the global and the local, too often understood as distinct and separated spheres. Glocalities, as we will learn, provide the main arena for democratic discourse in people's life. The presence of multilingualism and the language use in glocalities deserves close attention. It is uncontested that when speaking about language, a close proximity to culture and identity is established — as a matter of fact, language is culture (Kramsch, 1998), with its strong relation to personal identity. For this reason, we will outline modes of language use in different spheres.

The ideas will be made applicable for education in establishing a new literacies approach in line with the developments of the 21st century. Thus, we will speak of classroom glocalities, within which "*21st century skills*" (Trilling & Fadel, 2009) should be pronounced, in order to support students in becoming active citizens within a democratic and transnational civil society. The transnational dimension in a global age prompts us to formulate an unambiguous plea for cosmopolitanism. In order to eschew its common elitist connotation, we will wrap up that section with the concept of relational cosmopolitanism (Baildon & Damico, 2010), enabling the genesis of organically-grown cosmopolitanism from below in our classrooms. Content and Language Integrated Learning (CLIL), building on a bi- and multilingual pedagogy, makes language a central pillar of classroom glocalities. All of these thoughts will be captured in a competence model for CLIL classes in the social sciences. In order to exemplify the competence model, we will present *#climonomics*, a multilingual EU parliamentary debate about climate change and climate action for about 200 students, at the end of the article. *#climonomics* demonstrates that our suggested pedagogy, synonymous with the promotion of 21st century skills, is not merely a vision. Rather, it can be regarded as a tangible concept, as we will elucidate in the optimistic outlook during the closure of the article.

Entrenching Democracy and Promoting Sustainability in Glocalities

The Vicissitude of Modern Globalization

With the end of the Cold War and the rise of information technology, the world has become an even more interconnected place, paving the way for globalization processes to gain a newfound momentum. Globalization is virtually felt in every niche of the world, not to neglect the borderless digital space. Not only has the world thus transmuted to something like a smaller place, because interactions between different people around the globe are increasing but also political, economic and cultural questions are becoming increasingly global in nature. We see this in the rise of international and regional institutions like the United Nations (UN) and the European Union (EU), and global efforts to combat climate change, and, more recently, to coordinate initiatives to find a vaccine against the Corona virus under the auspices of an internationalized regime.

Most of all our 21st century challenges (like combatting climate change, eradicating poverty and fighting inequality, promoting human rights, and living together in a multicultural world) are global in nature. It is true that someone's own concern can be the same concern of a person ten thousand and more miles far away. While, no matter where, fighting for survival, clean water, access to education, in a broad sense for human rights and sustainability, that individual or group is never alone. The discourse about these challenges happens both at the local (e.g., community) as well the global level (e.g., UN, state and other summits, NGOs, increasingly in the digital space). Of course, this also applies for the intermediate space (e.g., the EU or nation states at a smaller level). Giddens (2000), among many others, has given an excellent account in his classic *"Runaway World"*, sketching the new form of global dynamics happening all over the world, being felt decentralized in localities. Robertson (1990; 1995) coined this idea with the much-echoed expression of *glocal*ization. Glocalization is equated with the emergence of glocalities that span around the world like a spider's web. They emit the potential and immediate need for new forms of

81

participatory and transnational democracy, to pay tribute to a *de facto* borderless society. The size of a glocality can vary, in accordance with communication structures given. Their emergence is not static but dynamic and not constrained to a fixed territory, because glocalities do not have clearly demarked but fluid and permeable boundaries. Even the world as a whole, or the digital space, can be characterized as a glocality under certain conditions, or said to consist of myriad glocalities during certain snapshots of our times.

Glocalities are characterized by the interplay of global and local forces. Sometimes the former dominates and deterritorializes their existence, sometimes the latter rather leads to (re-)territorialization. At present, we can witness different political forces on different levels, like the civil society as well as the governing administrations. On the one side, people in different glocalities are exerting pressure on authoritarian governments to democratize political structures (e.g., in Hong Kong, Belarus, Sudan). On the other side, many 'experienced democracies' are feeling new counterforces of nationalization and chauvinism (e.g., USA, India, Turkey, Brazil, the UK, to take Brexit). They are increasingly been pushed to the verge, following the surge of populism on a global level the last years. Social media, always bearing a potential of revolutionary force (be it democratic or anti-democratic), plays a significant role. Thus, the question how to entrench and improve democracy in glocalities, and promote transnational democratic structures becomes pressing in our times.

Social movements by the transnational civil society to realize the Universal Declaration of Human Rights (UDHR), and to (re)define and revitalize democracy and sustainable living conditions, are on the rise. This is concomitant with making prosperity a realistic concept and a human right for the entire world population. Such counterhegemonic forces are at first positive, as they can be equated with the emergence of transnational democratic networks. As a matter of fact, they want to render the opportunities encapsulated in globalization more human — increasingly also in the global north, to deconstruct the myth that development as a shallow concept only applies to less economically developed countries (Evans, 2003). The vicissitude and dynamics of globalization *per se* are most obviously felt by the world population in their respective localities, negotiated and (re)interpreted at that very place in first instance, transforming the local sphere into glocalities.

Realizing that we live in one world, the need to improve our existence and habitat mutually and together arises. We need to foster ways of *"thinking and acting both locally and globally at the same time"* (Karliner, 1997b, p. 199) — thus per definition in glocalities. The emergence of the digital cyberspace has had a tremendous impact on the understanding of glocalities the last decades, making them borderless. Glocalities are now less confided to physical space as in the past, because interaction can now theoretically happen between all individuals and groups. This requires engagement in a dialogue on eye-level with other world citizens, as ultimately cosmopolitanism and togetherness include many opportunities for conflict settlement and universal peace, for poverty eradication and sustainability in general. Promoting global discourse competence among the world population in pioneering educational ventures and making democracy of the 21st century a living and participatory construct, is set as a milestone. The role multilingualism occupies in glocalities needs not to be underestimated, as we will see in the following section.

Multilingualism in Glocalities: the Role of Languages

The role of languages and the increase in multilingualism within globalization has so far mainly been a domain of humanities and cultural studies. For transnational agency, communication across linguistic groups must be facilitated, simultaneously embracing participation of people in their most dominant language or other languages they feel most comfortable in. Fusing the valuable insights of applied linguistics with globalization from a social science perspective illustrates the dynamics of a fluid language use within glocalities *per se*. To lead to the concomitant genesis of glocalities, we will take one small step backwards and imagine distinct layers. We can contemplate that global discourses happen, roughly speaking, mainly on two levels: in the (1) global and the (2) local sphere.

We should turn to each of them separately and deliberate on the respective modes of languages.

Global Space

Occasions: Discourses within the global sphere can be witnessed during personal encounters, e.g., during family and friends' visits, migration, traveling, living away from home, conferences, workshops, within formal and informal networks. This can be physical, but also increasingly digital, within the global media, in the cyberspace, and especially within social networks, more or less with your smartphone in your pocket.

Language use: In general, global discourses are held multilingually. It may happen that family members or friends who grew up together meet again and speak in their first language (L1). Or speakers with different L1s have a common proficiency in another second or foreign language (Lx)[1] and hold their discourses in the relevant language of common proficiency. In many cases, as a result of modern globalization, these discourses happen in English as the global *lingua franca,* especially if people are unknown to each other and from different regions of the world. 1.27 billion people speak English as their L1 or equivalent Lx (Eberhard, Simons, & Fennig, 2020). The emergence of a digital space and digital media, and its political impact, further fuels the uncontested omnipresence of English as the main language of global discourse, as compared to the consecutively ranked world languages of L1 speakers, namely Chinese, Hindi, Spanish, French and Standard Arabic (Eberhard et al., 2020).

At a trade exhibition or international conference, English will be the quantitatively most spoken language. Against this trend, it is not unlikely, that e.g., Spanish, French, Hindi/Urdu or Chinese

---

[1] During the last decade, it has become a norm during the last decade to speak about L1 (first language) and L2 (second or foreign language) in distinguishing different roles of languages with individuals. To pay tribute to the emergence of multilingualism, and the difficulty of mapping a clear language history with individuals, we adopt Dewaele's (2017) suggestion to refer to Lx for any language other than the most dominant language of an individual.

speakers with the relevant L1 may use the same at. In digital communication, like with social media, when people are willing to reach the widest audience possible, English is a likely reference, or an English translation for reaching a larger audience is provided (common caption of posts: *"for the English version please scroll below"*). Other languages, both national or regional *lingua francas*, or minority and indigenous languages, are used nevertheless. Although everyone wants to speak English for a good reason, the policies of international or supranational organizations like the United Nations (UN) or the EU, promote linguistic diversity (e.g., Council of Europe, 2018).

Local Space

Occasions: Multilingualism in local spaces is as much a common phenomenon, even in regions with only one official language. Discussions happen formally at gatherings, festivals, workshops, and so on. Informal occasions offer another important space of unstructured discourse, as at cultural events, in bars and pubs, private homes, at associations, and many more get-togethers. Media and the virtual space like social networks, instant messengers, *etc.*, also play an important role. Election hustings and democratic franchise serve as a very prominent example. But smaller settings need not to be neglected.

Language use: As with the global sphere, *de facto* multilingualism as a characteristic of local discourses is common, with some significant differences though. The surrounding dominant language, e.g., German in Germany, occupies the place of the *lingua franca*, as with English in global spaces (of course, it can also be English, or any of the 'Englishes' in their different variations). The surrounding local language can be the L1 or the Lx of a speaker, even in *de jure* monolingual regions. We can observe an overall decentralization of multilingualism and transculturality to the very local and thus a wide array of different L1s in localities. It is hard to imagine of any locality without a multilingual reality, be it by language variety and dialects, or even completely different language families. A speaker may take part in global discourses at the local level in his or her L1 and/or Lx. A mixed language use, in different frequencies, has become a quotidian phenomenon.

This twofold distinction models the multilingual presence of global discourses in the two different spheres, called glocality when fused within one framework. As languages play a significant role during the construction of the glocality and its intensity, the well-known postulate *"the limits of my language are the limits of my world"* (original: *"Die Grenzen meiner Sprachen bedeuten die Grenzen meiner Welt"*, by Wittgenstein, 1963) brings it to the core. This scenario will now be exemplified with the German setting, not only for contextualizing the last and practical part of the article, but also for understanding the transformative power of glocalities in general. Per definition, German is the only official language (with some minority language protection in Sorbian and Frisian areas as well as for the Danish minority in the region bordering Denmark). Most of the public discourse about global challenges in the localities takes place in German, the dominant surrounding language, especially in the media and social networks. Nevertheless, we do not want to neglect that many topics are discussed in other languages, namely, minority languages, during different unofficial or private occasions. Ethnic minorities, for example Polish and Turkish L1 speakers in Germany, with German as Lx, illustrate this train of thought. The *"multilingual reality"* (Mohanty, 2019), and processes of transculturality (Welsch, 1999) have transformed, more or less, the concept of unequivocal *lingua francas* to be more blurry in the global age. A language might be dominant, but not necessarily decisive when it comes to the formation of individual political and economic judgements and decisions. We should now turn to education and in particular to everyday school classrooms, for assessing their potential of multilayered multilingual approaches to our global 21st century challenges. We will learn that constructing 'classroom glocalities' needs to be embedded within a framework of an education for cosmopolitan citizenship.

Classroom Glocalities in Education

The given framework of the preceding section outlined how global discourses about our 21st century challenges are negotiated in different spheres, with a differentiated and multilingual language use. It is apparent that glocalities constitute a microcosm and bring global discourses close to people, feeling and experiencing these challenges every day. The role of education becomes instrumental in providing the coming generation with knowledge and facts, preparing them for an active participation and their agency within a democratic and transnational civil society. Classrooms serve as an apt arena for the construction of glocalities with tailored pedagogies and a problem-based approach. The goal can be defined to engender *classroom glocalities* as a space for the seamless promotion of global discourse competences, with integrated *"21st century skills"* (categorized in *"learning and innovation skills, digital literacy skills und life and career skills"*, according to Trilling & Fadel, 2009). This can be regarded as prerequisite for the sustainable future of present and coming generations.

About Cosmopolitan Visions

We will develop an argument for all pedagogies within classroom glocalities, during our turbulent global times, to require one decisive characteristic: a purely cosmopolitan nature. An excursus why cosmopolitanism is juxtaposed with the genesis of glocalities in classrooms will follow. By no means do we have the space for a complete overview about the field of cosmopolitanism.[2] Rather we will select the most salient thoughts of a very contemporary body of literature in order to relate it to our concept of glocalities and classroom cosmopolitanism.

---

[2] Nearly every one of the cited publications contains a history of cosmopolitanism from ancient Greece via the epoch of enlightenment with special reference to Kant to the new post-Cold War world order. The edited reader by Brown and Held (2010) offers an excellent set of texts with general and mor specific accounts for obtaining an idea of an academic field in transition.

The idea of *cosmopolis* is an ancient Greek idea and was rejuvenated during the age of enlightenment. The renaissance of cosmopolitanism as a modern academic field of study occurred after the end of the Cold War, same as with the attention the sociology of modern globalization attracted. Mendieta (2017, p. 253) argues that *"[i]t could be claimed that we live in an age of cosmopolitanism, just as Kant can be said to have lived in an age of enlightenment."* What can already be called classical accounts of the two decades after the fall of the iron curtain, have in turn opened the arena and set the stage for present-day debates, mainly launched in the last decade. Academics from all over the globe have been critically tracing and examining the presence of everyday cosmopolitanism in everyone's live, in an endeavor to omit its initially elite character and to design conceptional accounts for our future on the globe. Many interdisciplinary 'from below approaches' have commenced to redefine the field, deconstructing the post-Cold War euphoria surrounding around ideas of a world government under institutional auspices of the UN. They challenge universalist approaches from above, often synonymous with a liberal and modernist western outline of the new monopolar world order (e.g., Fukuyama, 1992) and thus an elite and privileged notion of the metaphoric frequent traveler (Hawkins, 2018; Ingram, 2016; Kurasawa, 2004).

According to this new and growing research strand, cosmopolitanism has its main roots in the local sphere, also explaining the genesis and the power of glocalities. Held (2010) argues that linking the global and the local has already been identified as one of the most important endeavors in our times. There have been voices suggesting that the purest form of cosmopolitanism organically grows at the local level. Especially, but not exclusively, modern migration with people in motion deserve special attention. This is because *"migrant cosmopolitanism"* plays a significant role within glocalities and their interconnectedness, as *"[t]he twenty-first century will be the century of the migrant"* (Nail, 2015, p. 187). This not only counts for controlled migration but is especially relevant for a large group of people having suffered forced migration, namely refugees. Refugees have to quickly adapt to new circumstances in the wake of their migrant trajectory, acquire language and everyday skills in their new environments, contributing an indigenous form of a cosmopolitan outline and surpassing any national-bound identity formation. Any personal encounters of 'new locals' with other people in their environment, who in turn may already possess alternate interpretations of cosmopolitan awareness, lead to a new form of exchange. Cosmopolitanism appears more as a way of life and thinking in a constructivist fashion, individually, sociologically and culturally. It has by no means ethnic hybridity or any other hard criteria as precondition but stands for an individual or collective philosophy. Hawkins (2018, p. 67) offers the lens of *"critical cosmopolitanism to integrate a focus on creating and sustaining just, equitable, and affirming relations with global (and local) others in global engagements and interactions through attending to the workings of status, privilege, and power between people and groups of people."* Building on her notion, the construction of glocalities, with physical and digital, real-time and asynchronous interaction, across time and space, trespassing language boundaries, constitutes a roadmap towards promoting critical cosmopolitanism. From the view of education, classrooms with commonly diverse student bodies constitute natural glocalities, calling for a tailored pedagogy to emerge the potential of students' inherent cosmopolitan knowledge and awareness.

To use Beck's (2006) popular title in context of the main principles of the EU, we will now sketch our *"cosmopolitan vision"* for today's classroom glocalities. It falls in line with a democratic outline of the well-established teaching and learning culture. Ingram (2016, pp. 68, 76) states that *"[...] cosmopolitanism must be contestatory [...] radically democratic."* Thus, such debate culture has its core in fact-based, open and controversial discourses about our 21st century challenges, recognizing the multitude of opinions. Mendieta (2017, p. 254) summarizes this overall train of thought: *"There is no single cosmopolitan vision, but a process of arriving at it through an engagement with a dialogical imagination that opens up the spaces of mutual transformation."* The presence of diverging cosmopolitan visions is felicitated, paving the way for unity & diversity and valuing the transcultural dynamics within our multicultural world. We as authors subscribe to the plural form cosmopolitan *visions* in sincerity, and value the uniqueness of every glocality, be it a global megacity or a small, more remote space.

Once again, Germany exemplifies the power of cosmopolitanism for the construction of classroom glocalities. Current demographics from 2019 tell us that almost 40% of all German students have a migration history (this category is relevant with at least one parent holding another citizenship than German). Compared to the numbers of 2005, this proportion has gradually been on a rise, with an ongoing trend *(Table 1)*. We have no official numbers about the first (L1) and any other languages (Lx) being spoken by these students. However, we can carefully infer that an increasingly multilingual cohort has become common in German classrooms today, with a wide array of different L1 and Lx that—directly and indirectly—find entrance into German classrooms, adding to the cosmopolitan spirit.

Table 1 lists the amount of students with a migration history, born in- and outside of Germany (data source: Bevölkerung mit Migrationshintergrund—Ergebnisse des Mikrozensus—Fachserie 1 Reihe 2.2—Statistisches Bundesamt: https://www.statistischebibliothek.de/mir/receive/DESerie_mods_00000020).

Year of survey	2019		2015		2010		2005	
Country of birth: DE – Germany OT – out of Germany	DE (%)	OT (%)	DE (%)	OT (%)	DE (%)	OT (%)	DE (%)	OT (%)
Students officially counted with a migration history	28.2	10.3	27	5.9	24	5.2	18.8	7.6
	38.5		32.9		29.2		26.4	

Glocalities cannot be automated with a cosmopolitan outcome, reasoning the need for a tailored pedagogical approach. How can we transform classroom glocalities into arenas of cosmopolitan citizenship? The resources and worldly knowledge the diverse body of students possesses from home provide as helpful for the outset of classes (e.g., *"my father was born in ...; "my mother grew up in and speaks Lx..."; "my friend was born in..."*). Personal encounters along with a dialogical nature from an early age also leads to cosmopolitan awareness and spirit with all remaining students with genuinely local roots, as ethnic diversity is no required criterion.

Classroom cosmopolitanism can be equated with praising diversity and looking beyond boundaries as a personal philosophy. Providing ample space for an organic growth and assembly of diversified forms of cosmopolitanism in educational contexts facilitates the transformation of classrooms into educational glocalities. A pedagogy making the existing cosmopolitanism visible and further promoting cosmopolitanism awareness and transnational spirit, thus amplifying the role of glocalities in combatting 21st century challenges sustainably, will be sketched in the following section.

Our suggestion to engender educational glocalities is an amended concept in accordance with Baildon and Damico (2010), proposing *"relational cosmopolitanism"* as a new literacy for 21st century challenges. Their approach resembles a pedagogy for education for sustainable development (ESD), because their pedagogy means to *"help prepare students to live in 'new times'"* (Baildon & Damico, 2010, p. 1), requiring them to mutually work towards identifying problems and deliberating on pathways for their solution within a transnational democratic framework. Moreover, also elucidating the role of the media and new technologies in the global world, this new literacy has a clear nexus to Trilling & Fadel's (2009) 21st century skills, we made an argument for before. Relational cosmopolitanism welcomes different local interpretations of global issues and promotes awareness for a shared global destiny. The term *relational* means that there is no universal cosmopolitan vision, building on contesting and perpetually (re-)defining plural cosmopolitan visions in glocalities within a global framework. The pedagogy moves along the following definition:

> Relational cosmopolitanism begins with an integrated view of knowledge within the social studies. Rather than understanding knowledge as segmented, disjointed, and fragmented, an integrated perspective helps frame social studies content and curricula in ways that understand various social, economic, political, historical, and contemporary issues and problems as interconnected and shared. [...] One particular way to promote a stance of interconnectedness is to integrate local dimensions of human experience with global conditions and concerns. For instance, a complex and multifaceted issue, such as poverty, pollution, immigration, income inequality, war, or climate change, can and needs to be investigated as it occurs in a particular place and it needs to be investigated as an issue that cuts across the globe in comparable and distinct ways. (Baildon & Damico, 2010, p. 26)

We will introduce a conceptual framework for CLIL lessons in the social sciences as panacea and put language, in particular foreign language education on eye level with the content of the suggested new literacy. Our approach follows the seminal work of Osler and Starkey (2015), arguing that foreign language education is education for cosmopolitan citizenship. Reference to L1 besides the school language as well as other surrounding or available languages constitutes another key feature of the suggested pedagogy, to foster multilingual skills for cosmopolitan visions in glocalities. After the presentation of the competence model, we will exemplify our thoughts with a practical example, namely #*climonomics*, a multilingual EU conference on combatting climate change.

CLIL and the Promotion of Global Discourse Competences: the *PolECulE*-Project

Realizing the potential of CLIL in the social sciences to transform classrooms into cosmopolitan glocalities, the *PolECulE*-project at Goethe-University Frankfurt was founded, yielding an innovative and symbiotic partnership of didactic research with school practice.[3] Thus far, no educational standards had been defined for any CLIL subject, despite the exponential growth of CLIL programs in the 1990s, mostly in English (Breidbach & Viebrock, 2012). PolECulE's first goal was set to develop a conceptual framework with a competence model for CLIL classes in Politics, Economics & Culture, adding culture as addendum to highlight the humanist approach. The second step foresaw the practical implementation of the conceptual framework with teaching methods, recognizing the demand for general and subject-specific CLIL didactics, and responding to the scarcity of CLIL teaching materials.

    CLIL in the social sciences with its globalization-related curriculum offers an apt arena for global discourses. The multilingual approach sets the stage for realizing a diversified language approach. The target language is English as the main language of global discourse. It needs to be clearly highlighted at this point, however, that the bilingual approach with English as foreign

---

[3] More about the project can be found online at www.polecule.com.

language and German as the official school language only defines the starting point of the project due to many different L1s of students. The teaching methods and material will incorporate multilingual facets beyond mere bilingualism, to pay tribute to the potpourri of languages in glocalities, as demonstrated during the presentation of #*climonomics* in the final section. The remainder of this section presents the most salient points of the competence model *(Figure 1)*, recognizing our envisaged promotion of cosmopolitan classroom glocalities from the preceding sections.[4]

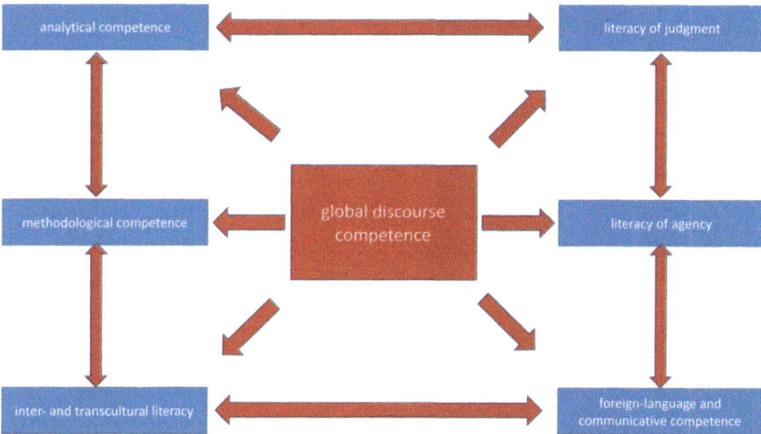

Figure 1 contains the competence model for CLIL classes in Politics, Economics & Culture for social science education (taken from Elsner et al., 2019, p. 24).

CLIL can already be regarded as an early effort of a reformist pedagogy, realizing its genesis out of a *"grassroots movement"* (Marsh, 2002, p. 56) in its initial stage of development. The transcurricular approach, combining language with subject learning, constitutes a more holistic view of education. The theoretical thoughts have been translated into **global discourse competence** as the main competence aim, summarized as the ability to understand, assess and act towards a sustainable future within a democratic, multicultural and transnational civil society.

---

[4] The full document can be found at Elsner et al. (2019). A closer analysis has been composed by Nijhawan (2019), and a review of the work written by Wohnig (2020).

The model builds on constructivist approaches to education, realizing the need for problem-solving pedagogies amidst the demand for 21st century literacies (Baildon & Damico, 2010). The grand innovation proposed by the model is the pivotal role of language, language learning and language awareness, juxtaposed with the inherent achievements of language didactics. This has been manifested with the foreign language and communicative competence as one subcompetence. In terms of the cosmopolitan outlook within the classroom as glocality, inter- and transcultural literacy, realizing the merits of foreign language didactics, embellishes the model. Interculturality mainly focuses on the relationship towards alternate cultural patterns (with the prominent development of the 5 *savoirs* by Byram, 1997). Looking deeper, Kramsch (1993) defines *"Third Places"* within classrooms, engendering during the negotiation of culture and meaning in foreign language classes. During cross-cultural communication, intercultural communicative competence develops herein. Her notion, to some extent, also includes transculturality and the genesis of both stable and dynamic third cultures.

Transculturality, as a concept or process, recognizes the dynamic and perpetual change of cultures in our modern age of global mobility, owing to the increasing encounter and mixture of people with different backgrounds and experiences (Welsch, 1999). It has been added to the competence model, to partly challenge the idea of interculturalism with its static notion of isolated, and often nation-state based cultures. The inclusion of more dynamic cultural models, felicitating the fluidity of culture during modern globalization and migration, thus questioning the definition of otherness and looking *"beyond other cultures"* (Schulze-Engler & Doff, 2011)[5], amplify the cosmopolitan design of the model. It highlights 'unity in diversity' as spirit, enabling togetherness and cosmopolitanism from below. Code-switching languages as well as constructed *"translanguaging spaces"* (Li, 2011), as common in cosmopolitan

---

[5] This edited volume is highly recommended as a source of inspiration to understand teaching concepts and practices that deconstruct the perception of otherness, still common in contemporary classrooms.

glocalities, play a significant role. Translanguaging promotes empathy and solidarity, using affect control as well as a balanced stance towards self-interest and altruism (Nijhawan, 2020b). This overall approach also manifests an opposition towards the surge of populism and nationalism by more recent communitarian trends (Merkel, 2017), with serious parochial, provincial and chauvinist threats to local and transnational democracy. The competence model we presented with its endeavor to construct classrooms glocalities with cosmopolitan visions can be seen as a further development of inter- and transculturality. *Figure 2* binds the preceding sections together.

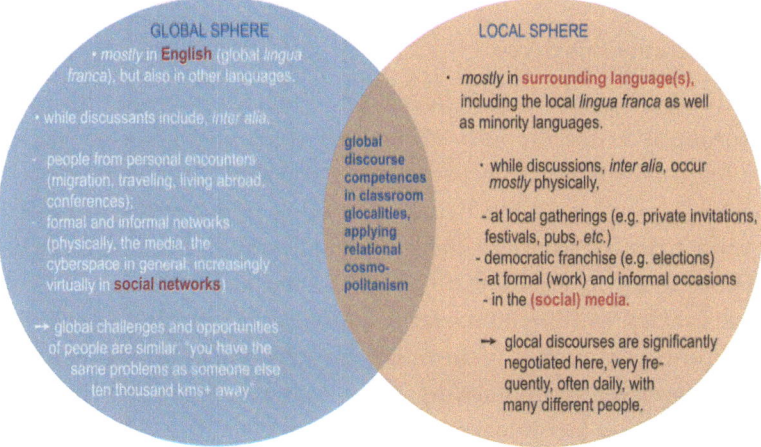

Figure 2 sketches different spheres of global discourses, with classroom glocalities as intersection for promoting cosmopolitan visions.

The next section will introduce *#climonomics* as a practical example for the implementation of the given framework. The roadmap was set to construct the conference room as a cosmopolitan glocality for motivating the students towards climate action.

A Cosmopolitan Approach towards Climate Change: *#climonomics*

Following the widespread media attention FFF is still attracting, *#climonomics*, a multilingual EU parliamentary debate about climate change and climate action, was designed by the *PolECulE* project. In October 2019, almost 200 students across Germany assembled and debated EU climate politics and developed masterplans for local, regional and global climate action, to promote their agency in the future. The large-scale event served as piloting exercise to refine the conceptual framework. We wanted to make *#climonomics* available also for later simulation in everyday classrooms as well as with larger student populations, across schools, and even beyond country borders, and ultimately also as digital project in the virtual cyberspace, to recognize that physical constraints of glocalities are abating. The following part presents the idea of the project, students' data, the proceedings and selected evaluation results.

Project and Objectives

The central objectives of *#climonomics* is to address two of the most burning and contemporary 21st century challenges in society with a tailored and integrative pedagogical concept: (1) climate change and (2) cohesion in the EU in promoting democratic awareness. Amidst the dynamics of the global FFF movement, *#climonomics* means to equip secondary school students across the age of 13-19 years with scientific climate facts. It offers a differentiated pedagogical concept to render widespread participation at related debates, and consequently students' agency possible. Moreover, noting with concern current disintegrating developments in the EU (i.e., Brexit and the surge of populist parties), *#climonomics* intends to frame the simulation of the EU parliamentary debate, in order to strengthen democracy in its core. The heart of *#climonomics* is the simulation of a multilingual debate, highlighting the merits of pluralism and transnational cooperation, mirroring the multilingual reality of the world.

For rather complicated scenarios related to the climate, games and simulations, both online and offline have proven to be effective tools. Wu and Lee (2015) were able to demonstrate that real world simulations, with an active engagement of students, help to engage a broader student population with the controversy. Bandura and Cherry (2019) highlight the role of social media and its reach and motivation for the youth when it comes to exerting pressure for an effective global environmental regime. With their model, they point out social-cognitive theory as a resource for *"children's innovative practices"*, leading to behavioral change as consequence of the global movement, with a variety of remedies in *"diverse social milieus"* (p. 6).

The idea to develop the project mainly resulted due to the evolution of FFF, involving young people globally to be engaged in their local communities. FFF's objectives, with Greta Thunberg initially refusing to attend school in order to protest for immediate climate action, have significantly transformed in due process. Not only have demands been expressed to combat climate change and promote a sustainable future for enabling human mankind a livelihood in dignity. But also FFF now goes further in urging far-reaching societal reforms up to a complete system change, away from the growth economy to a more solidaric societal outline. There has been criticism that FFF has an 'elitist character', with supporters mainly from the youth of the educated middle class, while large parts of students from mostly marginalized backgrounds do not have access to the discourse gravitating around climate change. Furthermore, recent populist movements, in its extreme form expressed in Brexit, indicate disenfranchisement with politics. In accordance with Held (2016), we can tie all of the objectives of #*climonomics* together, in arguing that cosmopolitanism, as the competence model envisions, would only be possible in a democratic and sustainable world.

One of the core features is the multilingual outline of #*climonomics*. On the one side, multilingual approaches can serve as positive resources and valuable scaffolding tools, enabling and supporting the seamless participation of a wider student community with native languages other than the official school language. On the other side, such an approach has also proven to be a modern pedagogy for foreign language learning. Here, the transformation of CLIL has undergone within the last decade to a problem-based pedagogy, as a solution for 21st century challenges (Coyle et al., 2010) plays into hands. The integration of content and language, constituting CLIL's DNA, has rendered it to be an apt approach for global discourses within glocalities, using novel multilingual methods for deeper cognitive processing of the content matter (Nikula & Moore, 2019). This idea is displayed in the competence model of the previous section.

In order to enable students of all competence levels and with different language proficiencies an active participation, a digital and student-reviewed conference reader was developed.[6] The reader organized the project threefold (*inter- and transcultural literacy* and *foreign language and communicative competence* as well as the *methodological competence* are promoted within all phases). The reader caters students' affordances and takes differentiated steps.

Knowledge and analytical competence
Equipping students with information on the EU and its institutions as well as scientific facts about climate change constituted the beginning of *#climonomics*. In a stakeholder-led exercise, optional multilingual sources were researched by students with other L1 than German and English. They served as differentiated and affordance-based supplement for students with various language histories, concomitantly highlighting different perspectives and the desired plurality of opinions. Perspective changes were initiated with role cards, prompting the students to enter the topic from their allocated role. As didactics suggests, they help students to form a legitimate and multilayered judgement during controversial discourses, also respecting alternative views along with a genesis of empathy. The majority of role cards represented EU parliamentary groups/parties, but also other important actors from politics and civil society beyond the EU were added to offer a more global view (e.g., Ibrahim Solih, President from the Maledives, Ram Nath Kovind, President of India, Greta Thunberg, Michael O'Leary from Ryanair from the private sector *etc.*). This underlines that

---

[6] A reworked version of the *#climonomics* reader, incorporating the experiences and evaluation results of *#climonomics*, is currently under review and nearly ready for publication by a renowned publishing house. It is a pilot project to broadly disseminate the project in the form of a hybrid product (digital/printed), to develop digital forms of teaching materials.

perspectives on climate politics are not unequivocal, while finding compromises in democracies is not as easy as it appears. The groups were mainly composed in accordance with language skills, amplifying the multilingual concept, and encouraging students to use less dominant languages as well. Moreover, this arrangement facilitated language learning.

Decision and literacy of judgement

The students proceeded to the EU parliamentary debate, also chaired by them. Half of the groups spoke in English the first half of the conference, the other in German. After half the time, they had to switch to the other language. Thus, they had to bilingually prepare beforehand during the group phase. Students were, however, encouraged to use any other language. Any such contribution was given priority, provided one group member was ready to immediately translate into one of the two main conference languages for all other participants. Students were able and actively requested to send real-time tweets from the accounts of their role to the main screen of the conference venue, in order to make the debate even more controversial, and also more realistic—keeping in mind that social media with its groundbreaking dynamics has become a decisive sphere of political discourse (see examples in the *Appendix*).

Literacy of agency

After the one-hour long debate, turning out to be very spectacular in its nature, the participants were supposed to turn back to their own personality. This last step was supposed to motivate students to become politically active, be engaged in a transnational civil society, realizing the merits of the EU as a citizens' network for peace, exchange and mutual understanding. Now, they were asked to develop local, European and global masterplans to combat climate change on different levels, in accordance with the knowledge they accrued the preceding phase as well as balancing the legitimate opinions of other actors. *Figure 3* visualizes the process of *#climonomics*.

MULTILINGUAL CONTENT AND LANGUAGE INTEGRATED LEARNING

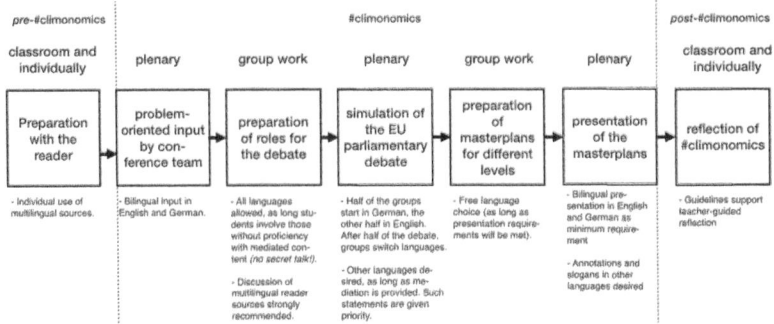

Figure 3 illustrates the outline of the *#climonomics* conference.

It deserves mention that the *#climonomics* conference had an attached teacher workshop, split in two parts. Participants had observation tasks and were requested to take structured notes. At a second session, the observations set the basis for the development of teaching models in terms of multilingualism and climate change in classroom glocalities.

Information and Data about Participating Students

An application to take part at *#climonomics* was open to every student in Germany. In some cases, teachers from schools requested to take part with their whole learning group. The set goal was to have at least 30% of students from secondary schools other than the elite *Gymnasiums*[7]. This decision had been made, because there had

---

[7] In most of Germany, students visit an elementary school for the first four years. In 2018/2019, about 2.8 Million children were at an elementary school. Thereafter, they continue either at a *Gymnasium* (40%), a *Realschule* (14%), a *Hauptschule* (7%), a cooperative comprehensive school (10%) with different models, an integrated comprehensive school with mutual learning (19%), a school for students with special needs (6%), or at another state-permitted school (5%). The *Gymnasium* as a traditional and elite institution is a classical grammar school, ending with the *Abitur* (A-level equivalent graduation, enabling to enroll in higher education) after either 8 or 9 years. The other schools are in general rather for weaker students, and often more practically oriented. Vertical movements of students exceeding or missing the expectations of each school type is possible. Numbers in brackets indicate the percentage of students enrolled at each of the school types in 2018/19 (data source: https://de.statista.com/statistik/daten/studie/3377/umfrage/anzahl-der-schueler-nach-einzelnen-schularten/).

repeatedly been concerns expressed that projects like *#climonomics* are in many cases exclusively addressed towards privileged students, leaving students with rather weaker socioeconomic backgrounds often behind. In total, 193 students registered for *#climonomics*. The detailed data, mainly the data on language proficiency, was used for the planning of the conference. *Table 2* shows the overall student profiles, also containing basic information on languages spoken by students.

Table 2 contains basic data that helped to plan and assemble groups for #climonomics.

Student responses in the registration survey (N=193)	
Age range	13-19
Average age / median age / standard deviation (SD)	16.05 / 16 / 1.3
Students from non-*Gymnasium* background	30%
Proficiency in number of languages beyond German and English (covering all competence levels)	29 Highest frequencies ≥5: - English: all students - French: 75 - Spanish 34 - Italian, 25 - Turkish & Kurdish, 13 - Persian, 7 - Serbian, Croatian and Bosnian: 5
Students with first languages other than German, or another (second) language proficiency close to a first language (often a language spoken at home)	59 students (31 %); 19 different first or equivalent second languages Highest frequency of first or equivalent other (second) language, ≥5: - Turkish: 12 - Persian: 7 - Polish: 6 - Portuguese: 5 - Serbian, Croatian and Bosnian: 5

Overall, the set quota of 30% students from non-*Gymnasium* background was just fulfilled. The data lets us observe an impressive pool of language proficiency in 28 languages beyond German and English. 19 of these languages were first or equivalent second languages of students. We should note the common fact that students do not have to have a proficiency in the first languages of their parents (even if both parents have the same first language). Noteworthy is that some students indicated in the survey's comment field their proficiency not only in other national languages, but also in certain regional or minority languages and dialects, respectively (e.g., Telugu, spoken in the Indian state of Andhra Pradesh). They indeed were willing to narrate and explain their personal language history and showed awareness and dedication. The given language diversity of the participants justifies #*climonomics*' multilingual CLI pedagogy for integrating students' L1 both as resource and additional perspective into the concept. In line with the theoretical account of the preceding sections, it facilitates the construction of the conference room as educational glocality. It not only constructs a realistic setting of transnational politics, but also promotes multiply of thought and arguments in line with the given notion of cosmopolitanism from below, rooted in diversity.

Proceedings

The group size was 8-10 students. In accordance with the concept, groups for the roles during the simulation were mainly assembled in accordance with the language competences students brought along, building on CLIL's meticulous approach to promote multilingualism with diversified L1 use. Especially when the number of students with L1 other than German or English were at least 5, their L1 constituted the majority within the group. The group work was quite concentrated, as the students were motivated with the prospects for the debate. Languages other than German or English were often spoken. At the same time, they were directed not to hold secret talks but to mediate their content in German or English to their group members not proficient in their L1. They apparently felt comfortable and even proud when using the multilingual source section of the digital reader with their electronic devices, to look at opinions beyond that of German and international English media.

We observed a very vividly held debate about a topic of immediate concern of the coming generation. Participation was strong, even though not every statement could be given during the 90 minutes debate. The natural adherence to the language rules after a couple of minutes, resembling a habit, made the debate truly multilingual. This is indeed natural when compared e.g., to the European Parliament, a UN summit, or other conferences. Mainly the contributions were in English and German, the main conference languages. Other contributions were also given in Polish (with both translations to English and German), Portuguese and Turkish. Some of these contributions came from non-*Gymnasium* students, emanating pride in demonstrating a competence not shared by everyone in the lecture hall. Here, we learned that CLIL's unique pedagogy with systematic L1 use results in a genesis of multilingualism and prepares students to feel comfortable within such environments. The contributions on Twitter were by times rational and fact-based, but at times sarcastic, satirical and humorous. They aptly mirrored the proceeding of the debate ending without a climate deal. The *Appendix* contains a selection of tweets that were projected in real-time on the main screen of the projector. Not even a minimal consensus could be reached due to conflicting positions.

The last and final phase was meant to equip students with hope and a sense of agency and enabled them to take an individual cosmopolitan perspective on the controversies. They could freely choose groups, in which they were supposed to negotiate either local, regional or global masterplans with measures they identified as appropriate to combat climate change. The language choice was free, but results had to be composed at least in both German and English. The results were handed to the patron of the conference, Mr. Peter Feldmann, the Major of Frankfurt, urging to act towards climate justice immediately. Since the concept of the conference was very innovative, and the topic of debate one of the prime topics in public discourse, media attention was tremendous. TV, nationwide newspapers and radio stations as well as other observers attended the conference and enabled a widespread news coverage.[8]

In all three phases, CLIL's distinction of being a genuinely transcurricular approach became visible. The multilingual methods employed not only resembled an authentic setting, but also caused students' deliberation of a more careful language use, to make sure they deliver their point appropriately and are actually understood. This clearly led to deeper cognitive processing to facilitate seamless de- and encoding, having a positive effect on the content. It appeared the multilingual climate facts offered security and scaffold to the group, since clear reference was given throughout to the material, mediating the content diligently. We believe this thwarted affective behavior and had a positive effect also on subject-based learning, which however was not formally assessed but can only be concluded from the overall proceedings and the final results of the last phase. For the entire conference, we felt the power of the glocality and the cosmopolitan visions of the students.

Evaluation

In order to gain insights for further research and development of the *PolECulE*-project, both for science and teaching practice, the students were asked to voluntarily participate in an evaluation at the end of the day. They were given a QUANQUAL questionnaire. 108 students gave their feedback (56%), summarized in the following paragraph. Detailed results are available in *Table 3* of the *Appendix*.

The quantitative part of the evaluation shows overall satisfaction with the multilingual concept of the conference. It does not seem that it disrupted the global understanding of climate change. As many qualitative comments indicate, it seemed to be a refreshing exercise, and helped the students to absorb the topic of climate change from different perspectives due to the higher use of cognitive resources necessary for following the conference. Some students indicated in the qualitative part of the survey that they had

---

[8] A conference video as well as the full media portfolio can be accessed here: http://polecule.com/2019/11/05/climonomics-so-lief-unsere-mehrsprachige-eu-klimakonferenz-fuer-schuelerinnen-25-10-2019/.

to concentrate more than usual, but in the end were able to improve language skills and language awareness, and to better understand the complexity of the subject. Disappointment about not being able to have ample speech time was expressed, as proxy for the overall motivation to actively take part in the proceedings.

Students were also asked to provide feedback with one emoji on their smartphones, in order to have a capture of their emotional state and feelings. A software tool was used to create a visual representation of the most frequently used emojis by size, while removing single-use emoji. *Figure 4* shows the result. We learned that many questions remain open, that further work is necessary, but also a certain state of confusion and even desperation, in accordance with the debate ending without an agreement. The positive smiley faces appear to indicate positive emotions and feelings about the project day. On the other side, also boredom was expressed, which should not be surprising considering the size of the conference.

Figure 4 emulates the emotional snapshot immediately after the conference, displayed by an emoji of choice.

The questionnaire as well as the immediate oral feedback serves as an incentive for refinement and project development for multilingual teaching concepts about 21st century challenges. It provides stimuli about how classroom glocalities can be constructed. In accordance with the informed consent of the students, the conference was fully videotaped. The close analysis of the footage will end in a more detailed videographic analysis. The digital reader has been edited and is in the process of publishing, to make *#climonomics* available not only for special events, but also for everyday teaching.

Looking to the Future: an Optimistic Outlook

From *#climonomics*, we learned that the construction of classroom glocalities with cosmopolitan visions in order to teach new literacies is more than just a theoretical model or a concept we had presented in the preceding sections. The development of both classroom and project-based teaching material, in accordance with research on sustainability didactics defining new literacies to prepare students for their agency towards 21st century challenges, remains an exciting exercise. We want to highlight that a theory-practice cooperation is essential for successful implementation of such ambitious visions.

Such a cooperation builds on the practical knowledge of stakeholders in schools (teachers and students), to render their pool of knowledge scientific, for further dissemination purposes. *PolE-CulE's* idea of thought were such partnerships, to produce sustainable teaching methods and material together with practitioners and students. Realizing often acrimonious debates about migration and refugees, to us it appears that a framework of seeing the positive sides of migration and cultural hybridity meets one of the main 21st century challenges, an epoch characterized by globalization. Classroom glocalities with cosmopolitan visions, mirroring the multilingual everyday reality, provide an apt conceptional framework for reformist movements in education. Both language skills and awareness as well as subject knowledge can be productively used by using student's knowledge and resources as productive starting points. ESD, as legally concluded by the member states of the United Nations Economic, Social and Cultural Organization (UNESCO), provides for a desired concept in line with the needs for coming generations. *PolECulE* as a project will end mid of 2021. Due to the demand in accordance with official political targets, funding for *"The Blue Planet"* as a follow-up project with the goal to promote a didactic for ESD in similar spirit has already been secured.[9] It seems that many young people have already understood the challenges that await them. The task of didactic and educational research is to provide them with tools to develop agency and meet these challenges.

As previously stated, we opened this article with two quotes from Greta Thunberg, as her voice exemplifies the importance of

---

[9] More information can be found at http://www.theblueplanetproject.de

youth speaking out about glocal issues, and now we will conclude with her powerful and pointed words.

> *"This is the year 2019. This is not the time and place for dreams. This is the time to wake up. This is a moment in history where we need to be wide awake."*
> [her speech in front of the United States Congress, Washington, D.C., September 2019]

Appendix

A Selection of Tweets during the Main #*climonomics* Parliamentary Debate

The following selected tweets, which on purpose remain uncommented for the readers of the article to develop own impressions, mirror the proceedings of the EU plenary debate of #*climonomics*.

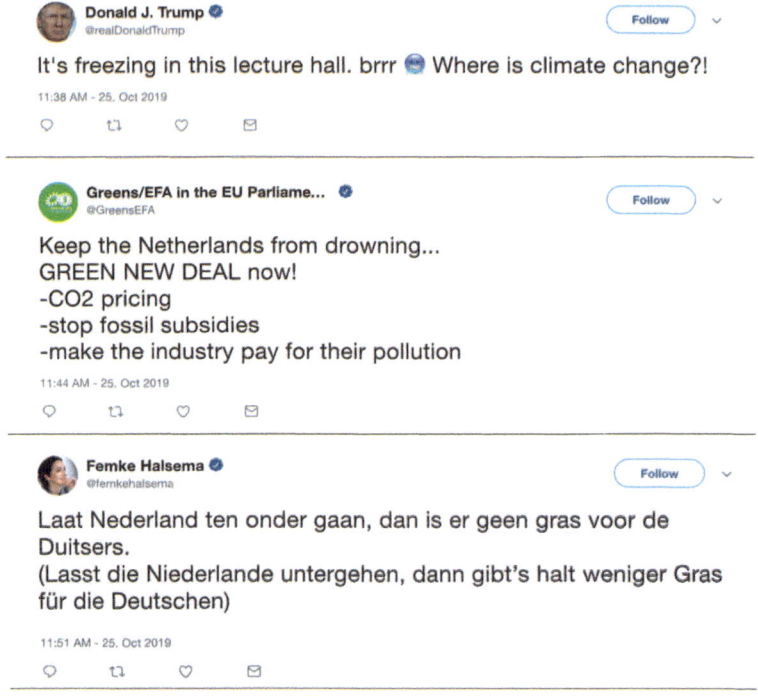

Evaluation Data of #climonomics

Table 3 lists selected quantitative evaluation results (N = 108).

Item	average	SD
I liked the digital conference reader...	1.8	0.8
I liked the multilingual concept of the conference...	1.7	0.7
4 point Liekert scale: 1 – very much; 4 – not at all *(positive scaling)*		

Item	Average	SD
I learned a lot of new climate facts...	3.3	1.1
The multilingual concept was instrumental for properly occupying my role during the debate...	2.9	1.4
I feel insecure answering in a foreign language in front of others...	2.4	1.2
Multilingualism actually led to miscommunication in groups and the plenary...	1.7	1
Using foreign languages lead me to see the topic more globally...	3.4	1.4
It was more difficult for me to persuade others in a foreign language...	2.7	1.2
I was able to note that my political judgement is different in a foreign as compared to my first language...	2.0	1.3
I listened more carefully during multilingual phases...	3.5	1.3
Switching languages also enabled me to switch to other positions ...	2.7	1.3
I could participate better, because I was allowed to use my first language besides German and English *(only for non-first language users of German and English: N=16)*...	2.8	1.5
I rather consider the multilingual part as unnatural...	2.2	1.1
Thanks to the multilingual concept, I was able to improve my English language skills in the topic area beyond my German knowledge	3.7	1.1
5 point Liekert scale: 1 – completely disagree; 3 – neutral; 5 – completely agree *(negative scaling)*		

Chapter IV

...about the science of practical knowledge...

Bridging the Gap between Theory and Practice with Design-based Action Research

Abstract

This article proposes design-based action research as an addendum to large-scale educational research. Placing design-based research together with teachers' action research into one single method, this study takes a pragmatic approach in accordance with Dewey's (1938) philosophy on democratic change in education. Its participatory methodological framework includes stakeholders directly into the discourse about educational improvements and reforms. To make my claims substantial, I will elucidate why teachers' practical knowledge is of paramount importance for bridging the well-known gap between theory and practice. I will exemplify the constructed method with a research project exploring the potential of The Simpsons for bilingual Politics & Economics classes. I will argue that the overall approach I offer makes practical knowledge become scientific. Additionally, considerations for including design-based action research as a methodological pathway into teacher education are mentioned.

Keywords: *design-based research, action research, mētis, pragmatism, teacher education, educational reforms*

Status: **Published**
Nijhawan, S. (2017). Bridging the gap between theory and practice with 'design-based action research'. *Studia Paedagogica: Special issue on Teacher Education and Educational Research, 22*(4), 9-29. doi:10.5817/SP2017-4-2

Listed in the bibliography as Nijhawan (2017).

Introduction

Latest with the launch of the triennial Programme for International Student Assessment (PISA) in 2000, large-scale empirical educational research has been dominating the discourse about educational reform. The use of standardized research tools generating a multitude of data sets for complex statistical analysis has triggered sweeping responses by policy makers. In contrast, methods that enable educators to directly intervene into educational contexts and thus consolidate theory with practice mostly remain a flash in the pan within this discourse.

What follows may at times be a bit personal, but it is nevertheless congruent with the overall approach of this article. It centers on the topic of how the voice and knowledge of the main stakeholders — i.e., teachers and students — can be embedded from inside the profession into scientific educational discourse. I firmly state that this article must have a personal dimension because I as its author occupy a dual role as a teacher at a secondary school and a research associate at Goethe University Frankfurt. I am part of the *PolECule*[1] project team that endeavors to develop theories of teaching and learning in bilingual Politics & Economics classes engendering from the practice of teaching. Indeed, it is the utmost objective of *PolECule* to consolidate theory and practice and fill that well-known gap. Especially the practical knowledge of educators teaching bilingual classes enjoys paramount significance as a gear of innovation within the ideological foundation of the project. Therefore, a proximity to the methods of anthropology, in the sense of field interventions in an overall natural environment, can easily be constructed.

When teachers are asked for advice to solve practical problems, statements such as the following are often echoed: "*This*

---

[1] *PolECule* is an acronym for politics, economics, and culture. The project was started in 2015 with the intention of developing educational standards for bilingual classes in this subject along with practical teaching and learning methods. The final version of a conceptual framework was completed in October 2017. The remainder of the project revolves around developing materials and methods for the practice of teaching. More at http://www.polecule.com.

method has always worked in my classes," "My impression is...," "In my experience...." To twist this argument a little, students in education and teaching at university as well as teacher trainees at school mostly ask me questions that can be put in bits and pieces into the following nutshell: *"Can you give us some practical tips and advice on what to do in such a situation that is not too theoretical?"* Students and teacher trainees usually then show due attentiveness and eagerly take notes and share their own humble experiences while displaying emotions and passion.

The outcome of similar discussions mostly ends in a cacophony of voices. On the one hand, this illustrates a large pool of impressive knowledge—often very personal but professional narratives that matter! On the other hand, this conglomeration of knowledge may—or may not—help in practice, but it hardly adds anything to theory due to a lack of a scientific essence. Experience alone does not necessarily suffice. Truly it can overwhelm any attempt at professionalism. Yet it would be a real pity and inappropriate to indulge in ignorance and reluctance because the stories teachers tell constitute notable vernacular narratives. In this vein, the following very emotional passage from five teachers highlights this train of thought:

> And teachers? We are characterised as unwitting participants in the system, lazy, not so bright, unwilling to accept responsibility for our failures, or sometimes, in ways taken up by Hollywood screenwriters, isolated and heroic. The current and most frequently suggested fix is to use tests and standards to make practitioners more accountable and offer 'research-based' guidance to those willing to improve. (Schaenen, Kohnen, Flinn, Saul, & Zeni, 2012, p. 68)

These five teachers articulate a valid concern. They want their case to be taken seriously within the educational discourse and their knowledge to contribute to theory in education. For this reason, I will proceed in the following manner. To begin, I will discuss the effect large-scale quantitative empirical research has had on education policy making and reforms, taking the so-called PISA effect as a starting point. My criticism is not directed towards any such initiative. Rather, building on Schön's (1983) famous distinction between technical rationality and reflection-in-action, I want to unfold more pragmatic research as a useful complement within the educational discourse and emphasize a plea for pluralism of methods in educational science. From Finnish success at PISA, we learn, *inter alia*, that the role of teachers in learning is seminal. I will therefore construct an argument referring to the modernist critique of science in the sense that practical knowledge, although ostensibly unscientific, matters. The next step consists of examining whether methodic pragmatism as a bottom-up methodology can be a harbinger of a science of practical knowledge. I will outline my train of thought in presenting my research project for the thesis requirements of my own teacher training a few years ago. The main part of this article is thus theoretical in nature. In a Weberian sense, it is an appeal to consider the dual roles of teachers as researchers because good scientists are good teachers and *vice versa* (Weber, 1919).

Who dominates the educational discourse? PISA and its Finnish paradox

In an open letter to Dr. Andreas Schleicher, the director at the Organization for Economic Co-operation and Development (OECD) responsible for PISA, more than 80 academics and educational experts from around the world expressed their firm opposition to PISA. One of the main criticisms was the exclusion of the main stakeholders, including students and educators. The authors of the letter further excoriated the method of collecting and analyzing data because it merely centered around economic aspects in public education (Meyer & Zahedi, 2014). PISA's logic consists of assessments in mathematics, science, and reading, with multiple data sets to rank countries' educational institutions globally. As the open letter pointed out, the steering committee comprises mainly external "psychometricians, statisticians, and economists" (p. 873) who design the tests, evaluate the scores, and put forward policy recommendations.

In some countries, PISA results have been met with cheerful joy. For instance, they constituted a positive surprise for Finland, whereas the United Kingdom showed pride in self-affirmation. In contrast, many other countries suffered from a PISA shock — in some cases such as Germany a quite strong one indeed (Grek, 2009). The bottom line is that PISA has led to ongoing, at times acrimonious, discussions and widespread consequences in education in many countries and has crucially changed education policies around the globe. Recognizing the paradigm shift towards a strictly numeric and "evidence-based policy agenda," Sahlberg (2006; 2011, p. 176) spoke of a new "Global Education Reform Movement" (GERM). He first acknowledged that GERM encompasses many progressive aspects. It is a positive attempt to react to the demands and challenges of the new global knowledge economy in providing students with key competences, such as "problem solving, emotional and multiple intelligences, and interpersonal skills rather than the memorization of facts or the mastery of irrelevant skills" (Sahlberg, 2011, p. 176). Furthermore, he endorsed the fact that in light of the United Nations Millennium Development Goals core emphasis is being placed on basic literacy and numeracy skills for the many people who had thus far been deprived of education.

However, he directed sharp criticism toward very crucial implications of PISA. He concluded that the backwash effect from merely focusing on "successful performance in standardized tests" (Sahlberg, 2006, p. 260) jeopardizes "creativity, flexibility and risk-taking" (2006, p. 275; 2011, p. 178), the driving forces for innovation in classroom teaching. The role of the teacher disappears in the quest to comply with GERM's prescriptions for performing well in comparative assessments. In sum, this erosion of teachers' creative leeway also stands in stark contrast with the demand for democratic participation by the authors of the open letter. Moreover, GERM has never defined a road map for best classroom practices for improving learning environments to achieve student success, not to mention dealing with the resulting insecurity, uncertainty, and pressure on educators.

Ironically, Finland, which emerged from PISA as the main educational showcase, has a culture of educational practice in diametrical opposition to the more universal and centrally planned GERM policies from external experts. The conclusions to be drawn from the Finnish paradox are that it is necessary to support a vernacularization of the global educational discourse, build on local solutions, and accept the pivotal importance of teachers in cooperatively designing and managing learning processes in the education system — see also Sellar and Lingard (2013), who trace the growing impact of the OECD on education in their review essay. Of course, this is by no means meant to be a call to jettison the methodology and findings of PISA *per se*. Rather, in defense of methodological pluralism, conclusions drawn from such large-scale studies can be supplemented by exploring certain issues and deficits from inside to ultimately establish a direct link to practice and natural environments.

As a consequence, and learning from Finland's longstanding "culture of diversity, trust, and respect" (Sahlberg, 2011, p. 182) in education, we should ask the question of how teachers as internal experts, knowing the dynamic field from their daily routines, can acquire practical knowledge in order to contribute to the discourse on educational reform from inside. This is something Goodwin (1994) would call "professional vision." The following sections will therefore explore the two fundamental sides of the coin. Why does practical knowledge matter so much? Can more exploratory and pragmatic methods be instrumental in providing teachers with the repertoire to sustainably develop practical knowledge? As a complement, can such methods bolster theory development for science, and thus for the discourse on educational reform, complementary to large-scale research? Let us first ask why a focus on the practical knowledge of teachers, comprising numerous personal narratives, is at all material to educational improvements and reforms, and why it needs to be at the same level as all findings and conclusions from large-scale studies.

Why practical knowledge matters: about mētis and educational innovation

In his book *Seeing like a State*, James C. Scott (1998) asked why so many policy programs by states, based on the most sophisticated and up-to-date scientific methods, have failed to improve human living conditions. To find possible explanations for the missing link between theory and practice, he turned to the ancient Greek concept of *mētis*, which he compared with a "rule of thumb" (Scott, 1998, p. 312). Mētis is acquired by experience, intuition, and stochastic reasoning with its basis in local vernacularism. It constitutes practical knowledge that addresses "the problem at hand." He continued by clarifying:

> Mētis is most applicable to broadly similar but never precisely identical situations requiring a quick and practiced adaptation that becomes almost second nature to the practitioner. [...] Mētis resists simplification into deductive principles which can successfully be transmitted through book learning, because the environments in which it is exercised are so complex and nonrepeatable that formal procedures of rational decision making are impossible to apply. In a sense, mētis lies in that large space between the realm of genius, to which no formula can apply, and the realm of codified knowledge, which can be learned by rote. (Scott, 1998, p. 316)

A comparison with farmers having defined the arrival of the Ice Saints over decades, and the adaption of farming and harvesting, may illustrate the general train of thought. In addition to Scott's use of mētis to provide conceptual policy approaches in the field of international development, a renaissance of mētis can be witnessed especially in the applied sciences. More specifically, it has been rejuvenated for improvements in, *inter alia*, management learning (e.g., Mackay, Zundel, & Alkirwi, 2014) and organizational theory (e.g., Letiche & Statler, 2005). These two articles provide a detailed and compelling genealogy of mētis from the Greek mythology and its adoption into modern thought by Detienne and Vernant (1978). Furthermore, we can learn more about the benefit of mētis for research and development in the sciences due to its potential to solve complex and situational problems and thus stimulate innovation while steadily maintaining a close proximity to the field. Letiche and Statler (2005, p. 4) went so far as to contend that mētis "cannot be ignored as a source of creativity or innovation." They emphasized its returns for solving problems in special and unforeseeable circumstances where the virtues of science often remain limited.

Against the backdrop of this and from Clifford Geertz' famous account (2000) about the virtue of local knowledge—or common sense—I want to borrow the concept of mētis to highlight the paramountcy of teachers' practical knowledge. Possessing and gradually developing mētis is highly relevant for a strong nexus between theory and practice in educational research and teaching and as an indispensable source of creativity and innovation, as Finland and its PISA success has illustrated. Teaching or studying mētis from textbooks, as Scott points out, is close to impossible. Thus, efforts are necessary to promoting the development of mētis already among teacher trainees through facilitating methods to closely observe the natural learning environment and engage in experimental activity. Trial-and-error logic occupies the foreground because any subjective theory develops by doing it yourself, reflection, and adaption — on a small scale.

There is no universal formula for mētis as such, as it is not static but fluid and defined in local varieties. However, teacher education can promote specific methodological competences — including something like a kit with a broad repertoire of tools — as a road map for developing mētis to remedy context-specific challenges and also contribute to developing theory. In other words, I see collateral expertise in teaching and scientific research as essential for educational change. In a broader sense, we can relate this plea to Dewey's theory of knowledge, and in particular to his book *Experience and Education* (Dewey, 1938). He was concerned about developing a theory of positive educational experience among teachers by which, per Scott, mētis develops. To engender such an educational experience, Dewey called for educators to inquire directly into natural environments. Interaction and an "experimental continuum" are, he believed, instrumental for the construction of knowledge. Additionally, such a process-based approach makes the discourse on educational reform and changes take place more among equals, empowering stakeholders to contribute to any innovations together with the GERM planners.

Dewey is often identified as one of the precursors of action research by teachers. His theory includes stakeholders into the overall discourse and is thus tantamount to an attempt to democratize and reform institutional arrangements pragmatically. The following section will deal with the question of how far these preliminary theoretical thoughts can work in practice. I will discuss methods of pragmatic research against the background of making it into a science in order to "evoke mētis ... in a cultural milieu that is replete with facile invocations of creativity, change and innovation" (Letiche & Statler, 2005, p. 13). At this point, let me clarify that references to mētis in the remainder of this article serve as a positive synonym for practical knowledge.

Anything goes? Almost! A science of mētis with design-based action research

In comparison with the laborious PISA and large-scale studies involving a large body of researchers, at first glance any idea to include individual teachers with their mētis into the educational discourse appears to have minimal impact. I contend, however, that the relationship between positivist approaches and more pragmatic ones does not at all constitute a zero-sum game. The question is how mētis can be made scientific and become an instrumental data set for educational discourse and professional teacher training.

At first glance, including teachers' mētis may sound like methodological anarchy. However, let me twist this argument in accordance with the ideas of Paul Feyerabend (1993). I argue that almost anything goes! Borrowing from Scott, the sum of all mētis is a unique body of knowledge instrumental for solutions in specific learning contexts. The business of teachers includes conducting numerous interactions and decisions during the quotidian vicissitude of classroom dynamics that are always unique and special. Juxtaposing Scott and Feyerabend, we have a high number of ad-hoc hypotheses with a need for an immediate however without much time for deliberation. Such ad-hoc hypotheses as well as the ensuing actions lay the groundwork for the genesis of mētis at a later stage. That means, "almost anything goes" if "professional anarchists" (Feyerabend, 1993, p. 12) systematically contribute to a science of mētis.

My use of Feyerabend's concept of professional anarchists is intended to establish a methodological guideline for teacher education and training to consolidate teachers' daily experiences with the need to contribute to innovative theories in the field of educational research. However, this approach should by no means restrict teachers in their exploratory and experimental liberty, as is implied by the word anarchist. Teachers' action research provides an apt starting point for engendering mētis. The analogy Scott constructs with reference to Charles Lindblom's famous expression of the "science of muddling through," or as I would put it "the art of teaching," mirrors this general idea. A central idea for action research is that the stimulus for taking the initiative originates with the teachers themselves with their incentive and interest to acquire further insights from a question or issue deserving deeper and more systematic scrutiny (Baumfield, Hall, & Wall, 2012).

There are many models of action research in various textbooks that are differentiated to various degrees. Their logic mainly consists of the following circular pathway: (1) identifying a problem and planning the intervention, (2) acting, (3) observing and collecting data, and (4) analyzing and reflecting.

The theoretical foundations can be explicitly traced back to Kurt Lewin, who set milestones for this method around the time of World War II (Lewin, 1946). The closeness of Lewin to Dewey's pragmatism and his endeavor to democratically reform educational institutions from bottom-up is quite clear (Stark, 2014; Thiollent, 2011). Pragmatism is, of course, a stark contrast to large-scale empirical research with its roots in the logic of scientific positivism and thus mostly relies on assessment in educational contexts.

During action research, the teacher isochronally occupies the dual role of a practical researcher. The inclusion of insiders, teachers, and students throughout the research process lies at the heart of the idea, as action research relies on their local knowledge and feedback during the teaching and research process. Adelman (1993, p. 8) emphasized that action research since Lewin "gives credence to the development of powers of reflective thought, discussion, decision and action by ordinary people." Thus, its proximity to the natural learning environment with the full involvement of all stakeholders constitutes its biggest virtue.

The literature on action research does not see a team structure among researchers as necessarily given. This means that action research can also be conducted proactively by one single researcher. However, some literature on action research strongly recommends a team of researchers to engender multiperspectivity (Fichten, 2005). Thus, a team of researchers and educators as an "ethical stance" provides the basis for a fruitful and "professional dialogue" (Baumfield et al., 2012), as opposed to lone fighters who are hardly able to systematically develop and especially theorize mētis outside a team structure.[2] Another benefit is that a team structure obviates the danger to bias the data collected and thus mitigates threats to scientific validity (Schaenen et al., 2012, p. 79). Argyris et al. (1985) termed this more experimental and inductive approach "action science" (cf. Adelman, 1993, p. 12). To conclude in accordance with Thiollent (2011), action research can provide a powerful alternative for scientific inquiry.

Nevertheless, action research is often still attacked for being not scientific because theory development must yield to practical application. This also explains why action research is clearly underrepresented in the literature on the educational sciences. As opposed to more mainstream methods, action research is mostly used in single cases without the findings being made available to the broader practitioner and scientific communities respectively. It is primarily employed to resolve very specific and contextual problems in local and very unique situations and settings. That means that the mētis acquired during the process could remain concealed and faint. Although we can infer from Scott's approach that the sum of all single cases produces a powerful pool of mētis, i.e. "knowledge that is *useful*[3] outside the scientific community" (Pålshaugen, 2009, p. 232), we need to find pathways to generate theories from this very useful knowledge. Or to put it better, the involvement of teacher training in similar activities for replication

---

[2] There are many practical handbooks on how to conduct action research in practice. It is important, however, to keep in mind that the use of such assistance as a result of individual motivation is rather unlikely because the matter of action research as such remains very complex and time-demanding against the background of teachers' daily work. Moreover, the question of the incentives for engaging in such projects at all remains unanswered from many teachers' points of view.

[3] Emphasis in the original.

purposes deserves serious consideration. Team structures comprising experts from various areas are doubtless a good starting point. Making mētis from single-case interventions available to the scientific community is therefore realistic, as Pa'lshaugen (2009) summarized. But how can we facilitate such a science of mētis?

A very similar, yet in some significant ways also very different, approach is design-based research, which also works within a pragmatic outline. This comparatively new methodological framework found its beginnings in the seminal papers of Brown (1992) and Collins (1992). Design-based research is used in natural learning environments with the ultimate goal of testing and developing grander learning theories. A close partnership between teachers and scientific researchers during the research process constitutes the main foundation of the methodology. Brown (1992) noted that design-based research produces reliable and replicable theories that work in practice:

> We must operate always under the constraint that an effective intervention should be able to migrate from our experimental classroom to average classrooms operated by and for average students and teachers, supported by realistic technological and personal support. (Brown, 1992, p. 143)

As the second popular representative of design-based research from its beginnings, Collins (1992) emphasized that its experimental character offers a great deal of distance from the grand theories of education. He nevertheless called it a science of education, pointing out that it is not a classical analytical science but a design science.

During the past 25 years, interest in and application of design-based research has been constantly growing (see Anderson & Shattuck, 2012, for an empirical analysis of the rise in frequency). Over this time span, it has been under close scrutiny regarding its value for scientific research in education and beyond. A decade after its advent, the Design-Based Research Collective (2003) concluded that design-based research had tremendously helped in the creation and dissemination of knowledge. The authors continued by stating that successful interventions by teachers were based on theoretically designed artifacts. It is no wonder why research on local interventions can contribute to the development of more general theory, as members of the research initiative clarified in another seminal paper: "Design experiments are pragmatic as well as theoretical in orientation in that the study of function—both of the design and of the resulting ecology of leaning—is at the heart of the methodology" (Cobb, Confrey, diSessa, Lehrer, & Schauble, 2003, p. 9). Similarly, Barab Barab and Squire (2004, p. 5) importantly noted that "a critical component of design-based research is that the design is conceived not just to meet local needs, but to advance a theoretical agenda, to uncover, explore, and confirm theoretical relationships."

An example of a very comprehensive design exercise from New Zealand should illustrate the approach. Timperley, Wilson, Barrar, and Fung (2007) argued from their research on teachers' professional learning that skills development alone does not suffice without any reference to theory. The overarching *Best Evidence Synthesis Programme*, originating from a policy initiative, serves as a powerful example of the link between academic educational research and its implementation in practice. Through a wide array of case studies, the process and results, along with implications for teaching, were presented. The authors evaluated the effect on teachers' professional learning as overtly positive (Timperley et al., 2007). Taking up the issue of sustainability and theory generation, they concluded that the approach "proved useful but cannot be considered adequate as a theory of professional learning. More work is needed" (Timperley et al., 2007, p. 228).

Despite the drive for innovation through the increase in design-based research, several shortcomings, as noted by Timperley et al. (2007) themselves, provide a *caveat* for scientific endeavors, possibly due to a missing link with mētis. At this point, we need to ask ourselves whether a more horizontal integration of teachers into the research and educational discourse could work. However, the largest problems includes the issue of researcher bias in design-based research. This is a common problem with methods directly involving the researcher in the field, as is known from traditional anthropological field research (Anderson & Shattuck, 2012). Bias in data selection, which means selecting cases that support claims and elucidate success stories at the cost of the average case, can lead to fallacies with more general theories during inference (Brown, 1992). This again suggests that design-based research provides more intellectual distance, albeit at the cost of the science of mētis being targeted. In order to cease going round in circles and yet arriving at a dead end, the sincere question I want to ask at this point may sound very trivial but at the same time it is fundamental: what value can more pragmatic methods such as design-based research and action research add to science and practice? Can researchers compensate for their shortcomings?

As often echoed, the unconditional application of grand theories in complex classroom environments does not necessarily lead to the desired success. We need reliable tools to verify whether mētis really works. Now, we could learn that design-based research is theory-driven and has the main feature of generating new theories from interventions into practice. However, the team's researchers do, in the end, act from outside. Changing perspectives again, action research emanates from challenges teachers face in practice with the ultimate goal of engendering pragmatic solutions from inside. It provides only a modicum of potential for a science of mētis because its link to science as such is now too little institutionalized and extracted. Action research, as many see it, fails to meet the criteria to be a scientific method because it is too embedded in practice (Richards, 2003, p. 26). Why not establish a powerful approach combining both action and design-based research into a pragmatic research method that aims theory development and mitigates the mentioned deficits?

The general idea is, of course, not a new one. In the area of information science and technology, Cole, Purao, Rossi, and Sein (2005) called for action design research. They pointed out the commonalities and basically suggested using parallel processes from both methodologies to synthesize two-way interchanges of information. Some of the aforementioned authors suggested in a subsequent article that action design research constitutes a new form of design-based research (Sein, Henfridsson, Purao, Rossi, & Lindgren, 2011). This means that their methodology is strongly biased towards design-based research.

I wish nevertheless to turn their proposition around. Earlier I argued that mētis enjoys a central role in developing practical solutions in teaching and made a plea for a science of mētis. Any combined methodology must be accordingly biased and focus on mētis as the matrix. For this reason, I wish to argue for design-based action research instead, with a light focus on action research. The features of design-based research have the power to transmute it into a strong science. I suggest that dovetailing the two methods gives teachers theoretical assistance in intervening with mētis into their real-world environments. The developed solutions can in turn be compounded into "something grander," meaning "contextual theories of teaching and learning with a medium degree of generality" (see also Fischer, Waibel, & Wecker, 2005; The Design-Based Research Collective, 2003).

We can find this overall idea mirrored in Cochran-Smith and Lytle (1999), who distinguished during teacher learning in communities among (1) knowledge-for-practice, (2) knowledge-in-practice, and (3) knowledge-of- practice. While the first can be equated with the body of science taught in university for direct application in teaching (formal knowledge, as in PISA), and the second originates from "wisdom in practice" (Cochran-Smith & Lytle, 1999, p. 265; practical knowledge, which means mētis). The last form of knowledge, knowledge-of-practice, as the authors emphasized, combines the first two. As the authors argued, a blurring distinction eliminates any hierarchy and "serve[s] to reify divisions that keep teachers 'in their place' — the separation of practitioners from researchers, doers from thinkers, actors from analysts, and actions from ideas" (Cochran-Smith & Lytle, 1999, p. 289). The core of their approach comprises both process-based action and design fashion amid a close collaborative structure within the school and with academic institutions for publicizing local knowledge with the objective of generating theory. Inquiry by teachers in a team structure consisting of direct stakeholders and outside experts, meaning "discourse-particular ways of describing, discussing, and debating teaching" (Cochran-Smith & Lytle, 1999, p. 294), in the end constitutes agency within a democratic and participatory setting. So the authors concluded:

> [R]ich descriptive talk and writing help make visible and accessible the day-to-day events, norms, and practices of teaching and learning and the ways different teachers, students, administrators, and families understand them. In this way, participants conjointly uncover relationships between concrete cases and more general issues and constructs. (Cochran-Smith & Lytle, 1999, pp. 294-295)

The commonalities between design-based action research and this account are obvious, as I suggested above. In order to exemplify how this approach can work in practice, I will now present my research project for my thesis as a teacher trainee.

Looking back to the future: how theory and practice can benefit from design-based action research

In the introduction, I clarified my dual role as a teacher and researcher, occupying a space between the two professions with my endeavor to contribute to filling the gap between theory and practice. Then, I showed how a science of mētis can become a powerful tool for discourse about educational improvement and reform. I strongly defended design-based action research as an apt method, as I believe it combines practice and theory. Now I will briefly exemplify this train of thought with my practical research project for my state examination towards my teaching license.

It was the following observation that attracted my initial interest in starting a deeper inquiry. While I was a trainee, I was given the opportunity to try my fortune in teaching bilingual Politics & Economics classes (German as the school language, English as a foreign language), an area with thus far a very modest body of teaching and learning theories. From my first contact with practice, I observed that, roughly speaking, there were two groups of learners who did not feel completely comfortable with bilingual teaching. A classroom conversation revealed the following: group 1 consisted mainly of students interested in the English language but with no motivation for Politics & Economics as a subject. Group 2 comprised completely opposite students, namely those possessing no motivation for English but great interest in Politics & Economics. Thus, there was a challenge to develop an approach to cater to all of the learners' needs and preferences, including those lacking in skills and motivation.

In a micro experiment, I started using *The Simpsons* in order to promote both language and subject learning. From my observations and a first round of open feedback, I could infer that group 1 seemed to particularly enjoy the content of the TV series, and, as a consequence, vividly participated in exercises surrounding the subject of Politics & Economics. Group 2, in turn, was caught by the interplay of semantics and visuals, despite their initial reluctance toward the foreign language. As the content, owing to their interests, initiated an unprecedented willingness to take part in classroom exercises, it seemed likely that the *The Simpsons* had the potential to increase interest, and thus also the learning outcomes, in the bilingual subject. Thus, the idea for action to design, evaluate, reflect upon, and theorize a more systematic use of *The Simpsons* in classrooms resulted in a project to fulfill my thesis requirement. I named it *A Visit by Five Yellow People from Springfield, USA, to a German 9th Grade: What Can The Simpsons Contribute to Bilingual Teaching in Politics & Economics?* (Nijhawan, 2013).

After developing the main idea for the project, a literature review directed me towards a significant number of accounts describing the potential of *The Simpsons* to teach the contents of politics, economics, society, and culture (e.g., Cantor, 1999; Hall, 2005; Kristiansen, 2001; Scanlan & Feinberg, 2000). Obviously, action research constituted the logical method for the thesis because teacher trainees are required to demonstrate that they can plan, evaluate, and critically reflect upon a classroom project. As my interest in the question became more intense, and I believed that discussing my approach and outcomes would add value to this inquiry's findings, I decided to establish a collaborative structure with interested colleagues from school and experts from university. The classroom atmosphere and student–teacher relationship had proven to be excellent, providing an outstanding opportunity to place the students' feedback at the center of the thesis.

Of course, such a project needs to go beyond merely watching the episodes in their full entity and having some unspecified classroom discussion. Rather, the real challenge was to make the students deliberate closely on the content, employing a progressive pedagogical concept. I therefore decided to use video sequencing as proposed by Swaffar and Vlatten (1997). In short, this includes reducing the input to 3–5 minutes per sequence and then combining it with task-based learning exercises in accordance with the relevant curriculum and the supply of designed material. In close consultation with the team structure I had established, I developed on four design cycles with the topics: (1) democracy, (2) social protest, (3) multiculturalism, and (4) the world of work.

I intentionally planned a full qualitative analysis of student feedback and output (observations, classroom discussions, and content analysis of written products). The analysis concluded with lessons learned from each design cycle as the first step towards a more comprehensive conclusion and the formulation of theories at the end of the study. For the final evaluation after the last cycle, I included a QUANQUAL survey also for internal triangulation purposes, thus ensuring the internal validity of the conclusions that developed during the continuous "action of designing, evaluating, and redesigning." *Table 1* gives an overview of the research process along with the lessons learned from each design cycle. The box at the bottom presents some data from the final survey. Since a full presentation of all results would have exceeded the scope of this section, I had to choose a small selection simply to demonstrate how design-based action research can look in practice. By no means do I mean to engage in academic cherry-picking with the data I decided to include. Rather, I am happy to provide further insights into the raw data upon request.

Table 1 Overview of the research process

setting/input/objectives	lessons learned from output and feedback
(1) Democracy (*Episode 8F01 (3/1991): Mr. Lisa Goes to Washington*) The first cycle included a session planned in the smallest detail comprising preplanned oral and written activities, such as a world café as a tool for language learning and visualizing the political concepts. Structured classroom discussions, including comparisons to Germany and beyond, were intended to deepen the content.	(1) need to try a more open arrangement (independent study); (2) more language work needed.
(2) Social protest (*Episode 3F06 (7/1995): Mother Simpson*) The second cycle included an openly planned lesson, with independent study at home as the main focus. Students were asked to explore a topic of interest with reference to social protest. They were prepared with historical input about anti-Cold War activism in the classroom. Core vocabulary with world fields was disseminated.	(1) vocabulary assistance is a must; (2) independent research needs structure as doubts about comprehension prevail; (3) risk of plagiarism needs to be actively addressed.
(3) Multiculturalism (*Episode 5F04 (9/1997): The Two Mrs. Nahasapeemapetilons*) The third cycle included a full set of elective and clear-cut research tasks along with the dos and don'ts of internet research. The research took place in pairs to find solutions together. Some of the research was supervised in the computer lab to address problems instantly. Online sources (vocabulary and content) were provided.	A lack of controversy – key for P&E lessons - made the exercise rather dull. The students suggested to supplement the exercise with role plays and other methods in the classroom.
(4) The world of work (*Episode 9F15 (4/1993): Last exit to Springfield*) In addition to research tasks, the last cycle included a number of classroom exercises to engender multiperspectivity. Creative writing tasks with optional perspective changes (along with language work) were introduced. The cycle ended with a written exam to monitor any change and progress in competences.	Subject and language learning improved. But there is a need for further micro methods. The feedback structure requires optimization. An emphasis on language correctness is needed.

Selected results from the final survey (N=23): (1) 17 students (74%) believed that the language work was more effective than lessons from the schoolbook, (2) 13 students (57%) confirmed that *The Simpsons* positively affected their interest in politics and economics, not a single student declared that they felt bored. **Example from the qualitative item [sic]:** (1) "I learned a lot of very important vocabulary I wouldn't have learned with the book. But my grammer never was the best but through watching and hearing how real americans speak (by the simpsons) I can build better sentences. I learned a lot of politics with the Simpson and i like that way because its not so strict and easy to understand.", (2) "I'm actually not very interested in Politics and Economics, but the Simpsons made me understand it much better."

The conclusions I summarized in my thesis mainly consisted of lessons learned from this contextual exercise. I then developed theoretical thoughts. Overall, I intended to show how an idea can be systematically implemented into the practice of teaching while contextually theorizing the findings along with recommendations for similar exercises. I could report ample evidence from this single case study the potential of *The Simpsons* to increase competences in both language and subject learning, and thus bilingual teaching. In accordance with the lessons learned, I recommended that similar projects be conducted and further work on a catalogue of episodes be done to establish a link to political and economic content. These would do well to provide ideas on how teaching and exercises could look. Furthermore, I argued for a focus on, *inter alia*, language correctness and the prevention of plagiarism through copying and pasting during independent research. To ensure the sustainability of my mētis, I published a journal article providing both theoretical accounts and practical advice for implementation purposes (Nijhawan, 2014). I therefore firmly believe that this design-based action research project contributed to the educational dialogue and further replication and development. To break it down to Schön's (1983) famous formula, it was "doing and thinking" at the same time.

Concluding remarks and outlook: towards an institutionalization of design-based action research?

In this article, I pleaded for mandating teachers have more space in educational discourse directed at educational improvements and reforms. The value of mētis is indisputable and therefore should not remain shuttered. This plea was put forward alongside an appeal for the further democratization of educational institutions. Policy requires clamorous large-scale educational research to induce systematic reforms, while the voices of direct stakeholders too often remain concealed.

Employing design-based action research, as I suggested and then exemplified in the research project about the use of *The Simpsons* in bilingual Politics & Economics classes, has another positive side effect. This article has revolved around teachers' mētis because we must never forget that the daily work of teachers is determined by close contact with students. Students will always remain the main stakeholders in schools. Group work as a symbol of classroom democratization, in combination with a feedback culture and a routine of evaluation within design-based action research, will ideally provide their voices with more authority also in the educational discourse. In a larger sense, it is a dual track strategy. Modern and critical pedagogy is based in constructivist theory. Therefore, constructing a science of teachers' and students' mētis from below, and more horizontal structures in science *per se,* should be a welcomed approach when thinking beyond bridging the gap of theory and practice in education.

To reiterate, I see a strong synergetic relationship between positivist and pragmatic approaches. Pragmatic methods can prompt large-scale empirical research and *vice versa,* if representatives of each approach reciprocally acknowledge the use of the ostensible diametrical opposite. Scott (1998) has a nice way of exemplifying the synergy; he compared the more pragmatic approach with the ability to speak and the more positivist approach with grammar.

Let me present one more case referring to pragmatic methods as an example of the status quo of bilingual teaching in Germany. Bilingual classes can be characterized as a worldwide success story in terms of language and subject learning. Large-scale research has provided ample evidence about their overall effectiveness—e.g., DESI-Konsortium (2006), as the largest undertaking in Germany, and the classic example from Genesee (1987) in the context of Canada, with its long history of bi- and multilingual programs. However, the availability of clear-cut material in accordance with the curricula is close to zero. Moreover, competences to promote a bilingual surplus have not as yet been defined. As a matter of fact, there is a serious lack of qualified and trained personnel. Bilingual classes in German schools can thus only work with highly motivated teachers who are willing to spend extra time out of pure intrinsic motivation. Many of these pioneers have developed inestimable mētis. This means that a lot of mētis exists within schools with bilingual programs, without it having yet been made into a science. It would be distressing if this mētis remained concealed. Indeed, questions like "How do you actually teach bilingually?" are anything but uncommon. Against this background, a bilingual research project, along similar lines as the project with *The Simpsons*, was launched at the end of 2017. The research question will be: Which teaching and scaffolding methods can concurrently promote competence development in both the school and foreign language in Politics & Economics? Beyond developing mētis for making a science, I hope to provide further insights on the question of whether design-based action research proves a viable method for improving both teaching and academic inquiry.

Promoting incentives for both young and experienced teachers and researchers to engage in design-based action research can, as I have tried to show, be instrumental in consolidating practice and theory in bilingual teaching, and of course beyond. Any effort to bring academics and practitioners together within larger research teams, with some occupying dual roles, would be appreciated and indeed enrich the discourse about educational improvements and reforms. For this reason, I want to end this article with a plea to include design-based action research into teacher training from its first phase at university. Methodological approaches that are directed towards consolidation of the gap between theory and practice need a sustainable treatment to democratically promote reforms from below and increase democracy and accountability. This, of course, requires equal openness from the scientific community and practitioners to take each other's voices and perceptions seriously.

Chapter V

...about a potpourri of languages...

Translanguaging... or 'trans-foreign-languaging'? A comprehensive CLIL teaching model with judicious and principled L1 use

Abstract

Amidst the demand for multilingual pedagogies with L1 use in CLIL, this article at first investigates the novel concept of translanguaging as a possible panacea. Translanguaging mainly refers to natural multilingual practices of speakers with multicompetences beyond their most dominant language. However, doubts need to be expressed whether students without adequate language resources in the target language can fully enjoy all benefits. Thus, the concept was adapted into trans-foreign-languaging (Trans-FL), making its distinctness also available for CLIL and foreign language (FL) teaching. Following a classroom intervention into a 10th grade CLIL Politics & Economics classroom (English: L2 as FL; German: L1 as school language), three different models of Trans-FL were designed together with the students as main stakeholders. Their genesis from triangulated data was reconstructed as thick description, elucidating different intensities of dynamic bilingualism within natural classroom dynamics. Finally, they were incorporated into one single and comprehensive CLIL teaching model for an affordance-based and differentiated approach to FL learning, recognizing the needs of various student types. The result is a tangible pedagogy for rendering the overall idea of translanguaging with the focus on L1 use into a daily pedagogical practice in various CLIL contexts as well as for FL learning in general.

Keywords: *CLIL, translanguaging, trans-foreign-languaging, bilingual dynamism, thick description*

Statement about the status of the article:
The article has been published by the journal *Translation and Translanguaging in Multilingual Contexts*. The version printed here is the "author <u>submitted</u> manuscript" that significantly differs from the "author <u>accepted</u> manuscript" after the common double-blind peer-reviewing process. For the *finally published version*, please refer to the bibliographic information below. Reprint rights were granted by John Benjamins Publishing Company Amsterdam/Philadelphia (January 28th, 2022).

<u>Status:</u> **Published** *(in a completely revised version)*

Nijhawan, S. (2022). Translanguaging… or 'trans-foreign-languaging'? A comprehensive CLIL teaching model with judicious and principled L1 use. *Translation and Translanguaging in Multilingual Contexts, 8(2)*. doi:10.1075/ttmc.00087.nij

Listed in the bibliography as Nijhawan (2022).

How do I say this in my native language?!?

> "*I never knew that sustainability is actually called Nachhaltigkeit in German!*"
> [a student of an elective CLIL course in Politics & Economics, around the time of her A-Levels *("Abitur")*, after in total almost four years of CLIL classes in English, at a school in Germany].

The quote originates from a student who has grown up with German as first language (L1) in a monolingual environment. At the same time, she is a very talented foreign language (FL) learner. The CLIL course of 25 students was *de facto* taught fully immersive in English (L2) by the author (the teacher researcher, in the following TR). Despite officially being called <u>bi</u>*lingualer Sachfachunterricht*, immersion into L2 with CLIL is, as a matter of fact, a common practice in Germany (Breidbach & Viebrock, 2012).

Out of that course, 14 students finally chose to submit a CLIL A-levels *(Abitur)* exam. For all those students, English was a FL.[1] By state law, students of CLIL classes are always permitted to submit their CLIL-*Abitur* exams in German. It therefore comes as a surprise that none of these 14 students opted for German as exam language. They unanimously stated their fierce belief of not being able to sustain in their L1 under exam conditions, because the content had previously been taught in L2 over two years. This 'hard decision' at graduation, indeed the most decisive time of school education, indicates a high personal risk assessment during exam conditions in L1. Consequently, all *Abitur* candidates elected L2 as language of assessment, although the subject competence alone, and not language proficiency, composes the decisive grading criteria. To further escalate: all those students belong to rather elite backgrounds,

---

[1] Furthermore, German, the official school language, is L1 of almost all those students. For the small multilingual cohort in that course with different L1 as home languages, German was a second language (SL), albeit with *at least* full L1-equal proficiency. Diversity of home languages mirrors today's global multilingual reality, leading to multicompetences in different languages during different occasions on different levels.

visiting a traditional and prestige ancient language school with a humanist program. Learning deficits due to marginalization or social factors can be completely excluded with this particular cohort.

What do we learn from this account for academic research in CLIL? First and foremost, one can assume a self-perceived absence of equipollent language development and thus less security in L1 following immersive classroom practices in L2. This article, to say it clearly, will however not deal with the question *if* immersion should be sacrificed for truly _bi_lilngual CLIL in accordance with recent academic positions (see e.g., Dalton-Puffer & Smit, 2013; Lasagabaster & Sierra, 2010) – or what Dailey-O'Cain and Liebscher (2009, p. 131) call *"First Language Use in the Language Classroom: The Great Debate"*. Rather, to fully recognize the given deficit, the article focuses on *how* to integrate L1 into CLIL. In other words, it only deals with the pre-stage of that *great debate,* at the end concluding with 'a comprehensive CLIL teaching model with judicious and principled L1 use' as result of empirical classroom research. To already provide an outlook, such a model, of course, can serve as basis to examine the popular *if*-question at a later stage.

L1 use in CLIL: the *status quo* in academic research and teaching practice

Amidst the steep growth in Europe since the 1990s, of what was labeled *"bilingual teaching"* before, Marsh (1994) coined the expression of CLIL, subsuming all kinds of subject-based lessons in any other than the official school language. During that period of time, the *White Paper of the European Commission of the* European Union (EU) communicated the target to promote plurilingualism among its citizens by the means of language learning, among that CLIL (European Commission, 1995). The EU itself takes a broad approach and defines CLIL as *"all types of provision in which a second language (a foreign, regional or minority language and/or another official state language) is used to teach certain subjects in the curriculum other than languages lessons themselves"* (Eurydice, 2006, p. 8).

Against this background, Dalton-Puffer and Smit (2013) amplify CLIL's prime focus on content from its initial outset. However, *de facto* CLIL is characterized by a language bias. In many cases the target language is a FL (Nikula & Moore, 2019). CLIL is often acclaimed as a modern and immersive approach to FL learning, explaining the exponential growth of, in absolute majority, English-speaking CLIL programs, the global *lingua franca* of the 21st century (Breidbach & Viebrock, 2012; Fuller, 2015; Nikula & Dafouz, 2016). Although CLIL and immersion are completely different from their ideological onset (Lasagabaster & Sierra, 2010) and have even been characterized as *"natural enemies"* by Genesee (1987, p. 187), most of CLIL in Europe is *de facto* taught immersive in a target language (Breidbach & Viebrock, 2012; Gierlinger, 2015; Lasagabaster, 2013) — without any allocated space for L1.

Historically, the quest for L1 use within FL teaching is well-known (e.g., Butzkamm, 1973; Cook, 2001). Ever since the increase in CLIL programs as serious competitor of traditional approaches to FL teaching, such debate has been receiving a very stark momentum, engulfing *bi*lingual education in its history of origins. The quest for multilingual approaches to CLIL has accordingly been propelling. In this vein, a short review in the following section descries the distinctive and innovative merits of translanguaging as a relatively young concept.

Moving to the avant-garde of translanguaging

The notion of *translanguaging* has attracted the attention of many scholars and practitioners within the last decade. Most prominently, its history can be traced back to Cen Williams' famous application in the Welsh context as minority language, au pair with English in the same bilingual classroom (for a detailed historical traceback, see e.g., Lewis, Jones, & Baker, 2012). Latest with García's seminal work (e.g., 2009; with Li 2014; with Otheguy and Reid 2015), translanguaging finally attained world-wide recognition. She offers insights into natural discursive practices of bilinguals as with the case of Hispanics as English SL speakers in the USA. Using a resource-based approach, the use of L1 Spanish is seen as symbiotic for the overall development of linguistic multicompetences. With some engineering and phantasy, her analysis can be synthesized as a new and innovative approach to language education also in FL contexts (see also Hornberger & Link, 2012). Metaphorically, we can frame her approach into the question Butzkamm (2011) names one of his essays after: *"Why make them crawl if they can walk?"*.

In the end, such a *de facto* amalgamation of languages is concordant with placing the subject at least on eye level in CLIL, because the main philosophy of translanguaging abates the focus on actual language and grammar use, retrenching in place of the negotiation of subject meaning. Echoing its increase in general attention, the number of very recent academic studies in applied educational contexts gravitating around translanguaging is on a sharp increase (e.g., Bieri, 2018; Daniel, Jiménez, Pray, & Pacheco, 2019; Erdin & Sali, 2020; Li & Luo, 2017; Lin & He, 2017; Nikula & Moore, 2019; Rabbidge, 2019; Rowe, 2018). Although some interpret translanguaging merely as a synonym of code-switching (e.g., Coyle et al., 2010; Marsh, 2002), it includes much more (García, 2009), namely looking beyond due to the important postulate of bilingual dynamism. An increase of bilingual dynamism is seen as ultimate goal in what Li (2011) calls the construction of *"translanguaging spaces"*. Translanguaging *per se* questions artificial boundaries between languages in an endeavor to blur them for the emergence of students' full linguistic repertoire (García & Li, 2014). Its theoretical assumption builds on one single linguistic system in the brain, in accordance with the common underlying proficiency (CUP) of Cummins' (1979, 1981) well-known iceberg theory.

Limits of translanguaging for CLIL: proposing a multilingual approach with trans-foreign-languaging

However, an important *caveat* exists in *"the tendency of multilingual scholars and researchers to romanticize the translanguaging practices of students"* (Canagarajah, 2011, p. 402). Most contributions to translanguaging originate from a SL learning environment. This demarcates its limits of applicability to FL learning. Lewis et al. (2012) summarize that translanguaging as a pedagogical strategy rather applies to contexts with children already possessing a progressed command of the respective languages. This is in concord with the well-known threshold hypothesis, because a CUP first requires the ability to crest a minimum language threshold (Cummins, 1976). Moore and Nikula (2016, p. 214) argue that *"studies are mainly situated in what we might term 'naturally multilingual contexts' [...,] not the typical CLIL scenario [...]"*. Hence, one can infer that any related practice of classroom translanguaging cannot apply to pure *foreign* language learning contexts without yet sufficient preexisting linguistic resources, when students still struggle with conveying their message at least halfway securely and appropriately.

This seems at first very logical, because a linguistic system thus far unknown to people is, as a matter of fact, something new for them. Take the example of students learning a completely new language script not common in their livelihood, for example Russian L1 speakers learning Hindi as L2 or *vice versa*. Any perception of the new script as *foreign*[2] appears just natural. FL learners can, until passing a certain threshold, never be called full bilinguals and thus not yield any benefits from natural translanguaging. Rather, we should describe them as possessing multicompetences at different levels in languages that require tailored promotion for expanding the full linguistic repertoire. This should also underline that even profoundly multilingual personalities can perceive any new language as foreign, i.e., unknown, at first exposure.

Nevertheless, with some adaption, the merits of natural translanguaging can be applied to different contexts as innovative and resource-based approach. In the following, a design for CLIL with L2 as FL will be constructed. In this vein, MacSwan's (2017) multilingual approach to translanguaging, with a holistic view on bilingualism, serves as contemporary starting point. Praising the legacy of, but similarly critically assessing the 'hyping up of translanguaging' in its original essence, he repudiates the denial of language boundaries, defending multilingualism and consequently

---

[2] With foreign, something thus far *unknown* or *unfamiliar* is meant — out of the students' eyes in the given example. "Otherness" as such in FL teaching has highly and rightly been criticized mainly out of post-colonial scholarship. Here, the expression foreign has been deliberately chosen, to distinct it from *SL* learning.

also clearly demarked code-switching practices by speakers. For CLIL, the merits of translanguaging, eschewing monolingual practices and facilitating multilingual approaches, have already been amplified (Moore & Nikula, 2016). Multilingual approaches explicitly value the existence of language diversity, among that the existence and preservation of minority languages, against the notion of completely fading them into one individual system within the repertoire of respective speakers. Fully cognizant of the ineptitude of applying natural translanguaging to FL contexts but explicitly welcoming its distinctive merits for pedagogical reasons, the genesis of a succinct CLIL pedagogy, valuing existent students' multicompetences, appears as desired. I propose the concept to be called 'trans-foreign-languaging' (Trans-FL), and define it as

"teacher- and student initiated, judicious and principled code-switching practices between students' FL, the dominant school language and/or other languages".

Trans-FL can be called something like a pre-phase of natural translanguaging. The approach is variable and includes smaller steps. It explicitly recognizes code-switching as first step to ultimately and actively have translanguaging spaces constructed by students themselves later. Following Lewis et al. (2012), this transformative pedagogy, in a FL context, should be teacher-initiated in its first stage. Trans-FL deliberately enforces code-switching within a clear-cut language policy. This includes tailored scaffolds as harbinger of translanguaging practices (Nikula & Moore, 2019). Synchronically, should existing multilingual resources already exist, students might engage in such practices themselves. As something like a joint component of code-switching and García's genuine version of translanguaging, Trans-FL builds on individualized dynamic bilingualism during CLIL with L2 as a FL, using an affordance-based and differentiated approach, gradually fading language boundaries in practice yet condoning distinct language systems. Any further existence of language boundaries *per se* must not be regarded upon as pitfall at all, especially with the recognition L1 as productive and by times very emotional resource (Nijhawan,

2020b). As a matter of fact, the proposal is in line with recommending teaching for transfer, challenging the two solitudes approach (Cummins, 2008), however recognizing any possible existence of several linguistic systems in people's brains within a superdiverse and multilingually scattered world society (Vertovec, 2007). Trans-FL as pedagogy for FL learning assists students in mastering several thresholds on their way towards becoming close to proficient bilinguals with a new language, using L1 as productive resource. The main assumptions and cornerstones of the proposed Trans-FL approach are displayed in *Table 1*. For demonstration purposes, natural translanguaging in its genuine form is compared and contrasted.

Table 1 Trans-FL as pedagogy for FL learning, as compared with translanguaging in SL environments.

CLIL target language	FL	SL
concept/ approach	Trans-FL as classroom pedagogy	room for translanguaging as natural phenomenon
cornerstones	- teacher-initiated policy with judicious and principled L1 use - affordance-based, offering scaffolds and challenges	- providing students with autonomy to use their pre-existing linguistic repertoire - affordance-based, offering scaffolds and challenges
ultimate goal	classroom as hybrid translanguaging space	

To date, research literature has failed to sketch any translanguaging pedagogy as a regular and integrated norm for multilingual classrooms. Scattered examples include, *inter alia*, Lewis et al. (2012, p. 646) for the communicative areas of speaking & listening, reading and writing, however rather resembling simple code-switching exercises. García and Li (2014, p. 131) even published a more comprehensive list of different recommendations, however not tailored to the dynamism of natural classroom processes in both SL and FL environments. Studies to date rather offer transcripts of classroom conversations, describing and analyzing students' and teachers' translanguaging behavior or the lack of it (Lin, 2013). But the black box about *how* translanguaging spaces can be actively initiated during FL teaching requires to be unlocked. Amidst this deficit, the next part of this article deals with my empirical fieldwork at a school. The goal was to develop clear-cut methods for Trans-FL during classroom practices for the genesis of a comprehensive CLIL model with judicious and principled L1 use.

Empirical classroom research: a judicious and principled L1 use in CLIL

Realizing the given deficits, the preceding theoretical framework has been translated into the following research question:

RQ: *How* can Trans-FL as classroom pedagogy with judicious and principled L1 use in CLIL promote the genesis of translanguaging spaces for different student types?

For the development of CLIL pedagogies, the resonating demand to engage in explorative classroom research has been expressed by numerous academics throughout, especially within the last decade (e.g., Breidbach & Viebrock, 2012; Cenoz et al., 2013; Corcoll, 2013; Dailey-O'Cain & Liebscher, 2009; Dalton-Puffer & Smit, 2013; Diehr, 2012, 2016; Erdin & Sali, 2020; Gierlinger, 2015; Pavón Vázquez & Ramos Ordóñez, 2018; Pérez-Cañado, 2012). As translanguaging gained its popularity mainly within the last decade as well, demands to exploratively develop classroom pedagogies have been posed accordingly (e.g., Canagarajah, 2011; Creese & Blackledge, 2010; Lewis et al., 2012; Lewis, Jones, & Baker, 2013; Park, 2013). In this vein, and very recently, an increasing number of authors has been advocating the close nexus of translanguaging with CLIL (Bieri, 2018; Lin & He, 2017; Nikula & Moore, 2019).

As a matter of fact, most existing classroom studies about multilingual teaching are rather descriptive than interventionalist, uncovering occasional practices, without offering any prescriptions or pedagogical functions. Lin (2013), in her review essay about classroom code-switching, utterly argues for breaking existing paradigm with researchers from outside merely analyzing classroom transcripts. Instead, she pleas for design intervention studies from inside in order to draw implications for a sustainable improvement of teaching practices. Contemplating the validity of findings and their relevance for practice, she appeals for an increase of teachers being synchronically researchers in their natural classroom ecologies, concomitantly providing ample space for students to actively contribute to research outcomes.

As part of these demands, the focal and eye-to-eye inclusion of stakeholders into research deserves more attention. The role of their *"lay beliefs"* has been underscored by e.g., Dalton-Puffer and Smit (2013, p. 549). Ultimately, students indirectly become lead researchers with their direct contribution to the results. Elsewhere, I have suggested to fuse action research with design-based research into design-based action research (DBAR), for theorizing stakeholders' knowledges, beliefs and practices, thus supporting Lin's (2013) strong plea. In that context, I proposed TRs to establish a broad team structure with both practitioners and academics, intervening into natural learning environments. This includes many small experiments within natural learning environments, often a result of lifelike and ad-hoc decisions with a variety in creativity resulting from such classroom dynamics (Nijhawan, 2017). Therefore, this study builds, as quite common with explorative research, on mixed methods. First and foremost, the development of models includes the beliefs and opinions of students from both formal and informal evaluations of classroom practices. The TR was assisted by four other observers from school, and two academics (investigator triangulation). Observations and classroom discussions were left open instead of defining fixed criteria, to expose all researchers to genuine and natural classroom dynamics without prejudice.

Information about the research context

The school and its CLIL program

The research took place in a German secondary school *(Gymnasium)*. For one year (9th grade, second semester; 10th grade, first semester), all students take part in a compulsory CLIL program in Politics & Economics *(CLIL for all)*. These lessons, an increase from two to four lessons a week in the subject, also substitute the regular English curriculum. For this reason, assessment within the *CLIL for all* program has been tailored accordingly: 50% of the grade is assembled by subject competence, and the remaining 50% by English language competence.

After the end of the *CLIL for all* program, students can enroll into an elective CLIL program in Politics & Economics, replacing the L1 subject requirement *(CLIL by choice)*. In the *CLIL by choice* program, assessment only takes place in line with the subject competences, in accordance with the recommendations of the *The Standing Conference of the Federal Ministers of Education in Germany* (KMK, 2013). As stated in the introduction, *Abitur* exams can be submitted in the CLIL subject, in either L2 or L1. Commonly also at that school, all CLIL classes are taught immersive. *Table 2* gives an overview.

Table 2 includes the CLIL program at the school of research.

	CLIL in Politics & Economics at the school	
	CLIL for all (one year, 9th and 10th grade)	*CLIL by choice* (from 10th to 12th grade)
description	all students receive CLIL for 4 hrs./week till 10.2, also replacing English FL lessons	students can opt for CLIL until *Abitur* in 12.2 (2-3 hrs./week), as a replacement for subject classes in L1
assessment	50% each subject and language competence	only by subject competence
comments	the approach of replacing the English FL requirement with CLIL in the form of L2 immersion was initially part of a field trial	can be selected as subject for the *"Abitur"* in either L2 or L1

Information about the research group, student types and learning arrangements

The case study took place in a 10th grade (N=22), the students' second and last semester during the *CLIL for all* program. The learning group was randomly allocated in line with the school planning and TR's research schedule. In this particular study group, L2 English was a FL for *all* students, while German as school language constituted L1 for almost everyone, or at least a SL fully comparable to fluent German speakers.[3] All students unanimously expressed their informed consent to take part in the research. Emphasis on research ethics defined a core. Surveys were taken anonymously to protect the participants' identity. This was meant as preventive measure to mitigate any concerns that the answers could have a negative impact on the final grade, recognizing that the research took place in a completely natural learning environment. Hence, participation at every stage of the research was completely voluntary, explaining the deviating N with different surveys.

For the affordance-based and differentiated planning, learner types were defined in a simple procedure: as the grade in this particular CLIL program is composed of 50 % each subject and language competence on a scale of 0 (failed) to 15 (distinctions), the students' grades from the first semester in each area, respectively, were consulted (N=22). In a quest to validate and locate this two-dimensional model within a broader context, their profile has been weighted against comparative data of 5 years of CLIL teaching by the TR (N=242). Such profiling is in accordance with Gierlinger's (2015) findings and his recommendations for researchers as well as with Abendroth-Timmer's (2007) categorization of CLIL students' motivational force as either content or language-driven. The model facilitates the provision of affordances and differentiated procedures, enabling the students to reach their zone of proximal development (Vygotsky, 1978). *Figure 1* visualizes the students' grades

---

[3] For this reason and for simplicity purposes, the study will refer to L1 and German and L2 as English, fully aware that some students have other L1s, with German actually being their SL, fully comparable to an L1.

and aggregates them into four different types.[4] In order to recognize the particularity of the standard distribution for every learning group, the median of both the English and Politics & Economics grade was set as benchmark for drawing the borders and constructing the four types of the left model, also making it applicable for other CLIL, and possibly even non-CLIL teaching contexts in its basic idea. The model on the right side is the generalized and simplified version of the heatmap.

---

[4] For informing present and future teachers about such settings, a short yet only descriptive outline of this model in a strongly abridged form has been published in Elsner et al. (2019).

TRANSLANGUAGING... OR 'TRANS-FOREIGN-LANGUAGING'?

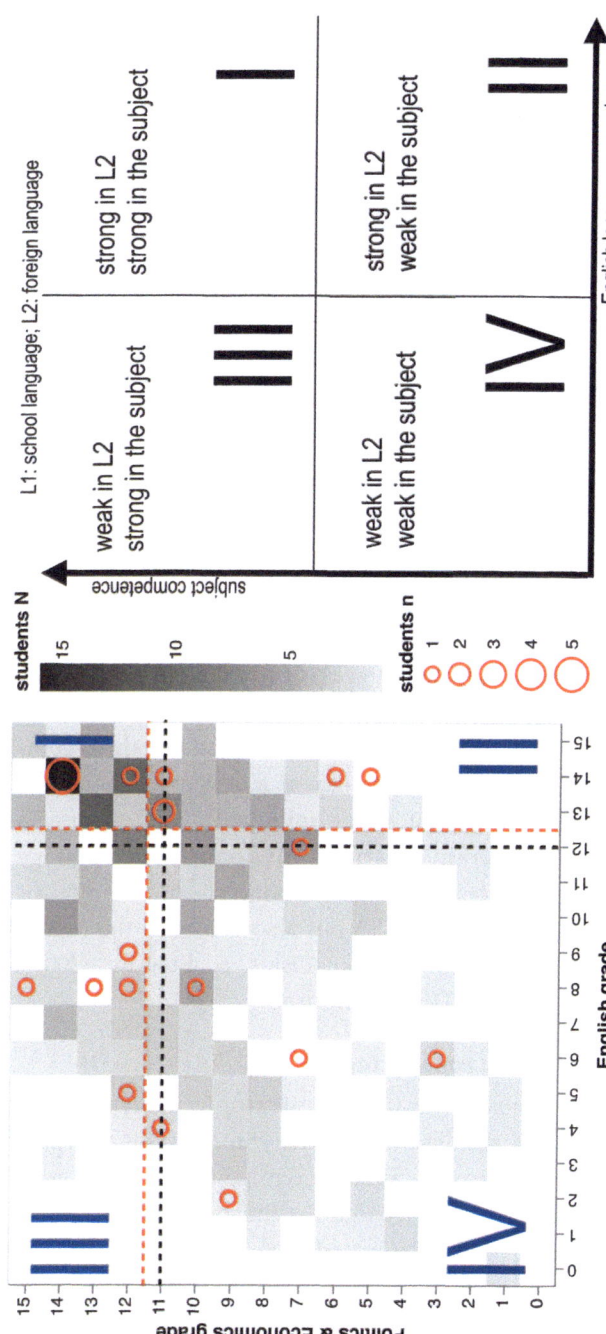

Figure 1 shows the grades in CLIL of the research group in circles (n), subdivided into English and Politics & Economics. The red dotted border defines student types I-IV. The shaded heat diagram is meant to compare it with data of five years of CLIL teaching by the TR (N), with the black line demarking different learner types. The model on the right side is the simplified and generalized version.

153

Table 3 briefly characterizes the student types more in detail, as they play a major role while describing the proceedings:

Table 3 **contains four different student types, as result from their assessment.**

Type III ("subject expert" with *language learning through content*): although the FL might impose a barrier, subject knowledge and interests define the prospects of Type 3 students' motivation for improving FL skills.	Type I ("overall talent and leadership"): students of Type 1 are achievers in both subject and language, often looking for higher challenges within CLIL.
Type IV ("below average"): students of this type require clear and distinct scaffolding tools, especially with assistance of L1, reducing complexity and excessive cognitive demand, respectively.	**Type II** ("language expert" with *content learning through language*): this group of students, in many cases, feels particularly motivated by the prospects of L2 use for improving subject knowledge, even if the subject interest is not necessarily as pronounced.

For the research, five groups of four students were randomized, however criteria-wise, composed by each of one student per type at an equal gender ratio. This setting makes group dynamics better and more comprehensively visible as well as the data analysis comparable across groups. In the end, it delivers a deeper and nuanced picture about different student types involved. Furthermore, a communicative and cooperative learning environment in language education has been identified as beneficial not only for translanguaging (Erdin & Sali, 2020) but also provides the democratic and participatory framework (Osler & Starkey, 2005), strongly desired during this DBAR venture.

Curricular provisions and content taught

Economics & the Environment was the semester topic. In line with the school curriculum, and amidst the ongoing climate crisis, the general aim of the full lesson row was set to equip students with relevant subject and language knowledge for their proficiency to express an appropriate judgment towards the famous *degrowth vs. green growth* debate. In accordance with Jackson's (2009) classic, the students were requested to evaluate the question *"can we have prosperity without growth?"* at the end of the lesson row.

Research design

The DBAR took was planned for six weeks. The students' opinion mattered first and foremost and served as a starting point for the circular research design. They were given a QUANQUAL questionnaire to formulate their opinion on CLIL and L1 use in the classroom. Their opinion was triangulated with the teacher's and team's observations during the further planning.

In total, the research unfolded three separate DBAR cycles, with one teaching method per cycle initiated and tested. Each cycle was followed by two larger evaluations with each one comprehensive QUANQUAL questionnaire. Formal assessment under rigid exam conditions with a bilingual exam defined the end of the research.

Information on models investigated

The following section contains a short overview on the three Trans-FL teaching methods that were developed during the research process. This section serves as a reading guide for better comprehending the consecutive data section as well as the *Appendix*. They will be called **(a) role-based model, (b) phase-based model and (c) mode-based model**. Each of them composed one single CLIL teaching model tested during the three cycles. They will be more closely elaborated in the empirical part. *Figure 2* visualizes the three models, with each four students per group.

> **role-based model (with half of the learners in L1 and L2) – RBM**

The role-based model (RBM) defined the starting point of the research. Each two students of every group of four occupy L1 and L2. They were supposed to code-switch languages after a certain time.

phase-based model (with mutual code-switching between different lesson phases) — PBM

The phase-based model (PBM) was the second tested method. All students within one group occupy the same language role. They code-switch together into the other language.

mode-based model (with learners speak in one, and write in the other language) — MBM

The mode-based model (MBM) allows the students to initiate individual codeswitches in accordance with the working mode, e.g., speaking on one, writing in the other language.

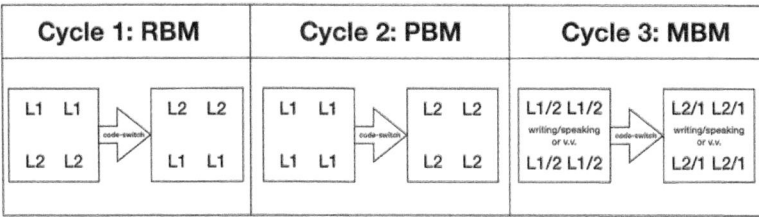

Figure 2 illustrates the learning arrangements of the RBM, PBM and MBM with four students per group, respectively.

Data

The triangulated body of data is assembled as follows:
a) student surveys at the beginning of the research, after each design cycle and after conclusion of the research;
b) leaner products and a bilingual exam;
c) observation data of the team, reconstructed as *"thick description"* in accordance with Geertz (1973) genuine account, to make natural classroom dynamics tangible and actively involve the readers into the research (Angele, 2015; de Boer & Reh, 2012). It should elucidate emotions and feelings of all stakeholders, in order to create a genuine, grasping and lively description for later inference, along with the decisions taken by the DBAR team. The thick description was reconstructed from detailed field notes over the six weeks research

period.[1] The full thick description was inductively categorized with MAXQDA, in order to condense it for the *Appendix* of this article. It helped to group the observations into relevant issues and identify both typical and atypical episodes of the classroom dynamics for later integration into the comprehensive CLIL teaching model.[2] Such combination of methods in the context of a thick description, by times resembling the grounded theory approach in accordance with Glaser and Strauss (1967), has been reasoned by a number of researchers, for omitting data overflow and making it operational (explicitly by Angele, 2015; but also by e.g., Roller & Lavrakas, 2015; Tholen, 2017; Vimont, 2015). Raufelder, Bukowski, and Mohr (2013) provide an excellent model for presenting such data in a concise form, adopted here accordingly. At occasions, transcripts alone were used to display the original reactions of the students. At other occasions, the description will look formal rather than interpretative. By times, there is a transition to a rather challenging and quite emotional writing style, to reason decisions taken during the research. *Figure 3* visualizes the research proceedings, with information on data sources. The focus in this article will be mainly put on the shaded areas.

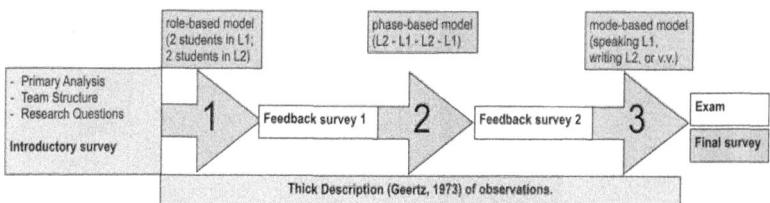

Figure 3 shows the research proceedings and indicates the data sources. The focus of this paper is set on the shaded areas.

---

[1] The final amount contains the volume of at least a single monograph, what means that only selected typical and atypical extracts are presented in the *Appendix*, considering the conciseness of this article.
[2] In total, ten different main topics with in total 28 subcodes were inductively developed. Each of the topics could be processed into single articles—like with Nijhawan (2020b), looking at emotional and rational learning in CLIL and the influence on political judgments.

The following part presents the research. It begins and ends with the introductory and the final survey, respectively. The thick description has been added to the *Appendix* as supplementary material, for being able to reconstruct the full DBAR.

Research proceedings and results

Results from the 1st survey (pre-survey ahead of the DBAR)

The first QUANQUAL survey (N=19) intended in particular to reveal (1) how the students had perceived lessons retrospectively during CLIL immersion in L2 *(Figure 4)*, (2) how they assessed their competence development in both L2 and L1 during the preceding semester *(Figure 5)*, and (3) how they believed the language use should look like the coming lessons *(Figure 6)*.

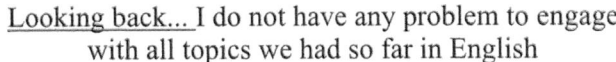

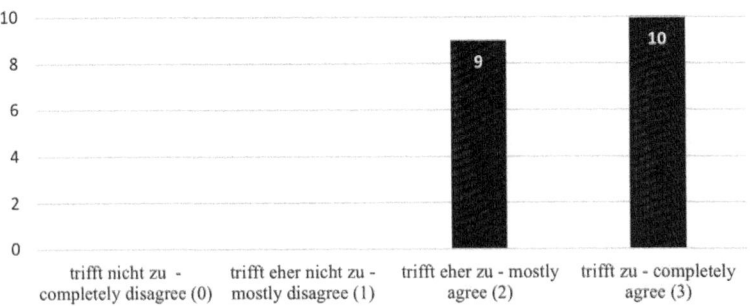

Figure 4 **includes the responses of the self-assessment of L2 competence development in CLIL classes of the first semester.**

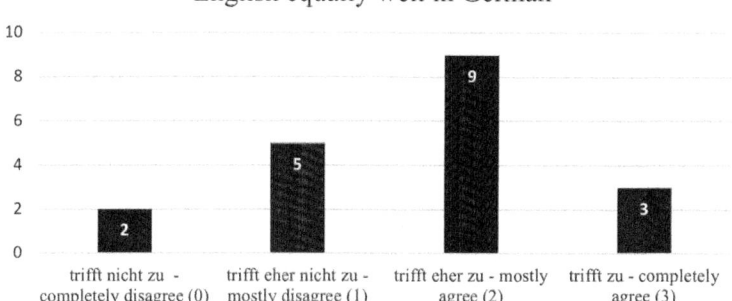

Figure 5 shows the students' self-assessment of equipollent language development in L1.

According to the students' self-assessment, we can unambiguously infer a positive effect of CLIL classes on L2 development from *Figure 4*. Contrary, *Figure 5* gives a different picture about an equipollent L1 development. Although a majority of students (12; 63,16%) answer affirmatively, about a third (7; 36,84%) do not feel as secure in L1, echoing the narrative of the article's introductory section. Remarkable are the detailed characteristics of affirmative answers. While in *Figure 4*, most of the students *completely* agree with the increase of L2 proficiency (see above), *Figure 5* shows a smaller number (3; 15,79%). These numbers inevitably are too high to justify any business-as-usual with immersion. Rather, they second the research question and the need to develop teaching methods respecting strengths and needs of the four different student types.

The next part of the questionnaire was intended to directly survey the students' opinions on a proposed L1 use in CLIL.

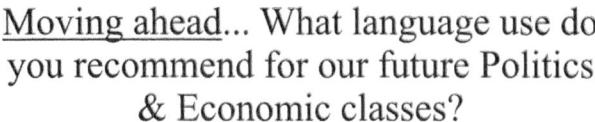

Moving ahead... What language use do you recommend for our future Politics & Economic classes?

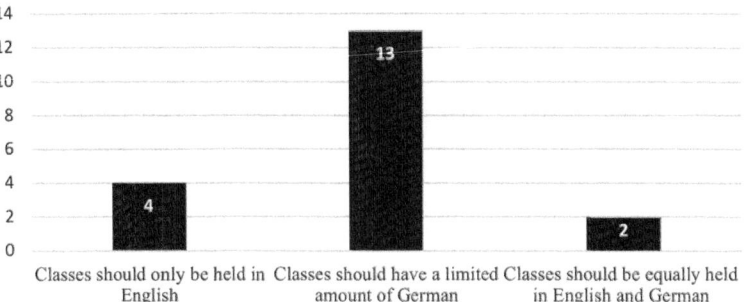

Figure 6 displays the language recommendation for future CLIL.

From *Figure 6*, we learn that the clear majority suggests L2 as dominant and L1 as ancillary language. In order to learn more about the detailed needs and expectations, *Table 4* shows selected verbal responses in relation to *Figure 6*. We can cluster these comments into two main categories: a considerable number of students reason the role of the L1 as scaffold, whereas almost as many students indicate a goal to become fluent in L1.

Table 4 lists a summary of the QUAL section with reference to Figure 6.

Please explain your choice with the previous item!		
Reason for limited L1 use	# of comments	Typical example
L1 as scaffold (support)	7	*In my opinion, classes should also have parts in German, because then it is easier to understand complicated contents, and you learn how some words are called in German, enabling you to use these words better.*
L1 to develop bilingual proficiency (equipollence)	6	*One should be able to talk in both languages about the topic.*

Analysis, students' views and planning of the first DBAR cycle

The analysis of the survey revealed a big span of opinions and thus manifold options how to design the classes. At first, students were directly confronted with the findings in the classroom, leading to a vivid and controversial discussion, whereby every single student was addressed individually by the TR to make sure that every voice had been heard. Asking repeatedly the question about suggestions how to ensure their concomitant L1 development *("So what do you suggest to exactly do?")*, the students were not able to express a clear-cut opinion. Suggestions ended in a cacophony of voices, ranging from starting in German (mainly *Type IV* students), to partly debating in German (mainly *Type III* students), up to simply repeating the content in German for 2-3 lessons after wrapping it up completely in English (mainly *Type II* students), or even letting German out totally (mainly *Type I* students). In other words, we were not able to agree upon a clear-cut and uniform masterplan how to proceed.

Developing the RBM as starting point

After careful deliberation and with the help of literature on strategies for children's bilingual language acquisition as first point of reference, the DBAR team took the decision to allocate individual language roles to the students in accordance with the RBM. The goal was to initiate and facilitate a mixed language environment in the classroom, as naturally quite common among multilingual speakers (e.g., Auer, 1984; García & Li, 2014). In a classroom with L2 as FL, on the contrary, we cannot rely on natural occurrences of code-switching but only engineer a clear language policy in accordance with students' affordances.

This form of language use, with speakers occupying a fixed language role during a conversation with another participant, can also be found in the literature on parents' language use raising bilingual children. Similarly there, no blueprint on *how* to facilitate equipollent bilingual language development could thus far be defined, as circumstances differ case-by-base. Rather, parents are recommended to experiment and finetune their language use (Byers-

Heinlein & Lew-Williams, 2013). Among these strategies, the one parent one language (OPOL) approach going back to Ronjat (1913), with parents and children occupying fixed language roles, has attracted considerable attention over the century. Byers-Heinlein and Lew-Williams (2013) recommend the exposition of children with significant time to each of the languages for their bilingual language acquisition. Such postulate offers interesting insights for FL learning in putting students with the RBM into fixed yet mixed language roles within their groups, followed by an initiated code-switch later for putting language production and reception in both languages into equilibrium. The next section presents the final survey. For reconstructing the classroom dynamics and the genesis of and experience with the three models, the thick description can be found in the *Appendix* as supplementary material.

Final survey: student evaluation of the three Trans-FL methods

At the end of the research, we took a final survey for being able to know more about the students' impressions and perceptions, and comparatively evaluate the three models. Furthermore, it allowed us to triangulate the findings with the thick description. The most salient results of the final survey will now be presented as a basis for the comprehensive CLIL teaching model and the final discussion.

First, we wanted to find out which of the models the students believed had been most demanding, to know more about any individually perceived bilingual dynamism *(Table 5)*.

Table 5 compares the three models on a more general level in terms of their difficulty.

N=16	PBM	RBM	MBM
Looking back: which model was the most demanding?	2 (12.5%)	3 (18.75%)	11 (68.75%)

At first glance, we see the observation confirmed that the MBM appears to be the most demanding. However, for a deeper insight, it may be interesting to compare the RBM separately with the other two models *(Table 6)*, because as indicated earlier, it had been set as the center of gravity of the envisaged comprehensive CLIL teaching model.

Table 6 intends to find out more about the RBM in comparing it with the other two models.

N=15	completely disagree (0)	mostly disagree (1)	mostly agree (2)	completely agree (3)	mean
The RBM was more demanding than the MBM	6 (40%)	7 (46.67%)	2 (13.33%)	0 (0%)	0.73
The RBM was more demanding than the PBM	1 (6.67%)	5 (33.33%)	7 (46.67%)	2 (13.33%)	1.67

Again, as with the first item, there is a clear tendency to classify the MBM as the most cognitively demanding one. Interesting, however, is the second item. Still a considerable number of students classifies the RBM as less demanding than the PBM. One can assume that the RBM constituted, more or less, a motivational force, an enjoyable space of (mostly oral) conversation and negotiation for the students. Moreover, after some time, the students who had already attained language and subject security before with the PBM apparently got acquainted with this method. As one could observe in the classroom, they now knew 'the rules of the game', looking forward to again emulating the RBM. Now, the evaluation of the three models in terms of separate language and subject learning is of interest *(Table 7)*.

Table 7 asks for skill building in language and subject competence, respectively, in the three models.

N=16	PBM	RBM	MBM
Looking back—which model was most suitable for the acquisition of subject knowledge?	9 (56.25%)	7 (43.75%)	0 (0%)
Looking back—which model facilitated bilingual language learning in the subject?	4 (25%)	10 (62.5%)	2 (12.5%)

163

With the first item, we see a similar outcome, albeit no significant difference, for the PBM and RBM. Without surprise, the MBM, already requiring the existence of a significant amount of subject- and language proficiency, does not receive any vote. The difference between the PBM and RBM in terms of language learning with the second item is significant, while even the MBM receives a small but significant number of counts.

It had proven as very insightful during the introductory and the intermediate surveys to look at their qualitative sections. Thus, the final survey gave extensive space for more individual data and a more appropriate interpretation of the research beyond the quantitative section. Instead of structurally presenting comments per response, all aggregated comments were used to generate inductive categories about what concerned students while providing feedback, i.e., what 'they wanted to tell and talk about'. Those vernacular accounts, as opposed to pregiven QUAN categories, open the stage how the students felt during and perceived the three cycles comparatively. The qualitative data analysis ended up with three main categories with each a positive and negative scaling, for (a) the intricacy of the method, its (b) promotion of skills, and (c) the overall learning environment. A count of the frequency rate tells us more about the students' overall evaluation *(Table 8)*.

TRANSLANGUAGING... OR 'TRANS-FOREIGN-LANGUAGING'?

Table 8 shows the count of comments per students with inductive categories for each of the three models.

intricacy		skill building		learning environment		comments / model
simple	complex	conducive	obstructive	encouraging	demotivating	
PBM						
1	0	6	0	0	0	7
RBM						
2	1	10	1	2	0	16
MBM						
1	6	5	6	0	2	20
∑ intriacy: 11		∑ skill building: 28		∑ learning environment: 4		total comments: 43

165

First of all, the number of comments received in sum for each model is an indicator for what students wanted to desperately tell. The PBM received the fewest comments, most likely because monolingual L2 and L1 teaching *per se* is nothing spectacularly new. The other two models received the biggest share of the comments we will investigate closer a bit later. The majority of 28 answers revolve around the question of skill building during each of these methods.

The PBM did not receive any negative comment at all. The replies indicate that it provides something like a 'protected space' for understanding the content matter with concepts and terminology separately in L2 and L1, as preparation for the more complex methods. To our surprise, the RBM did receive only one single comment declaring it as a difficult approach. As said, it seems that its complexity was seen as positive challenge, owing to individual learning progress. The MBM in turn was often qualified to be a demanding approach. Difficulty should not be seen negatively *per se* but can also be more positively construed as challenging with a high complexity. In terms of its productive output, five comments acknowledged its conduciveness. On the flipside, six comments declare the opposite. Latter comments sounded deeply annoyed and even acrimonious, even using by times swearing words. Two comments from the last categories classified it as rather discouraging. In terms of offering a positive challenge for learners, however, we can infer from the response rate to the categories intricacy and skill building that the MBM offers a high learning potential should certain conditions be met.

Discussion and presentation of a comprehensive CLIL teaching model

Putting the lessons learned during the three cycles with the RBM, PBM and MBM into three main categories, the following comparisons of *Table 9* provide as instrumental for further consideration:

Table 9 shows a comparison of the three models after the full data analysis.

category/model	RBM	PBM	MBM
main function	subject learning (languages moves into the background during the negotiation of meaning)	language and subject learning (concepts, content & terminology in safe spaces)	(optional) challenge for mainly stronger learners to increase their learning experience
dynamics of bilingualism / use of cognitive resources	high to very high because of L1/L2 arrangement within groups	low due to monolingual phasing	very high on an individual basis
type of code-switching	receptive and productive code-switching with a high frequency	controlled code-switching per phase (L2-L1-L2 or *vice versa*....)	productive code-switching with a very high frequency

The analysis of the full data, mirrored by the thick description of the *Appendix*, resulted in the following comprehensive CLIL teaching model *(Figure 7)*.

MULTILINGUAL CONTENT AND LANGUAGE INTEGRATED LEARNING

Model 1: Mixed groups with student types I–IV

			III IV I II
			III IV I II
			I II III IV
			I II III IV

input	affordance-based and differentiated working phase: three different models for engendering translanguaging spaces through *trans-foreign-languaging*		
warm-up: Either bilingual or scaffolded L2 input enables problem definition. Phase focus: acquisition of requisites for the cooperative working phases	**monolingual preparation:** Guided code-switching is initiated through two-way mediation (L2-L1-L2) with differentiated options (increased L1 use and writing in the opposite language). Phase focus: content and terminology	**bilingual consolidation:** Guided and differentiated as well as receptive and productive code-switching happens continuously throughout all interaction and negotiation processes. Differentiated option to write in the opposite language can be availed of. This arrangement constitutes the ultimate heartbeat of the model and thus also the longest phase. Phase focus: subject content (language mainly as resource only)	**optional intensification:** Autonomous and productive code-switching can be either teacher-guided or selected by individual choice. Phase focus: subject content and language

trans-foreign-languaging

TRANSLANGUAGING SPACES
level of bilingual dynamism, overall complexity and use of individual cognitive resources

very high | high/very high | low/medium

phase-based model (all L2/L1)
knowledge/understanding
Mutual code-switching from L2 to L1, or vice versa (i.e. starting with L1), should be planned by students or teacher.
for I–IV

mode-based model (optional: can be used as a tool of differentiation)
analysis/judgment
Can be combined and applied during the above phases by *individual* students. An indication by student type is given when students' use is recommended at the *earliest* point. At the end, all students can use this method cooperatively and choose alone which language to speak/ write in, either together or individually.

I *(autonomous start by choice or teacher recommendation)*

role-based model (two in each L2/L1)
analysis/judgment
Type I & IV students can start in the L1, but the exact assignment of language roles can be experimented across the groups. In the middle of the phase, all students should switch their languages.
for I–IV

II & III *(autonomous start, if students feel secure and comfortable, or if teacher motivates them)*

IV *(can join other students, with assistance from I–III)*

Optional

Teacher-driven bilingual, or L2 input with multimodal and multilingual L1-affordances

Figure 7 shows the findings of the comprehensive data analysis merged into a comprehensive CLIL teaching model.

The model incorporates the lessons learned of the three design cycles into a comprehensive framework, indicating different levels of bilingual dynamism. It includes recommendations on the proceedings of CLIL classes, in accordance with different student types, juxtaposed with Vygotsky's (1978) zone of proximal development. The RBM as fulcrum constitutes its absolute center of gravity. The PBM serves as preparatory tool for its achievement, whereby the MBM provides as an optional addendum to individually increase bilingual dynamism at any time. If circumstances allow, it can even constitute a separate phase for an increased learning arrangement. The PBM can be imported into the plenary when separate groups end their group work, effectively alternating L1 and L2, thus recommended as transition for launching the RBM in the next group phase.

All in all, the model builds on a gradual increase of bilingual dynamism, concordant with the increase in language and subject competence, entraining students for trespassing language thresholds. The suggested and consolidating approach of Trans-FL earmarks to emulate natural translanguaging, because simple code-switching at the beginning with the PBM fades into a more fluid overall language use. In the end, the FL ideally becomes an inherent part of the students' integral language grammars. This is in line with the CUP (Cummins, 1976), for enabling students one day to enjoy the 'idealized romantics of translanguaging more naturally'. Importantly, as it was recently recommended by Daniel et al. (2019), and had earlier been identified as a desideratum by Lin (2013), the model moves beyond the use of scattered scaffolds only at certain occasions or only lesson wise. It rather makes translanguaging a fully integrated norm and policy in the classroom, also abating the common issue of curricular pressure.

Focus on different student types

The cooperative arrangement enables *Type I* students to assume leadership functions throughout. The optional challenge with the MBM increases their individual bilingual dynamism and use of cognitive resources, coming closest to natural translanguaging. As the thick description of the classroom data in the *Appendix* shows, *Type IV* students' negotiation of meaning is facilitated with the pedagogical tools during the cooperative learning environment. The L1, especially during the PBM, serves as an active scaffold, reducing bilingual dynamism and preventing cognitive overload, under the condition that students do not completely fallback into it. Furthermore, code-mixing, if limited and within the more rigid language policy, can be a legitimate intermediate step to facilitate the merits of the teaching model. To prevent unplanned code-meshing and complete fallbacks, e.g., wildcards can be provided throughout to *Type IV* students (and possibly other types as well), permitting them to 'legally breach language rules' occasionally, instead of falling into complete silence.

Type II, and in particular *Type III* students, not defining extremes, deserve equal attention. For the former, language is the motivating force during CLIL *(content learning through language)*. Similar as *Type I* students, we should regard upon L1 phases as an amplifier of their subject learning capabilities and their equipollent promotion in the sense of a cognitive academic language proficiency (CALP). L1 moreover also has scaffolding purposes. For *Type III* students, in turn, the content leads to an increase in motivation for learning the language *(language learning through content)*. The reference to L1, as thick description in the *Appendix* illustrates, not only reduces complexity, but also motivates their participation, with positive spillovers into L2 phases.

The teacher

First engineering, then managing, finally observing
All options the model encapsulates imply a strong teacher role within CLIL classes for engineering the classroom policy. This includes closely observing and monitoring the classroom dynamics and supervising the progress of the students. Further fueling this train of thought, it is important that initial planning and design of classroom code-switching and translanguaging, here in the form of Trans-FL, is actively done by the teacher during the onset, knowing strengths and needs of the students (see also Corcoll, 2013; Creese

& Blackledge, 2010; García & Li, 2014; Lewis et al., 2012; Li & Luo, 2017; Nikula & Moore, 2019; Rowe, 2018). Normally, teachers, ideally reflective practitioners (Schön, 1983), know their learning group well, as context matters for the practical implementation of the suggested CLIL teaching model. Nonetheless, an integral part of the CLIL teaching model includes mechanisms for delegating many of the choices and options to the students, like language choice or initiation of new phases. Gradually, after students have achieved method competence and appear fit, teachers are advised to decentralize decision-making and correspondingly equip students with autonomy, with the ultimate goal of fostering students' empowerment through a *"transformative pedagogy"* (García & Li, 2014, p. 92; Li, 2017, p. 15). In other words, the overall approach is liberal, finding an appropriate balance between teacher- and student initiation and choices, respectively.

Teacher's language use: L2

During this research, the TR remained strictly in L2, for acting as a role model, underlining the FL objective, also recognizing the achievements of immersion in general (see also Lasagabaster & Sierra, 2010). Moreover, a planned use of L2, providing spoken language input, scaffolds, new vocabulary and language tools have been identified as instrumental. Not only the results of the students' surveys, acknowledging the TR language use for setting a positive example, but also longer group feedback rounds at the end of the research, confirm such procedure in line with the recommendations of Coyle et al. (2010). Admittedly, it has not been investigated in how far teacher code-switching might serve a positive purpose — which however would be an interesting venture when replicating and further developing the model.

Exemplary adaption of the model

Various forms of differentiation

Various forms of internal differentiation of learner groups are possible. Whereas the model recognizes different student types, it needs to be said that such models are never carved in stone and should be adapted, in accordance with needs teachers diagnosed with their particular learning groups. In some situations, e.g., *Type I* students may look for more eye-level discourse, while in turn *Type IV* students may feel more comfortable and safer in a group with similar learning levels. Thus, am exemplary second model has been designed and represents an altered, yet not evaluated version, for a setting with groups of homogenized student types *(Figure 8)*:

TRANSLANGUAGING... OR 'TRANS-FOREIGN-LANGUAGING'?

Model 2: Homogeneous groups with student types I-IV

input	affordance-based and differentiated working phase: three different models for engendering *translanguaging spaces* through *trans-foreign-languaging*		
warm-up: Either bilingual or scaffolded L2 input enables problem definition. Phase focus: acquisition of requisites for the cooperative working phases	**monolingual preparation:** Guided code-switching is initiated through two-way mediation (L2-L1-L2) with differentiated options (increased L1 use, phase increase and writing in the opposite language). Phase focus: content and terminology	**bilingual consolidation:** Guided and differentiated as well as receptive and productive code-switching happens continuously throughout all interaction and negotiation processes. Differentiated option to write in the opposite language can be availed of. This arrangement constitutes the ultimate heartbeat of the model and thus also the longest phase. Phase focus: subject content (language mainly as resource only)	**optional intensification:** Autonomous and productive code-switching can be either teacher-guided or selected by individual choice. Phase focus: subject content and language
	I II III IV	I II III IV	I II III IV
			I II III IV
			I II III IV

trans-foreign-languaging

TRANSLANGUAGING SPACES — level of bilingual dynamism, overall complexity and use of individual cognitive resources

- very high
- high/very high
- low/medium

phase-based model (all L2/L1) *knowledge/understanding*
Mutual code-switching from L2 to L1, or vice versa (i.e. starting with L1), should be planned by students or teacher.
for I–IV at the beginning
(group decides cooperatively, or teacher recommends phase transition)

role-based model (two in each L2/L1) *analysis/judgment*
Students decide who begins in which language. In the middle of the phase, all students switch their languages. Below, the *earliest* point by student type is indicated for entering the phase.

| I | II & III | IV |

mode-based model *(optional: can be used as a tool of differentiation)* *analysis/judgment*
Can be combined and applied during the above phases by *individual* students. An indication by student type is given when students' use is recommended at the *earliest* point. At the end, all students can use this method cooperatively and choose alone which language to speak/ write in, either together or individually.

| I | II & III | IV |
| *(autonomous start by choice or teacher recommendation)* | *(autonomous start, if students feel secure and comfortable, or if teacher motivates them)* | *(individual choice, if students feel secure and comfortable, or if teacher motivates them)* |

Teacher-driven bilingual, or L2 input with multilingual and multimodal L1-affordances

Figure 8 offers an alternative comprehensive CLIL teaching model with homogeneous groups.

173

Here, learner autonomy might be easier to implement, because groups can more seamlessly take decisions, once certain, e.g., criteria-based milestones, have been achieved by groups of similar student types. For instance, the PBM can be planned significantly longer for or by *Type IV* students for properly preparing and not excluding them from the RBM. Rather, it might provide them with a safe space, to mutually engage in exercises, while more extensive code-mixing may be permitted in the beginning.

Further possible variations: what about
'natural translanguaging'... randomization...?

The design of the alternative second version should underline that such models should be adapted to specific local contexts. They should provide scope to react to different circumstances, e.g., the multilingual reality of the world. Even in a *de jure* monolingual country like Germany, *de facto* an increasing heterogeneous student population in terms of diversity in first languages can be observed. Often, cohorts of students with same first languages gather together, enabling the scope for more natural translanguaging and valuing language diversity, in the end promoting the EU approach towards plurilingualism (García, 2009). Thus, in such a scenario, groups can be composed according to same L1s (Erdin & Sali, 2020). In such a safe space, first languages can even vary while promoting the target language *and* the official school language German concomitantly, opening the model for real multilingual teaching. However, it is important that in a common space like the plenary, common languages of mutual discourse should be applied (official school/target language), to prevent other students to be excluded from 'secret talk' as well as accidentally promoting communitarianism instead of inclusion and diversity.

Further examples of adaption include, *inter alia*, randomization as tool of real cooperative learning, experienced group compositions, or any other criteria worth for the group composition (like 'best friends').

Limitations of the research

The suggested CLIL teaching model underlies certain restrictions and limitations. Measures to counter such general objections and reduce the *caveat* have been, where possible, planned from the beginning, and will be listed where applicable.

As a matter of fact, such exercise with English as the target language, with a group of rather privileged students, is of course a rather thankful venture for researchers. English, the global *lingua franca*, is omnipresent young people's lives around the world, reducing the general threshold, as opposed to the other extreme, e.g., teaching minority languages as FL. Moreover, this particular research group was comparatively homogeneous, rendering this research to have 'lab-like elements', in turn helpful for the genesis of the clear-cut yet elastic CLIL teaching model.

The very contextual setting with the small N has to be interpreted and generalized carefully. For that reason, a second version as well as ideas for reapplying it in other contexts have been given for demonstrating its elasticity. The weakness, at the same time the strength, might be that the design of the model came from a completely natural learning environment within an ecological classroom culture. Certain factors (illnesses, stress from exam in other subjects etc.) were not controllable, however constitute the daily reality and thus rightly had an impact on the results. This, it can be argued, makes the model even more robust (Lin, 2013). Furthermore, building on Brown (1992), the merits of interventions into natural classroom environments for the development of genuine research results is inestimable, which does not downscale large scale research at all. Such rather small DBAR research initiatives may pave the way for something grander in the future.

Talking about the role of the TR, the researcher bias has been mitigated with the given team structure through investigator triangulation. The research also serves as a best practice how subjective theories can be modelled and provided for further scientific investigation.

Looking back, but moving forward: what has to happen next?

In the introduction, the paper promised to open one of CLIL's biggest black boxes in presenting a comprehensive CLIL teaching model with a judicious and principled L1 use. It presented the main theoretical pillars with Trans-FL as a classroom pedagogy to enable the genesis of translanguaging spaces in an environment with an FL as target language. Thereafter, selected data from the DBAR was presented, triangulated and made more transparent with the thick description in the *Appendix*.

The research concludes a first step to answer the given research question, amidst the expressed desideratum for developing CLIL teaching methods. The two versions of the comprehensive CLIL teaching model do not claim to be a blueprint. Rather, they lay the groundwork for further application in similar and other contexts for validation and refinement, to investigate whether the model and its inherent pedagogy withstands teaching practice in multiple contexts. Therefore, evaluation criteria, ideally within a mixed method framework, need to be developed. Such evaluation criteria can also pave the groundwork for large-scale replication with large N populations, and possibly controlled group comparisons, to measure the effectiveness of the three singular models as well as the CLIL teaching model as a whole. With reference to the overall effectiveness, videography, replacing the thick description, would indeed be welcomed.

Moving forward, the model opens the space for many new research questions, first and foremost with similar DBAR initiatives, but also and similarly with more evaluative or other methodological approaches. Among other questions, to give an example, the question on the quantitative proportion of L1 use in CLIL appears very accurate. The research of this article presented a milestone for related research initiatives, because, as Gierlinger (2015, p. 350) rightly argues, first questions *"about the actual methodological mediation and ownership of this* [L1 implementation] *space"* need to be explored, before investigating how much L1 is appropriate during CLIL and possibly FL teaching.

At the beginning of the thick description, the student' acknowledgment of being a crucial part of such research—or this more 'game-like exercise' — was narrated. We should optimistically enable coming generations of students more initiatives to integrate their voices into the discourse, promising that the game will never be over.

Appendix: Offering classroom insights with the thick description: the RBM, PBM and MBM

The following thick description offers insights into the natural classroom dynamics of the research. Names are completely fictional to make the observations personalized and thus more readable. As a positive side effect, converting real names with an algorithm into pseudonyms helped to establish distance to the students during the analysis.

A new bilingual dynamism with the RBM

Proceedings

There was a natural but quite loud noise of rumbling and murmuring after announcing the group composition and the individual language roles for the start. This reaction obviously mirrored the excitement about the new way of teaching, deviating from the common hitherto immersion classroom practice, i.e., 'something new', as if we were to play a game. Consider following longer episode of the very first group work during the RBM, nicely exemplifying the new form of bilingual dynamism that had organically developed.

> *Observation scene #1*, with focus on Kim (Type I; L2), Ben (Type II; L1), Frieda (Type III; L1) and Arnold (Type IV; L2)
>
> *Extract from a group discussion about the question: Is there a universal definition of wealth?*[1]
>
> The groups were supposed to agree upon a universal definition of wealth during their group work. Frieda, the note-taker of the group, mumbled about the intricacy of having to express everything in L1 all of a sudden. We could observe her being fully concentrated while making meaning of the group discussion and putting it into

---

[1] Dialogue reproduced from Nijhawan (2020b).

written, by times seeking confirmation especially from Kim. While taking notes from the mixed L1/L2 conversation of the others, she mentioned accidentally having used the English grammar for the German text, demonstrating at a sentence she had just written.

Frieda [reading out loudly a written sentence she had translated from Kim, *Type 1, L2*, as an appraisal of the group result]:

"Wohlstand wird verschieden angesehen von vielen verschiedenen Leuten [Kim orig.: *"Wealth is seen differently by different people"*]. [Mumbling] *Das ist voll schwer, alles in Deutsch zu übersetzen! [...] Oh, jetzt habe ich ja die englische Grammatik benutzt!* [editing and reediting the sentence, then reading the result loudly to the others] *"Es gibt in der Welt verschiedene Ansichten und Meinungen über Wohlstand"* [In the world there are different perceptions about wealth.]

Kim [answering immediately]: *"Yes, and for me, I want to earn enough money to afford all the things I like."*

Frieda: "*Du hast eben gesagt, dass du Wohlstand vor allem mit Geld in Verbindung bringst. Ich finde, auch andere Sachen wie Freunde und Familie gehören dazu.*" [You just said you associate wealth in particular with money. I believe, also other things like friends and family are part thereof.]

Kim*: "You just said that you believe that wealth has to be also defined beyond material things."*

Frieda: "Aber du hast eine sehr einseitige Definition von Wohlstand". [But your definition of wealth is very one-sided!]

Kim*: "Because I associate wealth with material things".*

Arnold and Ben, having listened eagerly throughout, finally intervened, because the controversy caught their attention and triggered their input. The discussion now simmered down, with two more people in two different languages. As one could unambiguously notice, the students were permanently busy in de- and encoding.

> To appreciate the contribution of the others, *"you just said; Du hast eben gesagt"* became something like an unspoken custom, no matter whether subsequent agreement or disagreement was expressed — however only among speakers communicating across L1 and L2.

We learn about the sensation of the new learning arrangement almost being treated like a game, thus a motivational force to try out 'something new'. Although Frieda admits being overwhelmed by the complexity of the new model, the outcome appears satisfactory, as meaning negotiation across languages was accompanied by language comparisons. Such comparisons within the new classroom ecology are seen as the desired bilingual dynamism through individual scaffolding (Creese & Blackledge, 2010; García, 2009; Königs, 2015). The example is particularly interesting, because Frieda, albeit a *Type III* student, points out the demanding practice of partaking in her L1. It teaches us that Trans-FL and scaffolding can be regarded upon as *"two-way street"* (Erdin & Sali, 2020, p. 6).

Particularly noteworthy was the observed behavior of all students to verify everyone in the group actually understood any personal contributions, also leading to an overall embellishment of a democratic and eye-to-eye level arrangement while negotiating their final result. Despite the language barrier, the content seemed to have served as motivating for Arnold as *Type IV* student, casting the pillars for a translanguaging space within the group arrangement. For Kim as *Type I* student, a more subject-based eye level dialogue with Frieda as a strong subject but very weak language student, otherwise often remaining silent during immersion, was possible. Within the proceedings, we see confidence developing with her, possibly owing to the banishment of a language barrier, being able to lucidly state her point. And in the end of the tirade between Frieda and Kim, when the discussion had become more heated, we noted that the actual language used by each speaker had occupied a secondary role. Not only scaffolds for weaker learners need to be offered, but also challenges and affordances for strong *Type I* students enable *"more effective learning due to cross- language semantic remapping that occurs when the encoded information in one language is retrieved to enable production in the other language."* (Lewis et al., 2012,

p. 650). This arrangement, as it became obvious, thwarted affective and ad-hoc behavior, with a more profound use of cognitive resources, also of Arnold.

Talking about Arnold as *Type IV* student, let us pay some extra attention to his negotiation of meaning, here constituent of CLIL in its idea and philosophy of thought, integrating content and language.

Observation scene #2, with focus on Kim (Type I; L2), Ben (Type II; L1), Frieda (Type III; L1) and Arnold (Type IV; L2)

Extract from the same discussion of observation scene #1

Arnold: *"In your example, it's a penner."* [hobo, tramp]
Kim: *"You mean a homeless person!"*
Arnold: *"Yes, a homeless, or a Bettler...."* [beggar]
Kim: *"A Beggar!"*
Arnold: *"Yes, beggar"*
Frieda: *"Nein, er meint nur einen Obdachlosen."* [No, he means a homeless.]
Arnold: *"No, a beggar."*
Ben (*Type II, L1*): *"Also einen Bettler, keinen Obdachlosen!"* [So a beggar, no homeless.]
Arnold nodding, showing approval.

At first, instance, Arnold uses a colloquial and rather insulting word in L1, obviously out of affective reasons, for clearly defining what he semantically means. Kim wants to provide him with language assistance. However, Arnold does not seem fully convinced. After receiving further assistance by Kim, Frieda intervenes, to decode the meaning back to L1, obviously trying to provide language support. Arnold however rebukes Frieda's intervention while strictly staying in L2. Ben, also in L1, finally confirms Arnold's choice.

Such negotiating of meaning in the weaker language has already been advocated by Cen Williams, as Lewis et al. (2012) note. Code-mixing, better than remaining completely silent, can be seen as legitimate strategy (Canagarajah, 2011), especially for weak *Type III/IV* language students. It can provide a valuable self-scaffold during the negotiation of subject meaning, overall exemplifying a conductive outcome at certain instances. However, it needs to be limited, and the main roles strictly adhered to.

As we noted, other groups showed similar experiences, albeit not in this intensity. However, there were also instances revealing the limits of the RBM that help to define its general scope, prompting to consider alternative pathways for enabling the secure participation of all. The following scene from another group tells us why.

> *Observation scene #3*, with focus on Mara (Type I; L2), Ludwig (Type II; L2), Andrea (Type III; L1) and Hannes (Type IV; L1)
>
> ***Observation from the same discussion, yet in another group***
>
> Hannes, who had been given the L1 role on purpose as the weakest student of the class, appeared completely lost by the mix of languages. The fact that he was allowed, and even actively encouraged, to contribute in German, did not alter the common group scenario at all. Another downturn occurred with Andrea as the other L1 student, normally quite loquacious. Both students had trouble to follow and then secure the content in L1 that had been delivered exclusively by the students in L2, namely Mara and Ludwig. This led to the latter two dominance, who after some time completely switched to L1, for explaining the content and the concepts to Hannes and Andrea. Otherwise, any negotiation would not have been possible at all—as Hannes and Andrea had seemed to have lost track completely while being caught in a mix of codes with L2 dominance attenuating the learning atmosphere. Both L2 students had first tried to mix languages, along with vocabulary help for the other two L1 students, albeit to no avail. This ended in the group discussion to be completely in L1 towards the end, at least bringing partial relief. Skepticism whether especially Hannes would ever be able to take part in a discussion during the RBM at all, even with tremendous scaffolding, is verisimilar.

We learn that Hannes and Andrea do not feel comfortable at all. Especially with Hannes, not even waiving language rules and permitting him space to contribute in L1, served its ends. The RBM at the beginning had cognitively overloaded him, leading to a zero comprehension and output scenario. However, in turn, we should try to think what further scaffolds, and that also includes a modified language policy, could serve its means to make his contributions possible. How can bilingual dynamism be reduced for him? We will take this up during the analysis at the end of this section.

Translanguaging is characterized by a fluid language use of multilingual students' languages. Trans-FL, as pre-stage, encapsulates a clear language policy which can also include language choices by the students (Nikula & Moore, 2019). A small experiment was planned for the next lesson, to compare whether students can, instead of having teacher-allocated language roles, be equipped with a language choice within their groups. Depending on the outcome, we might gain insights what could help Hannes, and weaker L2 students in general—but also how to cater affordances to stronger L2 students.

> *Observation scene #4, and conversation with Frieda (Type III; L2), Ben (Type II; L1), Jens (Type II; L2) and Tanja (Type III; L1)*
>
> *Observation of group decisions about the negotiation of language roles during an introduction to the GDP*
>
> The last phase of the lesson was meant to introduce the students to the GDP. Before the actual group work started, students were requested to negotiate two speakers in each English and German themselves. The outcome across the five groups, in accordance with student types, was as follows:
>
> *Type 1: L1: 0; L2 5;*
> *Type 2: L1: 2; L2: 3;*
> *Type 3: L1: 3; L2: 2;*
> *Type 4: L1: 5; L2: 0.*

The results here lie more or less in the range of expectation. *Type I & IV* unanimously chose L2 and L1, respectively. The outcome with *Type II & Type III* is quite similar, although it was anticipated that actually all *Type II* students select L2, and all *Type III* students L1. To know more about why this deviation took place, the students of the groups were asked by the TR after class about their motives:

Conversation 1:
TR: *"Why did you [Frieda] choose English, and you [Ben] choose German?"*
Frieda: *"Because I am more used to speak English in our PoWi-lessons! And it is easier for me, because I do not have to translate."*
Ben: *"I was OK with German or English, it didn't matter to me, and wanted to leave Frieda the choice!"*

Conversation 2:
TR: *"Why did you [Tanja] choose English, and you [Jens] choose German?"*
Jens: *"Tanja and Lukas [Type I] insisted on speaking English!"*
TR: *"And you were fine with that?"*
Jens: *"I can still better speak in German, because it is my mother tongue!"*
TR: *"Tanja, and why did you insist on speaking English?"*
Tanja: *"Because it is a good opportunity for me to improve my English! PoWi [Politics & Economics] in English is not so boring as our regular English lessons!"*

From *observation scene #4*, we learn that learner autonomy with respect to language choices and preferences can be an essential supplement for the success of translanguaging in CLIL lessons. Ben puts the choice of the language in the background, indicating his focus on the content. At the same time, speaking in L1 is not a decision against L2. In turn, Frieda highlights a language learning objective as CLIL self-concept. This self-concept seems to play an important role. This again underscores the importance of code-switching, to make students use both languages during lessons. On the other side, any teacher-initiated language policy needs to carefully unlock such preferences, and earmark to build an affordance-based classroom ecology with an environment that helps different student types to prosper in the bilingual mastery of the subject content.

Lessons learned from the RBM

From the thick description, triangulated with the data of the RBM's concluding survey, the following was analyzed. The RBM defines a valuable model for subject learning with a high degree of bilingual dynamism and fluid language use, almost engendering a unified language system within groups. It imposes a high challenge on all types of students, concomitantly a high use of cognitive resources. Given a differentiated language policy *(observation scene #1 and #2)*, it builds on the interplay of receptive (hearing) and productive (speaking) code-switching, with a focus on the negotiation of content meaning. In many cases, L1 fallbacks are intercepted by the cooperative environment with stronger students assisting weaker students. The 'game-like feeling' even perpetually prompted students reminding each other of their language roles. As Arnold's example taught us, limited code-mixing, instead of fully falling back into resignation, can be regarded upon as legitimate strategy *(observation scene #2)*.

The RBM thus should be defined as a main goal of bilingual teaching, owing to its potential and overall approval by the learners as main stakeholders. It does enact a close to realistic scenario of a multilingual world, with speakers having opportunities to aggrandize their overall linguistic resources during conversational settings. The pedagogy included at certain instances the assignment of language roles to students, at other instances the opening of spaces with free language choice. Hence it serves as a catalysator for resource-based language learning *(observation scene #4)*.

However, as the data indicated, there is the need to prepare mainly weaker learners with bilingual language tools for the RBM and provide scaffolds for reducing bilingual dynamism and delivering security at the beginning of classes. Security to receive subject proficiency can be mainly achieved with L1 as scaffold (Lewis et al., 2013; Moore, 2002; Nikula & Moore, 2019; Pavón Vázquez & Ramos Ordóñez, 2018), whereas L2 learning would be a next step. This calls for a potential test run of consecutive monolingual phases in both L1 and L2, as also the debriefing in the DBAR team recapitulated. The literature gives certain recommendations on such phasing of classes by simple code-switching (e.g., Baker, 2011; Butzkamm, 2010; Lewis et al., 2012), to prepare the emergence of translanguaging spaces. Here, in such safe spaces, students can warm up, learn the main concepts in L1 (Biederstädt, 2013) and later focus on language learning and mediation into L2. Benefits of such a 'sequential immersion' for language learning should also evade the 'language-potpourri', possibly imposing more harm for especially cognitively swamping weaker students in some instances *(observation scene #3)*.

The next cycle thus describes the experience with the PBM. It should already be noted here that the PBM goes beyond mere repetition of the content in the other language (Böing & Palmen, 2012). Rather, it provides a concept to integrate code-switching into regular classroom proceedings, however with a decreased degree of bilingual dynamism.

Reducing bilingual dynamism for subject and language learning: the PBM

Proceedings

A bilingual input was given by the teacher to provide students with the main terminology in both L1 and L2. Mainly, we paid closer attention to the immediate needs of especially *Type IV* students, but also pronouncedly encouraged *Type III* students to take a more leading role during the consecutive L2 phase.

> *Observation scene #5: Developing a strategy for L2 learning during L1 group work; focus on Frieda (Type III), Pascal and Sabine (both Type IV)*
>
> **_Observation of student-initiated code-switches in groups during an introduction to Malthus' Principle of Population_**
>
> Ample time was provided to bilingually acquaint the students with the multifaceted relationship of population, energy demand and GDP growth. The first group work started in L1. The students were told that we will enter the plenary after the group work in L2, so they had to prepare a strategy during the L1 phase for being able to participate in L2 later. The following could be noted: the students quite quickly and efficiently went through the material in both languages, an extract of Thomas Malthus' *Principle of Population* (Malthus, 1806), comparatively made available in L1 and L2. All the five groups unanimously and independently decided as their strategy to initiate a code-switch into L2 at the end of the phase, to be able later to mediate their results later. For instance, one could note Frieda whispering: *"Wir müssen das auch in Englisch können, lass uns das mal auf Englisch beantworten!"* [We will need to know this later in English, so let's answer the questions already in English!]. The voluntarily code-switch, in line with a determined yet liberal language policy defined the second, student-initiated monolingual phase in the alternating language.
>
> Some particularities across the groups should help to deliver a nuanced picture of the classroom dynamics. Throughout the writing process in L2, Pascal and Sabine (both *Type IV* students) conspicuously consulted the material in the L1 as an individual scaffold, for being able to follow and also actively contribute to the discussion of the tasks. The other students, including *Type III* students here, most of the time used L2-based material most of the time, but occasionally also gleamed on the L1 material, engaging in occasional code-mixing.

The monolingual design of the tasks with the bilingual material, however, seemed to provide them with security while catering individual affordances. They could concentrate on the content, concepts and terminology first and foremost, setting a clear roadmap for their later language use. That the clear language policy seemed to have determined a productive code of conduct in the classroom, as opposed to previous L2 immersion with perpetual fallbacks. As it appeared to us, the L1 material, in turn, did not only provide scaffolding purposes for continuing the work in L2 but also assisted the content comprehension as well as the proficiency in both languages.

For the next lesson, we wanted to test the difference of starting the working process in L2 or L1 across groups, thereafter code-switching to the plenary in the alternate language, thus *de facto* resulting in a bilingual setting with the RBM across groups. Two groups each were randomly selected to start their working process in L1 and L2. The fifth group was given the choice. As input, at first two videos (L1/L2) acquainted the learners with the topic in both languages. Thereafter, they were given the material in both L1 and L2 and were instructed to use the material as per their own affordances for developing an equipollent L1/L2 proficiency. After the group work, the students code-switched and discussed in the plenary. The following scene reveals how the PBM can be a preparatory method for the RBM, if carefully integrated.

> *Observation scene #6*, with focus on Mara (Type I; L1), Jens (Type II; L1), Carla (Type III; L2), Ilse (Type III; L2) and Sabine (Type IV; L2); bilingual plenary after monolingual group work (L1/L2 by choice)
>
> ***Observation of a plenary session after a group work in the PBM about population, wealth and emissions***
>
> Mara:
>
> "*Es ist unfair, wir leben im Luxus, fahren in den Urlaub und haben Yachten, und andere nicht mal sauberes Wasser!*" [It's not fair, we live luxury, have vacation and yachts, and others not even clean water!]

Jens: "I agree with Mara. We live im, ähm, Überfluss..."

Mara: "Wasn't that ... affluence, right Mr. [Teacher]?"

TR: "Yes, affluence!"

Jens: "Ja, we live in affluence and should also think about others!"

Mara: "Ja, das ist voll unfair! So viele Menschen haben auch keinen Zugang zu Bildung. Es ist kein Wunder, dass die Geburtenrate in den Ländern höher ist, weil die Menschen Kinder zum Überleben brauchen!" [Yes, that's not fair! So many people lack access to education. No wonder that the birth rate in those countries is higher, because the people need kids to survive!]

Jens: "In Germany, the... Geburten... birth... ähm..."

TR: "Birth rate!"

Jens: "Ja, die birth rate is so low, because people want to keep their lifestyle. This is very egoistic!" [...]

Carla [emotionally activated]: "Can I say it in German?"

Teacher: "No."

Carla [unpertubed]: "OK. But we have to say that people should have the own ... uhm, Freiheit?"

Ilse: "Freedom!"

Carla [unperturbed]: "Yes, freedom, to decide how to live!"

Ilse: "This is what I also wanted to say. We have to understand that the people there have other problems than we. But we should also be more... uhm, umsichtig?"

TR: "Considerate!"

Ilse: "yes, considerate, with our resources!"

Jens: "Yes!" [Mara nodding to signify her approval]

Carla: "We can see that CO_2 [se-oh-two] rises with the population growth."

TR [intervening]: "Carla, in English, we commonly call it carbon, rather not CO_2."

Sabine [interrupting]: "And the carbon will be very high in the future."

Frieda [without raising her hand]: "Es gibt auch die <u>Limits des Wachstums</u>!" Das hat doch dieser Club of Rome gesagt! Dass das <u>GDP</u> nicht endlos wachsen kann!" [There are limits of growth! This Club of Rome said that! That GDP growth is finite!].

[...]

We can note here that in the beginning of the plenary, two strong language students *(Type I/II)* interacted *de facto* with the RBM, then joined by two weaker language students *(Type III)* at a later stage in L2, who in the end had a monolingual and pragmatic conversation. Then, <u>Frieda</u> was desperately willing to deliver individual knowledge, code-mixed. Remarkable is that the students stuck to their language roles during the plenary discussion, receiving language assistance from their peers and the TR, however indicating that a mix of languages appeared almost natural to them. Again, limited code-meshing, or here actively asking for language assistance in a rather emotionally heated atmosphere, appears as a legitimate *ultima ratio* at instances. It appeared that the language spoken as such moved to the background with the development of security in content and terminology, as the extract shows. Some pauses while researching words did not really disrupt the conversation flow. Rather, they provided as instrumental for language learning during the bilingual arrangement and thwarted affective responses, most probably also for the listeners. And even Carla was not irritated when banned from speaking in L1. She accepted language aid from her peer as well as the TR's input. Even Sabine as very weak *Type IV* student intervened, with a conspicuous interest to contribute.

Lessons learned from the PBM
The clear difference between the PBM and the RBM became visible immediately, also mirrored by the concluding survey results. However, they are by no means diametrically opposites. Rather, the PBM looks like a supplement, constituting another piece of a puzzle for a comprehensive CLIL teaching model. We noted that the students were able to focus more on emerging the subject content synchronically developing equipollent language competence in L1/L2 during monolingual phases. This comes along with the reduction of bilingual dynamism and the multilingual perspective on translanguaging, recognizing different multilingual competences in L1 and L2 (MacSwan, 2017; Moore & Nikula, 2016). The PBM provides a safe space to acquaint students with content, concepts, and terminology in both L1 and L2. It offers students with ample room to first develop language competence and, on a meta-level, language awareness, also comparing and talking about language (Corcoll, 2013) for really understanding and digesting the topic *(observation scene #5)*. It appears as a prerequisite for passing language thresholds and increasing dynamic bilingualism with the RBM later. Hence, learning and understanding the concepts in the respective language without losing time and energy in a mélange of languages, and with the help of existing language resources, was facilitated, as preparation for the RBM thereafter.

In an informal conversation, Carla, today eagerly motivated to personally narrate her stakeholder's opinion to the DBAR team, told the observers after class that she noted students in L2 tended towards speaking more dialectically, so other students having worked in L1 before were able to better comprehend their input.

She argued that these speakers were aware of the need to include L1 speakers. This is a further option: to initiate a plenary in L2 with the focus on language learning but permit weaker L2 students to contribute in L1 at exceptional instances (according to some rule, like a wildcard). This can prevent both fallbacks as economical option, commonly but not exclusively chosen by weaker students as well as resignation in silence, in the end obstacles towards language learning. This option can indeed be added to any further exercise if the teacher deems it appropriate, to reduce the language threshold for weaker learners (Moore, 2002). Language choice can be a key, but too much autonomy can also be counterproductive, calling for balanced teacher- and student-initiated code-switches. The example with Carla and Sabine *(observation scene #6)* however shows that sometimes, students need to be constrained to L2 use, for also realizing the language objective of CLIL.

The PBM is mainly, but not exclusively, useful for weaker students. However, we should always keep in mind the needs and desires of stronger students (mainly *Type I*), cater them with affordances as optional challenges, and make the CLIL teaching model more comprehensive. Here, the recommendation of Lin (2013), arguing for integrating mode-switching into code-switching practices defines a possible pathway. As Diehr (2012) puts it, the function of L1 should be seen beyond mere scaffolding for weaker students but rather as an eye-level partner with L2. Liebscher and Dailey-O'Cain (2005), referring to Auer's (1984, 1995, 1998) seminal work, point out discourse-related functions of each language among bilinguals. Transferring this idea on mostly strong bilingual learners, we should discover in the following the merits and disadvantages of the MBM in the last cycle.

Providing optional challenges mainly for strong learners: the MBM

Proceedings

Seamlessly continuing in the PBM the next lesson, the classroom discourse was now in L2. The endeavor to prevent mainly *Type I* students from falling into boredom and realizing their affordances accordingly prompted for an investigation of the MBM as a model worth investigating. Only the extensive writing tasks were supposed to take place in L1. The students were at first supposed to talk about the first text they had prepared at home in L2. Then, they had to summarize, not translate, as a group, "in a nutshell" in L1, but continue talking in L2.

> *Observation scene #7*, with main focus on <u>Kim</u> (Type I), <u>Ben</u> (Type II), <u>Frieda</u> (Type III) and <u>Arnold</u> (Type IV), speaking in L2, writing in L1
>
> *<u>Observation of a group work in the MBM (speaking in L2, writing in L1) about the Club of Rome</u>*
>
> Before starting the groupwork, all groups were asked about difficulties with the L2 material, concordantly classified as easy. But e.g., <u>Mara</u> as *Type I* student, anticipating the group work process, clearly stated that it would be difficult to summarize it in German, because *"you have to translate."* It became immediately very clear that the students felt very challenged, along with deep cognitive processing of the contents, but also overwhelmed during mediating into <u>written</u> German. The students 'softened' the rules after some time. In the beginning, they clearly adhered to the rules, which was time-consuming and elicited resonating frustrations, but during writing, actually all groups all of a sudden switched towards speaking German, especially while researching the terminology needed. The atmosphere can be described as completely silent and concentrated, with whispering interrupting this allegedly tranquil yet chimerical peace. In particular, they read the passages of the material step-by-step in English, then spoke in German as a self-directed intermediate step (discussing the words needed) before writing. Thus, the group work comprised code-mixing as such, indicating complexity with the MBM. However, on the positive side, we were happy to note how <u>Arnold</u> as *Type IV* student was able to use the latter strategy to improve his language competence, significantly contributing to the group result. The following minutiae reveals the bilingual dynamism, which, by the adopted procedure of the students to take intermediate steps, was artificially slowed down.

Frieda [reading the paragraph of the material]:

"The team tracked industrialisation, population, food, use of resources, and pollution. They modelled data up to 1970, then developed a range of scenarios out to 2100, depending on whether humanity took serious action on environmental and resource issues. If that didn't happen, the model predicted "overshoot and collapse" – in the economy, environment and population – before 2070. This was called the 'business-as-usual' scenario."

[silence, everyone concentrated and noting on paper]:

Kim [starting to write silently, and then reading the first sentence, without speaking before about the content]:

"So können wir anfangen: Die Entwicklung der Welt bis 1970 war die Grundlage, verschiedene Szenarien für 2100 zu entwerfen, je nach dem, wie ernst die Menschen die Umwelt nehmen." [Let's start like this: data on the world development until 1970 was the basis for designing different scenarios for 2100, depending how seriously the people look at the environment.]

Arnold:

"Ja, das ist gut. Und dann weiter so: 'Wenn das nicht passiert, sagt das Modell es gibt einen Kollaps vor 2070!'. [thinking] Ah, das heißt also business-as-usual scenario, das heißt, wenn alles einfach so weitergeht, ohne dass irgendwas passiert!" [Yes, that's great. And then continue: if this doesn't happen, the model says there will be a collapse before 2070! Ah, that's what business-as-usual scenario means, it means, when we just continue without anything happening!]

Frieda:

"Genau! Das Business-as-usual heißt einfach weiter wie bisher! Und das wird kritisiert" [Exactly! Business-as-usual just means let's continue! And that's criticized!]

Arnold:

Dann lass uns doch so schreiben: *"Um zu verhindern, dass die Welt vor 2070 untergeht, muss sich etwas ändern!"* [Let's write it like this: to avoid a collapse of the world before 2070, something has to change!]

Ben:

"Ja, das ist gut! [Yes, that's great!]

[everyone else showing approval through nodding and mumbling; silence, everyone concentrated and noting on paper]:

Kim: [reading out the full summary of that paragraph]:

"Die Entwicklung der Welt bis 1970 war die Grundlage, verschiedene Szenarien für 2100 zu entwerfen, je nach dem, wie ernst die Menschen die Umwelt nehmen. Um zu verhindern, dass die Welt vor 2070 zusammenbricht, muss sich etwas ändern, sagt der Club of Rome!" [The world development till 1970 served as the basis to anticipate different scenarios for 2100, depending on how serious people treat the environment. The Club or Rome pleas for new pathways.]

Frieda [whispering]:

"Scheiße, das auf Deutsch zu schreiben, das ist anstrengender als auf Englisch". [It's shit to write this in German, it's harder than in English!]

We learn from *observation scene #7* that code-mixing within the mode-based model can be a useful strategy to master the mediation for weaker students, as L1 plays a significant part in the meaning making process of L2 material. Arnold needed the intermediate step and the space to first communicate in L1, to order his thoughts. A seamless transition as with Kim was not possible. Other *Type I* students were observed using a similar behavior as Arnold, albeit on a much smaller scale. Frieda admits that the task requires more cognition as opposed to classical immersion. Very interesting in the group was the swift from using *Kollaps,* the literal translation to *zusammenbricht* (transition from noun to verb), along with a more genuine sentence structure in L1, as opposed to 'importing the common English structure'.

> *Observation scene #8,* with main focus on Jens (Type II) and Carla (Type III), speaking in L2, writing in L1
>
> Experiences in the other groups were similar. Carla *(Type III)* presented her work: *"Der Club of Rome ist eine Assoziation [...]:"* Jens pointed out that association is an anglicism in this instance, which indeed are common, and suggested to use *Vereinigung,* which Carla accepted. She appeared to have reached her limit, but also admitted that she had to concentrate more due to the *"vocab overshoot"* with a result in deeper cognitive processing. She concluded that this procedure is actually a conductive way to learn L2 in that area, i.e., presenting topics of interest, challenging with language work but providing ample room for L1. Jens, in turn, read out the sentence: *"Das Zusammenspiel von Ressourcenknappheit mit Bevölkerungswachstum [...]".* This indicates that the content as such has been understood, and the student was able to mediate, albeit with typical L2-chunks and structure. Moreover, it appeared that they invested more effort than compared to L2/L1-only lessons, where notes are often carelessly taken. L2 terminology, when missing the counterpart in L1, was often described with fine words. Looking for expressions to generate L1 output in written after L2 input or L2 speaking is complex and cognitive demanding. The high frequency of productive code-switches in speaking and writing was used as possible explanation.

It appeared to us that, under certain circumstances, the MBM can be a very useful tool for language learning, especially for imposing a challenge for *Type I* students *(observation scene #7).* Seamless switching within the mode-based model can impose a — both positive and negative — challenge for all students. Thus, it seems to be a viable tool for the differentiation of lessons.

Nevertheless, we should register that the MBM can be destructive in phases with cognitive overload *(observation scene #8)*. We were permanently able to witness comments of students, complaining about the burden imposed of writing in the other language of speech. Hence, the MBM should be used with care, rather as an optional challenge at the end of a thematic cluster, in phases when students have already experienced adequate exposition to and proficiency in the subject and language. For strong students, depending on their development, it can already be provided as an individual option.

Lessons learned from the MBM

What became most obvious with the MBM was the high frequency of productive code-switches, from speaking in one, and writing in the other language. The recommendation to clearly explain this teaching model, however leaving students the choice to enter it, is in the foreground. In particular, *Type I* students can be encouraged to consider it as positive challenge, but other types should not be excluded as well. The role of the teacher as manager here to overview and set up such processes for pedagogical reasons, what García and Li (2014, p. 91) call *"official translanguaging"*, becomes instrumental. As we know from past research, individual language choices play a major role with translanguaging (Nikula & Moore, 2019). In FL learning, this can be equated with an individual language learning objective, comparable to the natural choices of multilinguals in their endeavor to apply their fully existing language repertoire. This assigns individual control over the amount of bilingual dynamism under regular circumstances outside of the classroom.

With a clearly delineated language policy by teachers directing their students into the MBM, even code-mixing and other intermediate steps can be helpful in mediation and meaning-making. The bottom line is that the MBM can be used as an addendum to foster certain learning objectives but needs to be applied with care.

Chapter VI

… about the virtue of emotions….

Finding the "perfect equilibrium of emotional and rational learning" in content and language integrated learning (CLIL) in the social sciences

Abstract

This case study investigates whether bilingual classes in the social sciences can engender a perfect equilibrium of emotional and rational learning. After introducing the topic, the merits of the emotional turn, welcoming the presence of emotions in science and education, will be discussed. Thereafter, the nexus to language learning will be established. These two parts will be integrated into a new competence model aiming to promote global discourse competence. Those theoretical pillars define the roadmap for a "design-based action research" in a 10th grade content and language integrated learning (CLIL) classroom in politics and economics. The data reveals that code-switching languages can balance emotional and rational learning as a cornerstone of a pedagogy addressing today's global challenges.

Reproduced with permission of The Licensor through PLSclear (PLSclear Ref No:61001), January 29th, 2022.

Status: **Published**

Nijhawan, S. (2020). Finding the 'perfect equilibrium of emotional and rational learning' in Content and Language Integrated Learning (CLIL) in the social sciences. In M. Simons & T. Smits (Eds.), *Language Education and Emotions: Research into Emotions and Language Learners, Language Teachers and Educational Processes* (pp. 181-201). London: Routledge.

Listed in the bibliography as Nijhawan (2020b).

Introduction: CLIL and emotions

CLIL in the social sciences: a response to global challenges

In Europe, the launch of CLIL programs was encouraged across the member states, to realize plurilingualism as a set target in a linguistically diverse region with many different mother tongues (Marsh, 2002). CLIL can be defined as "all types of provision in which a second language (a foreign, regional or minority language and/or another official state language) is used to teach certain subjects in the curriculum other than languages lessons themselves" (European Commission, 2006, p. 8).

However, besides this "language objective" (Lasagabaster & Sierra, 2010, p. 372), potential benefits for subject learning have for long, more or less, been ignored by both research and practice, also because CLIL still mostly falls under the scope of language didactics. In terms of globalization-related topics, CLIL in the social sciences naturally provides for an apt arena to enter other perspectives through other languages, as intercultural education suggests. This is highly relevant for, *inter alia*, second or foreign language teaching in English, undisputedly the global *lingua franca* of the 21st century. Thus, a bilingual surplus, beyond "only" promoting the development of a cognitive academic language proficiency (CALP), also exists in CLIL's unique pedagogy.

A short excursus depicting the merits of the so-called emotional turn (see later in this chapter) underlines the motivation of this study. At the very latest, the two summers of 2018 and 2019 unveiled the urgency to uplift a global challenge on the top of the political agenda: climate change. Its effects are felt worldwide in daily life. Climate change illustrates how the global and the local constitute a unified phenomenon, also called *"gLocalization"* (Robertson, 1995; own emphasis and capitalization). Debates happen, *inter alia*, at a local level in the surrounding language as well as at a global level, mostly in the *lingua franca* English. Apart from climate change, typical global challenges include poverty and inequality, multiculturalism, domestic and transnational power relations, demography, resource (mis)management and human rights.

Currently, the Fridays for Future movement demonstrates this train of thought: protests happen at several localities all around the world, albeit with a globally networked agenda. Participants who are very engaged or interested usually engage in both their L1 and the L2 (mostly English), respectively.

The emotional turn

The reference to climate change exemplifies that political action needs to consider positions beyond personal and national interests (Engartner & Nijhawan, 2019). Our times require not only to "think global and act local", as the slogan says, but rather think and act globally and locally at the same time (Karliner, 1997a), recognizing the unifying force of g*Local*ization. It is necessary to know how others are thinking and *feeling* and to deconstruct the well-known *us vs. them* distinction.

Our state of emotions affects our thinking and consequently our actions in society. From theory and research on the sociology of emotions, we know that empathy cannot sprout without emotions (Davis, 2006). Empathy again comes as harbinger and starting point of global justice and solidarity (Flam, 2005; Korte, 2015). Against this background the impact of the *emotional turn* of the 1970s offers the opportunity to open the *"black box"* and provide insights on how humans *really* think and *feel* (Stets & Turner, 2006). Research over the last decades has taught us that emotions as a matter of fact do not preexist as innate character traits. Rather, they are a learnable social construct (Weber, 2016), rendering the emotional turn particularly attractive for education (Barbalet, 2002), especially in the social sciences with reference to our contemporary global challenges.

On the flipside, we know that emotions in their lone and uncontrolled form can also cause illegitimate outcomes and thus their irrationality. *"Trumpism"* serves as a perspicuous example of the effects of uncontrolled emotions, with tweets followed by opposing voices demanding the return to facts and rationality. However, rational choice in its pure form defies *homo economicus* as an ideal type of an actor, negating any emotional foundation of judgment and human action (Detjen, 2017). But emotions and rationality, often wrongly classified as having a diametrically opposite existence, are in reality closely juxtaposed. As a matter of fact, "*[e]very cognitive frame implies emotional framing*" (Flam, 2005, p. 24). Here, the merits of Heise's (1979) affect control theory become applicable. Emotions serve as stimulus for human action; nevertheless they need to be internally controlled.

To promote global justice and solidarity as essential features for a sustainable future in the 21st century, an argument for the genesis of a *perfect equilibrium of emotional and rational learning* will be constructed. The question how to control emotions, or, in turn, fill rationality with feelings, leads us to consider the functions of language and bilingualism.

Bilingualism and emotion

Although there is no unique CLIL approach and pedagogy applied in teaching programs across the EU, one similarity can be discerned. *De facto* a strong bias prevails towards CLIL as a modern approach to foreign language learning in the form of "*additive late partial immersion*" (Breidbach & Viebrock, 2012, p. 6).

The earlier section indicated that decision making and political action are strongly related to one's emotional condition. The visibility of emotions in the social sciences and their controlled application during learning processes thus become a central aspect in education and deserve deeper diligence. A pivotal assumption for questioning the strict monolingual practice and instead following a real bilingual approach with an intended L1 use as a main pillar for CLIL classes in the social sciences can be constructed in line with evidence from experimental psychology. After several game theoretical experiments, Keysar et al. (2012) claim that humans are biased towards more emotional decisions in their L1, while decisions taken in an L2 (a less dominant language) show more rational features following deeper cognitive processing. A similar train of thought has been adopted in therapy and counselling for decades. Drawing on the experience of specialists, Martinovic and Altarriba (2013) assign the language employed with bilingual patients an instrumental role. They argue that code-switching languages to extract emotions in the L1 can be central and desired during any session. Emotions, counterproductive in their pure and lone form, can be rationally controlled while systematically employing the L2 (here mostly the *second* language as the less dominant). Rationality is equally central to therapy as well—but again, never in its pure essence.

As appraisal, it can be anticipated that switching languages within a CLIL arrangement as well can have a significant impact on learning outcomes and judgments in the social sciences, as "therapy for global justice and solidarity". The theoretical thoughts of this and the preceding section have resulted in the construction of a competence model for CLIL classes in the social sciences.

A theoretical framework for uniting emotional and rational learning

A competence model for CLIL in the social sciences

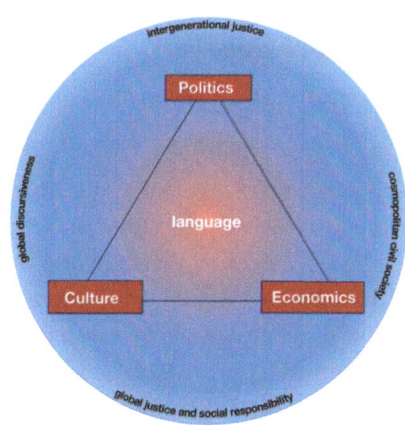

Figure 1: The triangle of Politics, Economics & Culture (Elsner, Engartner, Nijhawan, & Rodmann, 2019, p. 9)

Due to the absence of educational standards in CLIL, a full-fledged conceptual framework has been developed by the *PolECulE*-project of Goethe University Frankfurt (Elsner, Engartner, Nijhawan & Rodmann, 2019; Nijhawan, 2019) for CLIL classes in politics and economics in English as L2 (exemplary for social science education). Language is not only seen as a mere vehicle but as central for the achievement of subject knowledge as well as harbinger of global justice, solidarity and a cosmopolitan world view *(Figure 1)*.

Global discursiveness defines the fulcrum of the new competence model. This train of thought has been translated into defining

205

global discourse competence as the main interdisciplinary bilingual competence for CLIL classes in politics and economics, with an integration of culture. The combination of six competence fields *(Figure 2)* includes at first all the four main competences from the subject politics and economics. The two remaining competences round the competence model out and define the L1 as instrumental for bilingual classes.

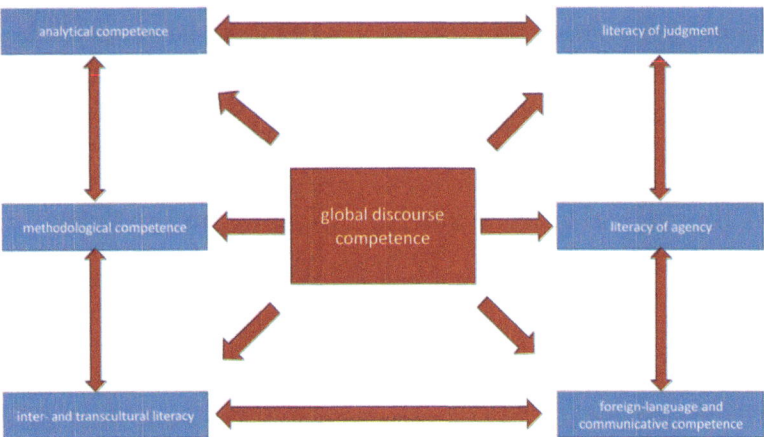

Figure 2: The competence model with the global discourse competence at the center (Elsner et al., 2019, p. 24).

Borrowing from foreign language teaching, *inter- and transcultural literacy* mainly envisages the understanding of alternative perspectives, along with the ability to feel unity and togetherness and develop empathy. Altruism should be considered as alternative to mere self-interest. *Foreign language and communicative competence* includes the ability of an equipollent L1 and L2 proficiency, requiring students to be able to code-switch languages at certain sequences within the subject content and to develop language awareness, ultimately instrumental for their participation during global discourses.

Is there an "ideal judgment for global justice and solidarity"?

To develop a more nuanced model of the ideal type of decision making, not only the distinction between *emotions* and *rational choice* is important but also the opposition between *self-interest* and *altruism*, as the preceding section revealed. These two extremes are again closely correlated with rationality and emotions, respectively, and help to distinguish the roadmap towards achieving global discourse competence two-dimensionally. Of course, a judgment never exists in its pure form, but contains features of the other criteria. In accordance with criteria for multilayered political judgment, the argument is brought forward that the ideal type of a judgment is well-balanced and thus in perfect equilibrium among four criteria. These **four** dimensions (efficiency [rationality], legitimacy [normative and moral questions], self-interest and perspective changes) belong to the main criteria for political judgments (Massing, 2003). In this context, Sander (2007) distinguishes between factual-based rational judgments and moral-based value-laden judgments. *Table 1* exemplifies this train of thought at the example of climate change policies and combines the two criteria of both dimensions into four possible categories. The inner box indicates the approximate location of an ideal judgment in perfect equilibrium of the four categories.

Table 1: Categories of forming a judgment about global challenges (e.g., climate change)

Example: Position towards climate change policies	
pure emotional self-interest	**pure emotional altruism**
The learner is (for or) against harder measures to combat climate change out of pure self-interest. S/he may have loved (or hated) the hot summer of 2018. Global justice and international solidarity are out of reach. *"Trumpism" and irrationality*	The learner is for (or against) harder measures to combat climate change, because in her or his eyes, quests for emphatic global climate justice are either supported or jeopardized. *references to the empathy altruism hypothesis (Batson, Duncan, Ackerman, Buckley, & Birch, 1981)*
pure rational self-interest	**pure rational altruism**
The learner is (for or) against harder measures to combat climate change after a jejune cost-benefit analysis, without considering other perspectives. S/he may have benefited (or suffered) from the hot summer of 2018. Any quest for global justice is jeopardized. *"homo economicus"*	The learner is for (or against) harder measures to combat climate change after a jejune cost-benefit analysis, because s/he realizes that sustainability benefits or disadvantages by global climate justice for everyone as a result. *references to social exchange theory (Homans, 1958) and effective altruism (Singer, 2015)*

The next section deals with the empirical classroom research. The focus is mostly directed towards the measurement of emotions.

Classroom research

Measuring emotions

Classification and measurement of emotions is a highly controversial venture (Thamm, 2006). Mauss and Robinson (2009) provide a critical review of different measures of emotions and group them into four main categories, two of them requiring complicated neuroscientific laboratory utilities and settings. As the research was set to take place in a completely natural learning environment, the following simplified procedure was adopted.

Rating system: self-assessment as starting point

After a comprehensive lesson series on *homo economicus*, along with different activities relating the concepts directly to the students' living environment (Nijhawan, Schmerbach, Elsner, & Engartner, 2020, pp. 12-13 includes an example), it was their task to range their own average personality on a 10-point scale. The extremes indicated their belief of being completely *ra*tional (0) or completely *emo*tional (10) persons *(RAEM)*. The exact middle (5) means the students see themselves in an absolute perfect equilibrium (50% rational; 50% emotional). Furthermore, the system was applied after every other activity for evaluating their own opinions to controversial topics. This very simple and easily applicable system was meant to help students monitor their inner self during the working processes. Moreover, these self-reporting values were used at a later point during the content analysis within a mathematical model. The same system was applied to the question of *se*lf-interest (0) and *al*truism (10), with the exact middle (5) again indicating an equal proportion of each extreme value *(SIAL)*. So the students' rating always consisted of a two-numbered pair from 0 to 10 on a two-dimensional scale (RAEM [0–10]; SIAL [0–10]).

Observations

The lead researcher (the author of this article) as well as the team members were set to observe one of the five student groups consisting of four students each. A handout defining emotional categories (e.g., facial expressions, vocabulary, rhetoric, voice characteristics) provided a guideline to classify students' behavior.

Content analysis

Bilingual assessment was scheduled for the end of the research, after seven weeks of teaching, making the written L1 and L2 use of the students comparable. A qualitative data analysis (QDA) with categories defining rational and emotional as well as self-interest and altruistic arguments was performed to calculate and scale scores of the essays as a whole on the two-dimensional RAEM and SIAL scale, respectively.

Research design

The preceding theoretical framework provided the guideline for a single case study in a 10th grade (N=22) of a German public high school at the end of 2017. The semester topic was "economics and the environment". The reason that exactly this group was chosen for the research in the given context coincided with the schedule of the *PolECulE*-project. The decision was taken to carry out the research in the second year of the initially three-year granted project, in the normal and natural teaching environment of the teacher-researcher. *De facto*, it is a random selection of the research group, because it was assigned independently by the school's planners. In this particular study group, the L2 English was a foreign language for all of the students, while L1 constitutes the mother tongue for almost everyone, or at least a second language comparable to fluent German speakers. All students expressed their informed consent to take part in the research. Surveys were taken anonymously to protect the participants' identity and to mitigate concerns that the answers could have an impact on the final assessment. Moreover, participation in the research was completely voluntary, leading to a different N at different times of the research. Furthermore, as it is common in natural learning environments, certain factors, for example, absence due to illness, are hardly controllable.

The research project was initiated as an answer to the desired teaching methods for the "judicious and principled use of L1" (Lo, 2014) in CLIL classes (e.g., Frisch, 2016; Gierlinger, 2015). This means that at certain times, the students had to work in their L1, at other times in their L2, in accordance with the teaching methods investigated. As democratic stakeholder participation—this includes students as well as the teacher-researcher—defined the cornerstone of the research, the outline was pragmatic in its setting. Hence, apart from a team structure established at university, a similar structure was installed at school to plan, design, test and redesign the classes. Putting action and design-based research together into one single framework prompts it to be "design-based action research (DBAR)" (Nijhawan, 2017), uniting features of both underlying methods.

This paper focuses on the research related to the possible emergence of a perfect equilibrium of emotional and rational learning as a "side effect" of testing the bilingual teaching methods (see Elsner et al., 2019, for three suggested affordance-based and differentiated models for a judicious and principled L1 integration). This is mirrored in the following research question:

RQ: Does an L1 integration into CLIL classes in the social sciences lead to a perfect equilibrium of emotional and rational learning?

Data

The body of data is assembled as follows: (a) self-assessment with the rating system; (b) surveys: students were requested to answer several surveys; (c) observation data of all observants, reconstructed as "thick description" (Geertz, 1973); (d) instant classroom feedback and individual as well as group interviews; and (e) QDA of a written bilingual exam.

Results

This section presents a synopsis of the results, containing a short introduction on the instruments used.

Survey responses

In the introductory survey, students appraised their previous CLIL experience, so far immersive in the L2, without any L1 use. Accordingly, their opinion whether L1 use in CLIL should find consideration was of general interest. In this context, one item, *inter alia*, asked whether students could discern any difference in decision making in accordance with the language they speak. The same question was asked in the final survey after the research had been concluded. They also had the opportunity to comment on their responses.

Table 2: Comparing decisions in the L1 and L2

Item: Comparing your decisions in English or German: do you see any significant difference in terms emotionality or rationality in the respective language you use (L1/L2)?		
Answer	I do not see any significant difference	I see a significant difference
introductory survey (N=19*)	16 (84%) *"I have the same opinion in both languages. I am not another person in the other language!"*	3 (16%) *"For me it's more complicated to express my feelings in English. That's why I rather have to refer to facts, whereby in German it is easier for me to express my feelings."*
final survey (N=16*)	11 (69%) *"I don't think anything changed while switching languages. Possibly because I always think in German and then translate."*	5 (31%) *"I think that my emotions are way more important for me when taking decisions in german. Depending on the situation it sometimes feels a bit like a game where I decide completely out of emotion in english."*

Table 2 highlights that not only a clear majority of the students negated any effect of the language on decisions but some even expressed surprise about this question at all. Only a small number of students responded affirmatively. It seems like a lot of awareness and reflexibility is needed to self-monitor any change. The students were thus explicitly requested during the research to pay due diligence to their nature of decision making in both languages, also with assistance of the rating system.

The final survey does not show any groundbreaking change. Although responses are slightly different, these results do not seem to be significantly different and could have also been caused by random effects in relation to the small population surveyed.

Group discussions

During the research period, we took up the issue several times, as a general rule spontaneously after a task, time permitting. The contributions were recorded in writing by the observers, to summarize them as a whole for the thick description as final product.

The students' responses mirror the results of the survey. Most students reacted with surprise to the recurring question whether they discerned any difference in their decisions in relation to the language they spoke. The language does not affect their personality and opinions, it echoed. The minority of students with a different opinion only modestly expressed their view, if at all. Such responses indicated that forming an opinion in the L2 took longer, as it was in many cases the process of internal making of meaning. That means that the decision making, as it was argued, happened in the L1, before translating and expressing it into the L2. Questions were asked whether this actually affected the nature of the decision. This minority of students did affirm that there is a lack of linguistic repertoire to express the same emotions they are used from their L1, explaining the more rational mirror of their opinions in their L2.

Observations by the researcher and the DBAR team

After close deliberation on providing a formal observation scheme (e.g., in accordance with the specific-affect coding system by (e.g., in accordance with the specific-affect coding system by Coan & Gottman, 2007), or using open observations, the decision for the latter was taken. The reason was to prepare for the reporting of the full classroom dynamics as a thick description for the overarching research project, requiring detailed field notes. Thus, any other form of structured observation beyond the employed procedure would have been beyond the observers' cognitive capacity. As preparation, all observers, each observing one student group of four, had a list of criteria (voice, face expressions, etc.) indicating whether any action by the students was rather emotional or rational and requested to record their observations and note any behavioral differences in the L1 and L2.

The observations during a mixed language arrangement (role-based model) with each two students in the L1 and L2, delivered a completely different picture as compared to the surveys. Affective responses and arousal were without any doubt stronger when students communicated with each other in the L1 (L1, translated: "*This is not true!*"). In turn, communication within the L2 led to a more rationalized picture ("*You just said that... I disagree with you*"), because students apparently needed more time to express thoughts and opinions, looking for the appropriate language and terminology. This thwarted the first affective seconds after the stimulus received. L1 speakers proved to be less acrimonious and impulsive as usual, and thus more considerate with their group members to ensure the meaning is negotiated properly. They expressed emotional words but made sure those students working in the L2 could participate equally. The setting was almost comparable to speaking with a smaller sibling. Students tended to show more patience and consideration with their input (L1, translated: "*But you need to consider that...*"). Reactions in the L2 usually took more time than in the L1.

Especially these mixed L1/L2 language arrangements indicated a stronger control of emotions and transformed the group discussions into a more rational form, with the requirement to invest cognitive resources for the benefit to be able to discuss under these more challenging conditions. The following extract from a discussion about the question "Is there a universal definition of wealth?" serves as a typical example of a mixed language arrangement:

Extract from a discussion about the question: Is there a universal definition of wealth?
St. 1 (English):   "*Wealth is seen differently by different people*"
St. 2 (German):   (*reading out loudly a written sentence he had translated and written from St. 2*):   "*Wohlstand wird verschieden angesehen von vielen verschiedenen Leuten*"   (*mumbling*): **Oh, jetzt habe ich aus Versehen die englische Grammatik benutzt!** [*Oh, I just used the English grammar by accident*]; (*editing and reading the edited sentence*): **"Es gibt in der Welt verschiedene Ansichten und Meinungen über Wohlstand"** [*In the world there are different perceptions about wealth*]
St. 1 (English):   (*answering immediately*): **"Yes, and for me, I want to earn enough money to afford all the things I like."**

St. 2 (German):	"<u>Du hast eben gesagt</u>, dass du Wohlstand vor allem mit Geld in Verbindung bringst. Ich finde, auch andere Sachen wie Freunde und Familie gehören dazu." [you just said ou associate wealth in particular with money. I believe, also other things like friends and family are part of it.]
St. 1 (English):	"<u>You just said</u> that you believe that wealth has to be also defined beyond material things."
St. 2 (German):	"Aber du hast eine sehr einseitige Definition von Wohlstand". [But your definition of wealth is very one-sided!]
St. 1 (English):	"Because I associate wealth with material things".

It shows us how the negotiation of meaning and content thwarts any affective dynamic of the conversation and rationalizes the same. Students mostly first repeated what the conversation partner had said in the other language. But then, in turn, the language used reveals the emotionally charged discussion about the topic, where both students desperately try to claim the truth.

To all observers it unanimously appeared that deliberation and the use of cognitive resources was deeper even as compared to monolingual arrangements, no matter whether in the L2 or — as it typically happens — in the L1. But the L1 enabled students to express more feelings, which were comparatively absent during discussions in only the L2.

Bilingual exam

In contrast to the hitherto presented data resulting from direct oral interactions, decisions taken while writing and under exam conditions, however, significantly deviate from observable behavior. In most cases, the latter results out of immediate and *ad-hoc* action-reaction sequences, while writing includes more room for careful deliberation. Thus, the last data set comprised a total of 19 bilingual exams as additional data source to investigate the research question. The exam topic was the popular debate *degrowth vs. green growth* to combat climate change. The students were given three different choices of comparable exams, all comprising a short text with three tasks in the customary order: summarize, explain and discuss (ending with a final judgment in accordance with all of the preceding tasks). In detail, the options were as follows (numbers indicate the choices made):

- Exam A: exam with material in the L1, and answers in the L2 for all three tasks (10 times);
- Exam B1: exam with material in the L2, a summary in the L2 in Task 1, an analysis in the L2 in Task 2, and a final judgment in the L1 in Task 3 (5 times);
- Exam B2: exam as B1, but with an analysis in the L1 in Task 2, and a final judgment in the L2 in Task 3 (4 times).

The issue of an appropriate measurement needs careful deliberation at first. The array of methods Mauss and Robinson (2009) summarize are only suitable for measuring emotions on the spot, that is, in the direct *presence of the investigated person or group*, evaluating any physical response and/or observable behavior. To my knowledge, any measure of how to discern emotions in a rather clinical written product, as a testimony of an intense and past deliberation process, has not been developed. And this exactly counts for exam conditions, during which students are requested to justify their line of argument accordingly using proper language, without being able to refer to emojis, initially invented to express emotions in, for example, short communications during instant messaging. Consequently, it needs to be asked: what constructs an emotional argument in a written product like an essay?

What comes first to mind is a close analysis of the particular words employed in the argumentative part of an essay. There have been suggestions of comprehensive coding schemes with keywords indicating an intensity of feelings. One of the most prominent suggestions includes the Geneva Affect Label Coder, defining affect categories and pertinent word stems (Scherer, 2005). However, a more holistic approach looks at the entire content of the argument, not just single signal or key words, is needed. As a useful guiding principle, Gilbert (1995, p. 7) argues that "[a]n emotional argument [. . .] is one in which the feelings being communicated by the participants are more important than the words being used to communicate those feelings." This means that analytical units need to contain at least one full sentence.

To analyze the exams, the following qualitative approach was adopted. Task 3 of the 19 exams was evaluated in the form of the QDA (in accordance with the guidelines of Kuckartz, 2016) with the MAXQDA software package. This exercise was performed in the following steps: typical examples were defined for emotional, rational, self-interested and altruist arguments separately, independent of the language (English/L2 and German/L1). However, as supposed to the 0–10 scales of the self-assessment, the weight of the scale was reduced to 0–2, with 1 defining an average, and 0 and 2 a low and strong intensity, respectively. It needs to be explicitly mentioned that a single argument can simultaneously contain features of up to all four categories, because the categories are *de facto* not always distinct and also often consist of more than one sentence, addressing different aspects. *Table 3* includes a list of typical examples for all four categories across the two languages, in accordance with all three intensity scales. Although the holistic content of the argument decided on the evaluation, some keywords/phrases are underlined.

Table 3: Categories for the classification of arguments on the REAL and SIAL scales, respectively

category / intensity	0	1	2
emotional	Nobody seemed to question this surreal development until the Club of Rome released a study in 1972 that predicted there was a limit to this madness and that it would be reached sooner than many thought or hoped.	So if we would live (lived) more sustainable with more new technologies (GND) and wouldn't se the nature, family etc. as our wealth and not the consumption we would have a better world– in my opinion.	Economic growth is what us actually destroys because this what we call "economic growth" is a capitalist growth, not a social growth. That means that there are some persons that makes profit out of this but also many that have to suffer-what isn't fair at all
rational	To support the environment we could recycle our trash etc, too.	Also they want higher prices for the usage of energies and carbon emissions. I think that is a good point to stand, but it will not be enough for completly stopping climate change.	In my opinion both strategies sound promising, though the "Club of Rome's" suggestions and main focus that our planet won't be able to sustain such a huge amount of population and it's its needs to continue living as we do these days, still seems more appealing to me.
self-interest	In my opinion a Green New Deal is a good way to reduce climate change but isn't enough to ensure a good future as pollution also harms our environment.	(Zudem sollte man nicht) das Argument des Bevölkerungswachstumes es „Club of Rome" vergessen. Denn gibt es zu viele Menschen auf der Erde, wird man auf Massenproduktion zurückgreifen und unqualitative Ware in Kauf nehmen müssen (Plastik etc.) nur um zu überleben.	Ich finde aber trotzdem nicht, dass sie diese Technologien an weniger entwickelte Staaten umsonst geben müssen/sollten. Die Herstellung und erforschen (Erforschung kostet (kostet) den Industriestaaten Geld. Wenn sie dann gezwungen sind ihre Technologien zu verschenken, wird ihnen ein wenig der Anreiz genommen

"PERFECT EQUILIBRIUM OF EMOTIONAL AND RATIONAL LEARNING"

category/ intensity	0	1	2
altruism	They also want to make a balance between speed and stability, <u>so that</u> the economy for example does not grow so fast <u>so that</u> it could get unstable (unsustainable) and harm the environment. The last point is a (the proposed) balance between equality and economic output.	So only the idea isn't enough – we need to make compromises with other countries, to rethink ourselves (our lives) to live more sustainable and so on…	die Technologien zu erforschen, weil sie „persönlich" nichts davon haben. That's why I am convinced that industrialized countries should act as an example a rolemodel and provide poorer countries with modern technologies for free, since a better world is everyone's benefit!

219

It was expected that all four categories would be nearly equally represented, as the theory suggests that code-switching brings *emotio* and *ratio* into equilibrium. Same expectations were formulated for self-interest and altruism, as code-switching helped to refer both to "us" in the immediate surroundings as well as to "them" on the global level. *Table 4* includes an overview of the sum of unweighted codes by category. It shows a very similar occurrence of all four types within the total of 346 codes applied within Task 3 of the 19 exams. It is necessary to keep in mind that the number 346 does not represent the total argument count, because each argument can be coded up to four times.

Table 4: **Arguments count by category**

Type of argument	count	percentage
rational argument	95	27.5
emotional argument	92	26.5
altruistic	83	24.0
self-interest	76	22.0
sum / percentage	346	100

The arguments then were counted for each essay and weighted in accordance with their intensity, to reach a score between 0 and 10 on the RAEM and SIAL scale. However, an intermediate step became necessary. In accordance with the initial self-assessment on the rating system, indicating the average sense of the self, the numbers were slightly adjusted. This step was taken to recognize that the average self-perceived personality by the students influences the score. In total, 90% of the score was composed by the essays and 10% by the self-assessment. The final scores were put into relation on the two-dimensional scale. *Figure 3* visualizes the final scores of the 19 essays. The axes represent the original scale of 0–10 in two dimensions (RIAM; SIAL). The intersection of the two axes means a 5 for all of the four categories. The central rectangle symbolizes the location of the perfect equilibrium. It is placed between 4 and 6, to allow a +/−1 variance. The outer rectangle suggests a possible larger tolerance between 3 and 7, allowing a +/−2 variance.

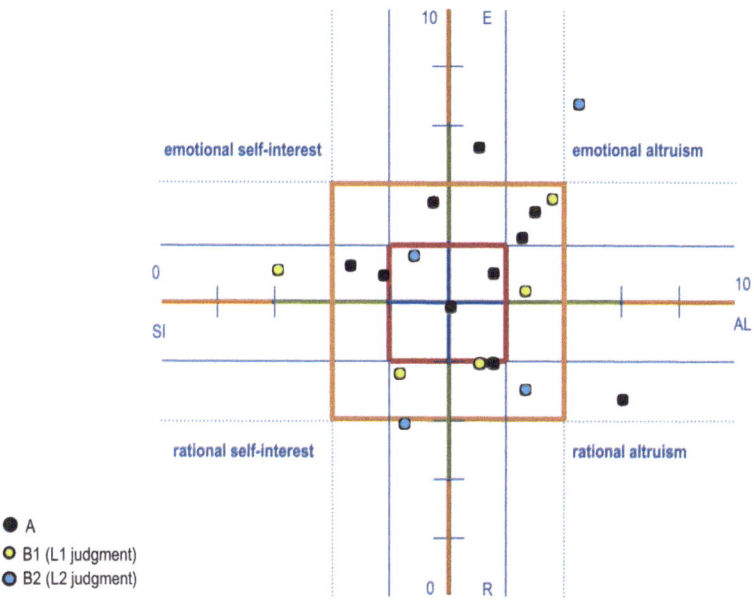

Figure 3: Location of the 19 essays on the RAEM/SIAL scale

From the visualization of this sample, one can infer that there is no significant difference among the three different exam categories. Thus, it is possible to conjecture that after long-term teaching during CLIL comprising code-switching as an integral part, the language employed does not have a significant impact on the classification of the judgment, supporting the approach of translanguaging (García & Li, 2014). However, only 5 out of 19 exams of all categories lie in the defined area. Hypothetically, if the circle was expanded by one unit into each direction, 16 out of 19 exams would be placed within. We should define this larger area not as the new perfect equilibrium, but in turn refer to the 3 remaining cases as outside of the desired norm. Nevertheless, as freedom of opinion is a set norm, of course even these results are fully legitimate.

An evaluative QDA in this field bears the risk of a significant high subjectivity by the rater, also keeping in mind that "there is no single gold-standard method for [emotional] measurement" (Scherer, 2005, p. 709). This prompts the need to objectify the results for abating the researcher bias. Thus, an interrater agreement has been conducted with another rater, neither part of the team structure nor involved in the research in any other way. The second rater received a training and independently rated the same data set. The Cohen's kappa score was counted for all identified but unweighted arguments and for each of the 19 cases separately.

On average, the achieved score of 0.5, with a standard deviation of 0.146 over all cases (the extremes defining 0.17 and 0.72 for individual cases, respectively), shows a moderate agreement of both raters. Although the number only indicates an approximate agreement of 50% of all segments, it offers a motivation to continue the research in the same fashion in this quite unexplored field.

Furthermore, the final results of the second rater, now including the intensity scaling, were arranged in the same way as with the first rater in *Figure 3*. The average deviation of the scores on both axes was calculated and is also represented case by case in *Table 5*. For the RAEM scale, the average difference of all scores is 1.73 with a standard deviation of 1.07. The SIAL scale shows an average difference of 1.83, with a standard deviation of 1.15. These scores mirror the moderate agreement of the Cohen's kappa. Hence, further refining the developed method of analysis in similar research initiatives is recommended.

Table 11: **Results of the interrater agreement**

Interrater agreement		Interrating	Difference between raters by case	
	Case number	Cohen's kappa	Difference RAEM	Difference SIAL
Exam A	1	0.62	2.3	3.3
	2	0.44	1.2	3
	3	0.37	1.95	2.8
	4	0.39	2.3	3.2
	5	0.67	1.3	2.9

		6	0.69	0.7	1.7
		7	0.43	0.9	1.5
		8	0.47	1	0.4
		9	0.35	0.3	2.5
		10	0.33	1.7	1.7
Exam B		11	0.67	0	1.7
		12	0.52	0.8	1
		13	0.56	2.4	3.4
		14	0.5	2.4	1.2
		15	0.17	3.1	2.7
Exam C		16	0.58	4.5	0
		17	0.4	2.1	0.25
		18	0.72	1.7	1.5
		19	0.6	2.3	0
	M		0.50	1.73	1.83
	Mdn		0.50	1.70	1.70
	SD		0.15	1.06	1.15

Conclusion and discussion

The triangulated data analysis delivers the following overall picture. At first, an impact of the language on emotional and rational learning and decision-making processes appears to be likely. All observers unanimously agree that the L1 made a stronger emotionalization of the classes possible at all. The negotiation of meaning with students working in the L2, however, rationally controlled emotions during language mediation. Since students had to listen and speak in the L1 and L2 at the same time and thus perpetually code-switch languages, this mixture provided the DBAR team with interesting insights. It could be noted that during such discussions, there was a quite balanced relationship of emotions and rational thought, as a facilitator for the envisaged perfect equilibrium of emotional and rational learning. The selected scene from the thick description illustrated several emotional control mechanisms.

The students' point of view from the survey data reveals a different picture. Any effect on the personality and decision making is negated by a clear majority of respondents. Especially the only slightly different outcome in the post-survey came rather unexpectedly, because during classroom discussions on that very topic, a more balanced stance could be discerned. A suggestive effect on the post-survey due to the increase in awareness was expected, as students were requested to carefully track their emotional and rational experience during decision making in accordance with the language role occupied.

The qualitative content analysis of a bilingual exam, making the L1 and L2 use of the students in terms of the content comparable, reveals further insights into this topic matter. The exam options all included tasks exacting code-switching. As the data shows, no significant difference among the three exam categories is discernable after long-term CLIL education with an L1 integration. Although only 5 out of 19 exams lie in the inner box defining the approximate location of the perfect equilibrium, we learn that all but 3 results lie within a more tolerable area of variance.

Besides, there is one major insight attained from the methodological pathway taken during the QDA. It looks like a first successful attempt for the goal to provide a roadmap for the emotional measurement of written texts, holistically and thus beyond simple word signalers. The definition of emotional and rational (as well as self-interested and altruistic) arguments deserves further attention in the future. For an evaluative QDA, the modest interrater agreement motivates to further refine the procedure, although a higher Cohen's kappa would have been desired.

Limitations

The limitations of the research present us insights for possible future replication. At the *Third International Conference on Language Education and Testing* (Antwerp, 2018), the keynote speaker J.M. Dewaele expressed the following utter appeal. He argued that more action research is needed to explore new grounds. However, he immediately confined its validity and clarified the following. For a stronger impact in education, one inevitably needs statistics to convince the planners in education policy.

Dewaele's recommendation defines the limitations of the findings. Both in terms of sample size and research design, they only provide first insights into the field. Redesign and replication to reach validity and a higher degree of generality are necessary. Although the results have been factored with the self-assessment of the students in terms of their personality on the REAM and SIAL scale, comparative data with another groups taught monolingually in the L1 or L2 is needed, along with longitudinal features.

Furthermore, random effects seem to be very likely. This could include, *inter alia*, a specific position towards the controversy asked in the exam that deviates from the average personality in the self-assessment. Although the interrater agreement mitigated the researcher bias, nevertheless it is not completely abated.

Outlook and implications for practice

As the discussion revealed, the language used during CLIL classes seems to influence emotional and rational learning processes and personal judgments, with an overall likelihood that CLIL with judicious and principled code-switching facilitates a perfect equilibrium of emotional and rational learning. Replication along with fine-tuning of all of the tools used for the emotional measurement is motivated, as well as the generation of larger data samples, more sophisticated methods and a team comprising experts from neighboring sciences to validate the findings. Especially the RIAM and SIAL scaling deserves close scrutiny, as they have proven to be tangible instruments for the students and easy to use. Criteria and a questionnaire development to assist students in their self-assessment are encouraged. The typical examples of the QDA for the argumentative categories need more fine-tuning, as the Cohen's kappa score implies. That value should be at least in the region of a high substantial agreement (>0.70). In order to validate the instruments, approaches in line with Mauss and Robinson (2009) should be considered.

It is suggested for teachers and researchers to rethink CLIL classes as an opportunity of a modern bi- and multilingual pedagogy, not only in the social sciences but also beyond. Emotional state of affairs of students have proven to be instrumental for the success of their learning experience. Close classroom observations are an apt starting point. Participating students at academic research initiatives as active stakeholders helps to make their learning progress and awareness more visible. Also, when discussing students' essays, the coding scheme can provide for a mutual basis to evaluate the integrity of arguments towards an effective pedagogy for realizing our 21st-century global challenges as a mutual opportunity.Further academic research along these lines can here supply modern pedagogy with convenient tools to emerge the potential of emotions, affect control and language learning.

Chapter VII

…about looking back in the future…

Discussion, Conclusion and Outlook

This last chapter will now conclude the results of the research. Each of the preceding chapters has already been discussed in detailed extent within the common paper structure they all originate from. Thus, this final discussion will tie the main findings together, for viewing at them as one contextualized entity. Results will be grouped into different sections, in accordance with areas in theory and practice the research project contributed to, structured according to the RDs of *Chapter II*. Furthermore, results will be overall qualified in terms of generalization, applicability and replication. The overall contribution to theory generation in CLIL research will be illustrated. An outlook about the future will conclude the work.

Educational Standards and Competence Aims for CLIL in Politics & Economics

Chapter II started with a survey on CLIL research and practice in Germany with several focus areas. It set the stage for both the conceptual work as well as the empirical interventions of the subsequent chapters. Particularly, the absence of educational standards and subject didactics, mainly from the administrative side, remains noteworthy. Gaps in CLIL research, like defining clear-cut didactical principles or methodological pathways, are remarkable as well. Against the new common ground of European CLIL research, differentiating CLIL from immersion as well as EU efforts to reconceptualize and harmonize CLIL, debates multilingualism and CLIL, in particular L1 use, have been propelling.

Despite the subject primacy as the most seminal official didactical principle, CLIL research, as it was shown, mainly has a language bias. Subject-specific questions, and this includes the bilingual surplus for subject lessons, find only little consideration. Especially CLIL in Politics & Economics, both in academia as well as in practice, has proven to be underrepresented, although the innovative literacy approach constitutes a logical field for CLIL with English as L2 as a response towards 21st challenges in an age of modern globalization. No conceptual framework has been outlined, not to speak about educational standards and competence aims for operationalizing the particularities of CLIL, neither in general nor with special reference to subjects like Politics & Economics.

With the conceptual framework *cum* competence model, *Chapter II* brought forward the sublime approach to, in general terms, global education and ESD. Global discourse competence as bilingual competence aim for Politics & Economics constitutes the center of gravity, amalgamating subject and language competences, respectively. Cosmopolitanism, with its roots in local identities, is one central pillar, highlighting unity in diversity and the need for admittedly suggestive approaches towards securing peace and stability, as part of ESD put forward by the UN. Here, L1 integration unveils many opportunities, also out of a subject perspective of Politics & Economics, as *Chapter III* reasoned in depth. To my knowledge, *PolECulE's* work is the first contribution towards clear-cut and subject-based educational standards in CLIL, even beyond Germany. Due to its innovative force and immediate needs of the administration, it has been adopted by the Ministry for Education and Religious Affairs of the Federal State of Hesse,[1] hence serving as a valuable contribution for teaching and also for future academic studies.

Cosmopolitan Classroom *Glocalities* through CLIL in Politics & Economics

In an effort to specify the meaning of global discourse competence, *Chapter III* subsequently explicated the conceptual framework in more detail. It closely linked the subject side with multilingual language use, insinuating the bilingual surplus of CLIL in Politics & Economics. *Chapter III* was also submitted with the purpose to disseminate the work of the *PolECulE*-project to a global community, because the general idea of thought can be equated with proposing

---

[1] The conceptual framework is hosted by the Ministry for Education of the State of Hesse at https://lernarchiv.bildung.hessen.de/sek/englisch/engl/news/pub/orientierungsrahmen_polecule_final.pdf

a new literacy as ESD towards our 21st century challenges, as the chapter recapitulates.

Chapter III closely elaborates on the most salient features of the conceptual framework in detail, with climate change as *leitmotif*, representing it as arguably one of the most pressing challenges of the 21st century. In line with the competence model, the focus was set to transform classrooms into cosmopolitan *glocalities*. Their genesis was intended at preparing students for their agency towards cooperatively identifying solutions for our 21st century challenges within a transnational civil society. Importantly, *Chapter III* highlights how cosmopolitanism can deviate from its original rather elite notion, because it is already omnipresent in an organically-grown form at the side of an increasingly heterogeneous student body. In sum, it mirrors the diversity of our multilingual world society. Classes valuing such resources, following modern constructivist approaches, can benefit from the global cultural knowledge inherent in classrooms. Relational cosmopolitanism, moving beyond inter- and transcultural literacy, thus provides as a new literacy for the 21st century juxtaposed with ESD, fully in line with the thoughts of *PolECulE*'s competence model, *Chapter III* argues.

Finally, data of the *#climonomics* conference illustrates that the ambitious competence model can be implemented into teaching practice when prepared accordingly with a didactical concept. Its multilingual approach was not only constructed but mirrored a realistic scenario. The conference organizers were happy to note that students in general approved of a multilingual setting and did not consider the same as unrealistic or destructive. Hence, the idea of defining L1 use as didactical principle for CLIL in Politics & Economics is fueled accordingly. Importantly, this includes L1 of students beyond German as official school language.

#climonomics was a big project, initially carried out as a one-day event after intense preparation along the lines of formal EU parliamentary rules. Yet it remains open to granularly design and develop such multilingual teaching methods with judicious and principled L1 use for daily classroom practice within the dynamics of natural learning environments. Therefore, research during daily and regular classroom teaching defined the field of the main

intervention. At first, *Chapter V* addressed such demands, with Trans-FL as a new concept to pedagogically use translanguaging beyond SL also in FL learning contexts, with data from empirical classroom research, – most importantly a thick description".[2]

A Comprehensive CLIL Teaching Model with L1 use

The main purpose of *Chapter V* was the development of teaching methods with judicious and principled L1 use, defining pathways for regular L1 use in CLIL classes, in accordance with the competence model of *Chapter II* as well as the deeper idea of thought of *Chapter III*. The classroom research was set amidst the delineated needs to make translanguaging a realistic concept and daily pedagogical routine also during CLIL teaching. Translanguaging is a relatively new concept which is a result of highly idealized modern thought process. However, it has limits for teaching scenarios where multilingual skills might not have been developed adequately yet, especially when the language threshold is too high. Consequently, questions how to embed the acquisition of the FL into any translanguaging pedagogy remain unanswered. Thus, translanguaging was modified as Trans-FL, enabling a pre-step and facilitating the acquisition of the FL. Within Germany, as *Chapter II* showed, the planned use of multilingual teaching methods is yet marginal. Moreover, for CLIL with L2 as FL, the lack of relevant studies defined a RD.

The empirical research of the DBAR[3] was planned along the lines of developing pedagogies together with the students as main stakeholders, grouping them into four different student types. One

---

[2] The design of #*climonomics* benefited from the research of *Chapter V*, composed and carried out before #*climonomics* was held. In order to make #*climonomics* also available for daily classroom practices, the digital reader was reworked and published by Nijhawan et al. (2021a).

[3] DBAR as research method, as *Chapter II* had already highlighted, constitutes a new and innovative approach used in both empirical *Chapters V & VI*, each also including a method reflection after the discussion. In the later part of this present chapter, the method will be reflected separately as well as in context of elaborating on validity, generality and limits of the findings, respectively.

Discussion, Conclusion and Outlook

of the main ideas of thought was also to look at L1 beyond just mere scaffolding for mainly weaker students but also to investigate any synergetic function of Trans-FL and L1 use for stronger students. The categorized thick description was chosen to reconstruct the genesis of the three different teaching methods within regular and natural classroom dynamics. That data source was triangulated with other data sources. The comprehensive CLIL teaching model is discussed in *Chapter V* in extent. Possible alternatives for other settings and contexts have been provided for extending the reach of this research beyond the given local settings as well, in a quest to make it globally applicable yet recognizing and praising diversity of context. Last but not least, it was suggested that the teacher remains in L2 during the classroom time, an oxymoron to the overall multilingual approach. Any research about possible teacher codeswitching in accordance with the presented CLIL teaching model would nevertheless possibly yield alternative solutions.

The single case outline of the study includes both merits and shortcomings as delineated in *Chapters V & VI*. A response to the shortcomings along with suggestions has already been given. On a broader level, the subsequent part of this final chapter, dealing with the validity and limitations of all findings, will take a more global approach. On the one side, it was the outspoken goal to inductively develop methods and theories that really work in practice, within the shape of a more comprehensive model with a holistic approach and an ambition to achieve at least a medium degree of generality. *Chapter IV* had already defended the overall chosen approach with DBAR as method within the given context. On the other side, such contextualized results need to be carefully interpreted. Models are never carved into stone, realizing the multiplicity of various contexts with myriad different student profiles. It should explicitly set the stage for further research initiatives to amend the mosaic under the overarching concept of translanguaging towards differentiation as well as generalization and thus wider application.

The Perfect Equilibrium of Emotional and Rational Learning

As a result of the altered language rules for the regular CLIL classes, a new form of bilingualism engendered. This brought up the question about any effect on the subject side. Accordingly, the approach of L1 use in CLIL from *Chapter V* generated interesting secondary data, wherefore more additional data was surveyed to look deeper into that topic area and answer the RQs of *Chapter VI*. The theoretical framework suggests that CLIL with L1 use, as result of the new competence model, can lead to judgments more in equilibrium with *emotion* and *ratio* as a harbinger of global justice and solidarity. Both emotions as well as rationality were postulated as important features of an ideal and multifaceted judgment, complemented by a second dimension with self-interest and altruism.

Emotions in multiple languages constitutes an intense field of research with a recent gain in popularity (e.g., examining the relationship of emotions and code-switching, Dewaele, 2013). In other words, this part took the announced subject turn, applied the merits of the emotional turn for education through diversified language use and asked about further bilingual surplus. Ultimately, this chapter even further extends the more conceptual *Chapter III* and its new 21st century literacies approach for more modern theories of learning, and inevitably integrates language and subject learning and research in accordance with CLIL's original idea of thought], with the purpose of contributing towards a holistic ESD."

Triangulated classroom data revealed the cleavage between students' self-perception and observers' impressions. In an innovative approach to look at written products in the form of exams and find emotional arguments, a new coding scheme was developed for making emotions measurable. Within three exam options with different language use, no significant difference was detected. Due to small N and the lack of comparative groups (taught monolingually in L1 and immersive in L2), of course no far-reaching conclusions could be drawn. However, the focus of this chapter was mainly to develop hypotheses and offer first tools of investigation in measuring emotions in written products and apply the same. The

DISCUSSION, CONCLUSION AND OUTLOOK

indication that CLIL with its bilingual dynamism, as examined in *Chapter V*, could influence the outcome on the subject side, is promising enough to be reexamined within a larger research design. Moreover, the contribution towards the established rating system for measuring emotions in written texts, deserves further attention, fine-tuning and validation.

New Remedies for Theory-practice Cooperation with DBAR: Reflecting the Method

Chapters V and VI were both based on DBAR with an axial TR, embodied in my person. DBAR offered an approach to consolidate theory and practice in the sense that all theories were generated inductively during regular classroom activities within a trans-institutional structure. As *Chapter IV* showed, both AR and DBR have many common features, mainly based on the origin and lead of the research either in university or school, respectively."

In *Chapter IV*, the nexus of DBAR with mixed methods was reasoned. The interventionist approach is mainly directed towards invention in education in the sense to render practical knowledge to be scientific. Still, one has to highlight that the views mainly are emic, such insiders' views coming along with a lot of knowledge and attached benefits. This is especially applicable for the practical relevance of the research. On the other side, etic dimensions are important, too, for mitigating the researcher bias for later validation purposes.

Especially for areas hitherto not explored, explorative research and its close proximity to the stakeholders serves as an important procedure to become acquainted with the topic matter and develop first ideas that in turn can be tested with more sophisticated scientific methods. I could experience that ventures and partnerships between universities and schools, juxtaposed with real eyelevel interaction of both institutions, define a much desired form of cooperation when it comes to the generation and dissemination of knowledge. This also calls for new pathways towards teacher education *('learning through research')*. It seems that the growth of method variety, coming along with the increasing application of

DBR in universities, is a result of the rise in demand for innovative and experimental research settings. [4]

DBAR offers new pathways as a plus for didactic research, intermingling it with practice in schools, realizing that field experience and subjective theories often add significant value to academia when systematized and theorized. On the one side, it is a very laborious exercise to keep a team from school and university working and cooperating properly, realizing the different work cultures, general methods and rhythms of action. On the other side, such forms of cooperation generate inestimable knowledge for academia, which in turn, after making it scientific, can be disseminated to practice again through various channels. As *PolECulE's* idea of thought was the result of close cooperation between scientific research and school practice, this short reflection of the research method also constitutes a significant part of this overall project. And for future research initiatives by academics together with teachers, or 'hybrids' as with my example, such methodological experientialism can offer fresh ideas and insights for future research and theory generation in CLIL and beyond.

Obviously, DBAR happens in very contextual settings, and mostly in single case studies as with *Chapters V & VI*, with the TR occupying a dual role. This calls for examining what impact the results can have for didactics and science in general, and about the quality standards of *Chapters V & VI*.

Quality Criteria, Generalization and Limits of the Research

This section evaluates the empirical work as a whole with relevant quality criteria. Questions about generalization, or other way round, the limits of the results, have already been discussed within

---

[4] There seems to be a lot of demand by mainly emerging researchers for step-by-step instructions and manuals how such concepts like design-based research, but also thick description etc., are carried out in practice — as many of the ideas are mainly disseminated in the form of theoretical academic contributions. The number of emails I received after publishing that article serves as a proxy for this conclusion.

the chapters. But they need to be answered on a more general level here as well, to evaluate the DBAR project as a whole. Furthermore, this section means to reflect on both methods and results more holistically. Their symbiotic relationship has already been emphasized various times.

Other than with experiments in lab-like settings and more quantitative research outlines, which inevitably are assessed by objectivity, reliability and validity, the quality of DBAR with mixed methods, and here with a bias towards the qualitative side, follows different standards. For mixed methods, the discussion about quality criteria still have not yielded any far-reaching consensus (Onwuegbuzie & Johnson, 2006). Looking at the literature of DBR, however, helps to qualify the results, because discussions about quality criteria have been part of the discourse from the beginning (see for instance Brown, 1992), to abate doubts by apostles of more quantitative philosophies. The Design-Based Research Collective (2003, p. 7) summarizes:

> Design-based research relies on techniques used in other research paradigms, like thick descriptive datasets, systematic analysis of data with carefully defined measures, and consensus building within the field around interpretations of data. By trying to promote objectivity while attempting to facilitate the intervention, design-based researchers regularly find themselves in the dual intellectual roles of advocate and critic. [...] In particular, design-based research typically triangulates multiple sources and kinds of data to connect intended and unintended outcomes to processes of enactment. [...] There is a trade-off here between the refinement of a particular innovation to maximize its success, and the generalization of findings from an ultimately highly refined enactment. The challenge for design-based research is in flexibly developing research trajectories that meet our dual goals of refining locally valuable innovations and developing more globally usable knowledge for the field.

Mainly, the interplay of local interventions resulting in more general applicable findings is spotlighted. This effectively refers to rich and triangulated data attained from carefully planned intervention into practice. One can infer that quality criteria for DBR deserve careful scrutiny, for entrenching the work against claims of a lack of scientific value.

In this vein, Reinmann (2005, p. 63), evaluating the merits of DBR for theory generation in science against more positivist notions, has a pragmatic suggestion. She recommends to define three relevant criteria, namely (1) newness, (2) usefulness and (3) sustainable innovation. Newness refers to innovation towards examining a RQ or solving a problem. With usefulness, the relevance for theory and practice is meant. Sustainable innovation, as it can be concluded, means that the new knowledge should not be singular within the context but be able to withhold in other contexts as well, coming close to generality and objectivity. She brings up criteria of the National Research Council (2001, 2002), which, *inter alia*, demands to *"replicate and generalize [the research] across studies"* (2005, p. 65).

Examining these criteria, at first, the results, comprising the comprehensive CLIL teaching model with L1 use *(Chapter V)* as well as the idea to use CLIL and its interplay of emotions with rationality *(Chapter VI)*, are new. Secondly, the innovation of both chapters, as outlined there, definitely is useful not only for practice, but also for the further scientific discourse. In *Chapters V & VI*, respectively, it has been reasoned that the innovation and the novel theoretical insights mainly define a first step to explore these relatively untouched areas. Lastly, sustainability of the innovation deserves attention. These very fresh results, however, can only be evaluated with further replication within other contexts which has not happened so far. Keeping the latter point in view, additional reference to more general quality criteria may prove to be helpful in this case, in an attempt to render the results more robust and indicate whether sustainability of the results is likely. Thus, as a further exercise, a short excurse about quality criteria for qualitative research appears appropriate, because the explorative and mixed methods interventions of *Chapter V* and *Chapter VI* are mainly biased accordingly.

For qualitative research, a consensus to refer to the criteria of Lincoln and Guba (1985) seems to be given. Richards (2003) makes their four criteria comparable to those of quantitative research *[in brackets]*, namely (1) credibility *[internal validity]*, (2) transferability *[external validity]*, (3) dependability *[reliability]* and (4) confirmability *[objectivity]*. Korstjens and Moser (2018) suggest viewing (5) reflexivity as an additional and separate criterion. Reflexivity is central in this research context with the given TR structure, in order to abate the researcher bias. Amidst the pioneering experience with DBAR as newly constructed approach, the research method as such has already been reflected above. The following part will examine the quality of the research along the four main criteria as well as with the annotations by Korstjens and Moser (2018) and Richards (2003).

Credibility

The research can be seen as credible mainly if the engagement with the study object or group has not been singular but based on long-term exposure, persistent observation, data triangulation and member check (Korstjens & Moser, 2018, p. 121; Richards, 2003, p. 286). With *Chapters V and VI*, all these criteria are met. The research not only lasted over six weeks during the regular teaching of the students but was joined by external observers throughout as well. Moreover, as the chapters show, different data sources were used, meeting the triangulation requirement. Lastly, all results include stakeholder responses and feedback. Both intermediate results of the cycles as well as final models that had been generated from the data were rolled out to the students as main stakeholders for perpetual respondent feedback. Also, group discussions were held regularly. All discussions were deep, which lead to slight modification of the intervention and the results thereafter, because the ideas and feedback given were original and valuable and thus enriching for the research. In the end, the responses of the stakeholders were fully included into the results. In *Chapter V*, this relates to the comprehensive CLIL teaching model. In *Chapter VI,* apart from the students' opinions, the interrater agreement has been presented as additional step for objectification, along with a *caveat* for careful contextualization and interpretation of the results. As a plus, data transparency was a set focus.

Transferability

Transferability, referring to the *"richness of description and interpretation"* (Richards, 2003, p. 286) for transferring and re-examining the findings to other situations, defines this criteria. Thick description as a tool of reconstruction for the entire research context is recommended as a method of data presentation and interpretation (Korstjens & Moser, 2018). In *Chapter V*, the thick description comprised the major data source, facilitating reconstruction and later replication. *Chapter VI* dialectically laid open the genesis of the analytical tools, also to have them critically examined by future research, fully aware of some of the shortcomings resulting from the absence of a design with group comparisons.

Dependability and Confirmability

Both Korstjens and Moser (2018) and Richards (2003) combine these two criteria and also juxtapose them with transparency, to enable others to reconstruct the findings seamlessly. Especially learning processes and their influence on the results of the research were laid open in *Chapter V*, also containing the full thick description as integral part within its Appendix. *Chapter VI* contains minutiae sequencing about the data analysis. Furthermore, the use of the methods, along with the decisions behind, was transparently outlined. A method reflection was added to the preceding section. Furthermore, as it was said in each of the two relevant chapters, replication is strongly desired for validation purposes also in other contexts, explaining the overall transparency and close description of the research *per se*.

Generalization and Limitations of the Findings

On the one side, I argue that the research presented is in accordance with respective quality criteria. On the other side, comments about the scope of generalization and limits should be made here for interpreting the results correctly. With mixed method research and the qualitative bias, it would be very ambitious to seek full generalization, which does not necessarily have to be a declared goal from the beginning for making the results valid. Furthermore, it always needs to be kept in mind that a part of the contribution here had a method focus, dealing with DBAR as a new best practice example for bridging the gap between theory and practice. It defined pathways how single case research can have a significant role in developing new ideas and didactical theories of teaching and learning, embedded within a more formalized framework.

Each of the two chapters already qualifies the research in the sense that such contextual single case research within a DBAR framework can never claim full generalization from the beginning, of course. Rather, as it was pointed out multiple times, the research marks a first step towards inductive theory generation in accordance with the RQs. For the results of *Chapter V*, the comprehensive CLIL teaching model with L1 use needs to be replicated, evaluated, fine-tuned and amended in similar and different contexts, also across subjects and student populations. However, it is firmly argued that a medium degree of generality for the validity of the model, as it was emphasized both in *Chapter IV* and *V*, would not be far-fetched, as the micro teaching methods of Trans-FL are quite elastic. But other contexts define new challenges. Would a tailored Trans-FL pedagogy as presented possibly repress natural translanguaging or other student-led creative approaches, and be less effective, even obstructive? This example should illustrate that nothing is carved into stone even as logical the conclusions might sound. *Chapter V* already concluded accordingly. On the one side, first alternatives were already offered in the form of slightly adapted models, illustrating the resilience of the model. On the other side, one of the main objectives was to define a best practice example in the sense to see such ventures as a source of inspiration for future research.

With *Chapter VI*, of course, the findings have clear limits, because such small sample from the described context can never be generalized on a larger population. But from the theoretical framework alone, indications that the proposed model can be applied in practice for the benefit of achieving the competence goals for CLIL in Politics & Economics seem everything but remote. Here, for validation purposes, group comparisons for the quantitative part now become necessary, along with further refinement of the proposed system to measure emotions in the classroom under natural conditions. Such very limited and contextual contributions, however, have an important value for science *per se*. To say it more colloquially, you need to first have the ideas and take the initiative to structure and formulate theories, before writing them on paper in accordance with scientific conventions. Thereafter, they can be further developed and validated, or eventually criticized and rejected due to certain fallacies, or for any other reasons. And even if a model is positively falsified, the contribution to science should not be neglected. Indeed, any further development with other methods and large-scale research would be highly appreciated. Small steps are nevertheless steps forward into the right direction.

Outlook

Generally speaking, the research contributed fourfold to research in CLIL with the (1) conceptual framework *cum* competence model and detailed annotations, (2) the methodological approach with DBAR, (3) the integration of multilingualism into CLIL in the form of Trans-FL, resulting in a comprehensive CLIL teaching model with L1 use, and (4) using multilingual approaches for the achievement of subject-based competences with real content and language integration. It should have become obvious that all these four areas, so far not explored enough, deserve much more investigation, both with direct relevance to the work presented by me as well as to other ideas, subtopics and research frameworks.

The single papers of *Chapters III-VI* were all submitted to English speaking journals, for increasing the reach to a global audience, and also in order to challenge the borders of national discourses within a globalizing world society. Rightly, on the one side, in *Chapter II* the endeavor was taken to clearly contextualize the research within Germany's context, as a pre-step to fit it within the local research context. But on the other side, entering the global debate about CLIL and multilingualism as well as with the given subject focus in Politics & Economics was an explicit purpose, also setting the ground for comparative work in CLIL beyond single case, or country-specific studies. All of the topics and questions asked in the respective chapters are relevant for a more general, global level, without questioning local contextualization. But it is desirable to exactly replicate this research in other settings, in order to validate results and increase their degree of generality. As a next step, large-scale and comparative research undertakings would deliver more robust results with a potential of withstanding rigorous statistical examination. Hence, further research in investigating and refining these findings from local intervention, in accordance with similar questions and methods, is appreciated.

This should not speak against suggesting a broader perspective for the outlook. The four areas the research, of course, deserve closer attention by other researchers, also using different methodological approaches. At first, this concerns, as demanded by the KMK (2013), the development of subject-based CLIL didactics. Common principles within the different subject fields could ultimately contribute to a more general CLIL didactics, also facilitating the development of more clear-cut didactic principles and teaching methods, as suggested by *Chapter V*. The consolidation of CLIL's potential as a modern reformist pedagogy and solution-based response towards globalization, as the 4Cs framework by Coyle et al. (2010) suggests, can benefit from such more inductive and stakeholder-centered research and development. Such initiatives are urgently needed to facilitate negotiation between academics and policymaking.

Ever since DBR has been proposed by Brown (1992), the debate about pragmatic methods intervening into natural learning environments has accelerated. The inclusion of the experience with AR, consequently suggesting DBAR as a modified approach, mainly had the purpose to consolidate theory and practice. Methods and models, as the suggested CLIL teaching model from *Chapter V*, survive on their further elaboration and development, calling for more clear-cut criteria and principles to refine such methodological approaches. Lastly, the empirical research was planned along the lines of DBAR. It would be interesting to have results from similar questions, however with different methodological approaches within this area of intervention (e.g., videography) — both using different methods within DBAR as well as alternatives to DBAR as a whole. And other way round, it would be interesting to investigate different questions with DBAR as a method, to investigate and further develop its application in practice. In this vein, and very importantly, this research displayed an attempt to contribute 'to a better world', in line with my professional and personal vision of *Chapter I*. *Chapter III* was detailed on this. There it has become apparent that reformist pedagogies like CLIL are severely needed in schools for equipping students with knowledge and — synchronically — intellectual and real-life competences like 21st century skills, relevant for their sustainable future and well-being.

To close the cycle and make a round affair of this monograph, reference will be taken to the initial questions of *Chapter I*, before having become an engaged CLIL researcher. In short, the question now would be: have these initial questions been answered? Browsing the questions step-by-step, but without going into singular details, this monograph contributed to each of them at different levels. The work inevitably took up some of the most important discourses on CLIL in Germany and beyond. It showed how the concept and its didactical principles have always been, and will always be, further developed, explaining CLIL's dynamic transformation over time, in line with societal changes. As arguably my main contribution from *Chapter V*, the comprehensive CLIL teaching model with judicious and principled L1 use has been designed in line with latest worldwide research on multilingual education, for making CLIL's benefits tangible for larger and geographically dispersed student populations. Furthermore, a robust conceptual framework for CLIL in Politics & Economics was offered, also investigating subject outcomes and establishing a nexus to the particular modes of language teaching. Whether the multilingual approach leads to a more sustainable lifestyle, also combatting climate change, is the *leitmotif* of my postdoctoral project, so more will be coming!

To make the affair short, the quick answer to the guiding question of *Chapter I* is: partly yes. For most of the questions I could achieve important insights for my future CLIL practice, develop theories and models, and hope to transfer those to other teachers and academics. But this does not count for all eternity, whereby it

DISCUSSION, CONCLUSION AND OUTLOOK

must be stated that more questions have developed during my personal and very intensive research venture. This is a common feature, starting with only a few questions, thereafter having many more and new interesting questions, defining a more positivist nature of research and explaining why there is *no end of history in human (academic) development*. This is what I really enjoy from the deepest of my heart!

And for me, to add a personal notch also during closure of this monograph, realizing the emotional last sentence of the preceding paragraph (see *Chapter VI* about how rationality requires emotional framing, and about the power of *emotional arguments*): it has become a personal interest to actively contribute to the development of multilingualism as a driving vehicle for the promotion of diversity and sustainability in the world. I am writing these lines in the midst of the Corona crisis. Unsurprisingly indeed, emotions play an important role here. Corona is the ultimate litmus test for our cosmopolitan world society, for a world in which, to name a few 21st century challenges, climate change threatens every one of us... where populism threatens to jettison democracy, not as entrenched as we have always been believing, realizing Russia's sudden war of aggression against Ukraine since February of this year... where poverty and inequality have ever since been a stress test for peace and stability... and living together in a cosmopolitan world in unity in diversity, *etc.*. Therefore — and now I would, same as with the opening, like to close with my personal perspective again — I hope that this small step I took will end in 'something grander' in the future. In line with the double-decker principle, it would be nice to integrate students as main stakeholders into further research and provide space for their voices and opinions, going as far as to say with the ambitious objective to entrench democracy and promote global justice and solidarity as a milestone for a sustainable future."

Bibliography

Abendroth-Timmer, D. (2007). *Akzeptanz und Motivation: Empirische Ansätze zur Erforschung des unterrichtlichen Einsatzes von bilingualen und mehrsprachigen Modulen.* Frankfurt am Main: Peter Lang.

Adelman, C. (1993). Kurt Lewin and the origins of action research. *Educational Action Research, 1*(1), 7-24. doi:10.1080/0965079930010102

Albrecht, V., & Böing, M. (2010). Wider die gängige monolinguale Praxis?! Mehrperspektivität und kulturelle Skripte als Wegbereiter der Zweisprachigkeit im bilingualen Geographieunterricht. In S. Doff (Ed.), *Bilingualer Sachfachunterricht in der Sekundarstufe - eine Einführung* (pp. 58-71). Tübingen: Narr.

Aljets, E. (2014). *Der Aufstieg der empirischen Bildungsforschung. Ein Beitrag zur institutionalistischen Wissenschaftssoziologie.* Wiesbaden: Springer VS.

Anderson, T., & Shattuck, J. (2012). Design-based research: A decade of progress in education research? *Educational Researcher, 41*(1), 16-25. doi:10.3102/0013189x11428813

Angele, C. (2015). *Ethnographie des Unterrichtsgesprächs: Ein Beitrag zur Analyse von Unterrichtsgesprächen über Differenz als Alltagserfahrung.* Münster: Waxmann Verlag GmbH.

Argyris, C., Putnam, R., & Smith, D. M. (1985). *Action science* (1st ed.). San Francisco: Jossey-Bass.

Auer, P. (1984). *Bilingual conversation.* Amsterdam: John Benjamins Publishing Company.

Auer, P. (1995). The pragmatics of code-switching: A sequential approach. In L. Milroy & P. Muysken (Eds.), *One speaker, two languages: Cross-disciplinary perspectives on code-switching* (pp. 115-135). Cambridge: Cambridge University Press.

Auer, P. (1998). *Code-switching in conversation language, interaction and identity.* London: Routledge.

Bach, G. (2010). Bilingualer Unterricht: Lernen - Lehren - Forschen. In G. Bach & S. Niemeier (Eds.), *Bilingualer Unterricht: Grundlagen, Methoden, Praxis, Perspektiven* (5th ed., pp. 9-22). Frankfurt am Main: Peter Lang.

Bach, G., & Niemeier, S. (Eds.). (2010). *Bilingualer Unterricht: Grundlagen, Methoden, Praxis, Perspektiven.* Frankfurt am Main: Peter Lang.

Baildon, M., & Damico, J. S. (2010). *Social studies as new literacies in a global society: Relational cosmopolitanism in the classroom.* London: Taylor & Francis Group.

Baker, C. (2011). *Foundations of bilingual education and bilingualism*. Bristol: Multilingual Matters.

Bandura, A., & Cherry, L. (2019). Enlisting the power of youth for climate change. *American Psychologist*. doi:10.1037/amp0000512

Barab, S., & Squire, K. (2004). Design-based research: Putting a stake in the ground. *The Journal of the Learning Sciences, 13*(1), 1-14.

Barbalet, J. (2002). Introduction: Why emotions are crucial. *The Sociological Review, 50*(2_suppl), 1-9. doi:10.1111/j.1467-954X.2002.tb03588.x

Barrows, H. S. (1996). Problem-based learning in medicine and beyond: A brief overview. *New directions for teaching and learning, 1996*(68), 3-12.

Batson, C. D., Duncan, B. D., Ackerman, P., Buckley, T., & Birch, K. (1981). Is empathic emotion a source of altruistic motivation? *Journal of Personality and Social Psychology, 40*(2), 290-302. doi:10.1037/0022-3514.40.2.290

Baumfield, V., Hall, E., & Wall, K. (2012). *Action research in education: learning through practitioner enquiry*. London: Sage.

Beacco, J.-C., & Byram, M. (2007). *From linguistic diversity to plurilingual education: Guide for the development of language education policies in Europe*. Strasbourg: Council of Europe.

Beck, U. (2006). *The cosmopolitan vision*. Cambridge: Polity.

Biederstädt, W. (2013). *Bilingual unterrichten - Englisch für alle Fächer [Sekundarstufe I]*. Berlin: Cornelsen.

Bieri, A. S. (2018). Translanguaging practices in CLIL and non-CLIL biology lessons in Switzerland. *E-JournALL, EuroAmerican Journal of Applied Linguistics and Languages, 5*(2), 91-109. doi:10.21283/23769 05x.9.142

Böing, M., & Palmen, P. (2012). Bilingual heißt zweisprachig! Überlegungen zur Verwendung beider Sprachen im bilingual deutsch-französischen Geographieunterricht. In B. Diehr & L. Schmelter (Eds.), *Bilingualen Unterricht weiterdenken. Programme, Positionen, Perspektiven* (pp. 73-90). Frankfurt am Main: Peter Lang.

Bonnet, A. (2004). *Chemie im bilingualen Unterricht - Kompetenzerwerb durch Interaktion*. Opladen: Leske und Budrich.

Bonnet, A., Breidbach, S., & Hallet, W. (2013). Fremdsprachlich handeln im Sachfach: Bilinguale Lernkontexte. In G.Bach & J. P. Timm (Eds.), *Englischunterricht* (pp. 172-198). Tübingen: Narr.

Bosenius, P., Donnerstag, J., & Rohde, A. (Eds.). (2007). *Der bilinguale Unterricht Englisch aus der Sicht der Fachdidaktiken*. Trier: WVT Wissenschaftlicher Verlag.

Böttger, H. (2016). *Neurodidaktik des frühen Sprachenlernens: Wo die Sprache zuhause ist*. Stuttgart: utb.

Breidbach, S. (2007). *Bildung, Kultur, Wissenschaft - reflexive Didaktik für den bilingualen Sachfachunterricht.* Münster: Waxmann.

Breidbach, S. (2013). Geschichte und Entstehung des bilingualen Unterrichts in Deutschland: Bilingualer Unterricht und Gesellschaftspolitik. In W. Hallet (Ed.), *Handbuch bilingualer Unterricht - Content and Language Integrated Learning* (1st ed., pp. 11-17). Seelze: Kallmeyer.

Breidbach, S., Lütge, C., Osterhage, S., & Prüfer, K. (2010). Die Forschungslandschaft im Bereich "bilingualer Sachfachunterricht": Eine Bibliographie 1996-2010. In G. Bach & S. Niemeier (Eds.), *Bilingualer Unterricht: Grundlagen, Methoden, Praxis, Perspektiven* (5th ed., pp. 177-324). Frankfurt am Main: Peter Lang.

Breidbach, S., & Viebrock, B. (2012). CLIL in Germany: Results from recent research in a contested field of education. *International CLIL Research Journal, 1*(4), 5-16.

Brown, A. L. (1992). Design experiments: Theoretical and methodological challenges in creating complex interventions in classroom settings. *The Journal of the Learning Sciences, 2*(2), 141-178.

Brown, G. W., & Held, D. (2010). *The cosmopolitanism reader.* Cambridge: Polity.

Bundeszentrale für politische Bildung. (2020). Dossier digitale Desinformation. Retrieved from http://www.bpb.de/gesellschaft/digitales/digitale-desinformation/

Bündgens-Kosten, J. (2020). Mehrsprachigkeit und CALL (computer assisted language learning). In I. Gogolin, A. Hansen, S. McMonagle, & D. Rauch (Eds.), *Handbuch Mehrsprachigkeit und Bildung* (pp. 273-277). Wiesbaden: Springer VS.

Bündgens-Kosten, J., & Elsner, D. (2018a). Multilingual call: Introduction. In J. Bündgens-Kosten & D. Elsner (Eds.), *Multilingual computer assisted language learning* (pp. xi–xxiii). Bristol: Multilingual Matters.

Bündgens-Kosten, J., & Elsner, D. (Eds.). (2018b). *Multilingual computer assisted language learning.* Bristol: Multilingual Matters.

Burns, A. C. H. (2013). Language across the curriculum. In M. Byram & A. Hu (Eds.), *Routledge encyclopedia of language teaching and learning* (2nd ed., pp. 378-381). London, UK: Routledge.

Butzkamm, W. (1973). *Aufgeklärte Einsprachigkeit zur Entdogmatisierung der Methode im Fremdsprachenunterricht.* Heidelberg: Quelle & Meyer.

Butzkamm, W. (2010). Über die planvolle Mitbenutzung der Muttersprache im bilingualen Sachfachunterricht. In G. Bach & S. Niemeier (Eds.), *Bilingualer Unterricht: Grundlagen, Methoden, Praxis, Perspektiven* (5th ed., pp. 91-107). Frankfurt am Main: Peter Lang.

Butzkamm, W. (2011). Why make them crawl if they can walk? Teaching with mother tongue support. *RELC Journal, 42*(3), 379-391. doi:10.1177/0033688211419830

Butzkamm, W., & Caldwell, J. A. W. (2009). *The bilingual reform: A paradigm shift in foreign language teaching*. Tübingen: Narr.

Butzkamm, W., & Lynch, M. (2018). Evidence for the bilingual option: Rethinking European principles in foreign language teaching. *Journal for EuroLinguistiX, 15*, 1-14.

Byers-Heinlein, K., & Lew-Williams, C. (2013). Bilingualism in the early years: What the science says. *LEARNing landscapes, 7*(1), 95-112.

Byram, M. (1997). *Teaching and assessing intercultural communicative competence*. Clevedon: Multilingual Matters.

Canagarajah, S. (2011). Codemeshing in academic writing: Identifying teachable strategies of translanguaging. *The Modern Language Journal, 95*(3), 401-417. doi:10.1111/j.1540-4781.2011.01207.x

Cantor, P. A. (1999). The Simpsons: Atomistic politics and the nuclear family. *Political Theory, 27*(6), 734-749. doi:10.2307/192244

Cenoz, J., Genesee, F., & Gorter, D. (2013). Critical analysis of CLIL: Taking stock and looking forward. *Applied Linguistics, 35*(3), 243-262. doi:10.1093/applin/amt011

Coan, J. A., & Gottman, J. M. (2007). The specific affect coding system (SPAFF). In J. A. Coan & J. J. B. Allen (Eds.), *Handbook of emotion elicitation and assessment* (pp. 267-285). Oxford: Oxford University Press.

Cobb, P., Confrey, J., diSessa, A., Lehrer, R., & Schauble, L. (2003). Design experiments in educational research. *Educational Researcher, 32*(1), 9-13.

Cochran-Smith, M., & Lytle, S. L. (1999). Relationships of knowledge and practice: Teacher learning in communities. *Review of Research in Education, 24*, 249-305. doi:10.2307/1167272

Cole, R., Purao, S., Rossi, M., & Sein, M. K. (2005). *Being proactive: Where action research meets design research*. Paper presented at the ICIS International Conference on Information Systems, Las Vegas, USA, December 11-14, 2005.

Collins, A. (1992). Toward a design science of education. In E. Scanlon & T. O'Shea (Eds.), *New directions in educational technology* (pp. 15-22). Berlin, Heidelberg: Springer-Verlag.

Conteh, J., & Meier, G. (2014). *The multilingual turn in languages education. Opportunities and challenges*. Bristol: Multilingual Matters.

Cook, V. (1996). *Second language learning and language teaching* (2nd ed.). London: Arnold.

Cook, V. (1999). Going beyond the native speaker in language teaching. *TESOL Quarterly, 33*(2), 185-209. doi:10.2307/3587717

Cook, V. (2001). Using the first language in the classroom. *Canadian modern language review, 57*(3), 402-423.

Corcoll, C. (2013). Developing children's language awareness: Switching codes in the language classroom. *International Journal of Multilingualism, 10*(1), 27-45. doi:10.1080/14790718.2011.628023

Council of Europe. (2010). Council of Europe charter on education for democratic citizenship and human rights education: Recommendation cm/rec (2010) 7. Retrieved from https://www.coe.int/en/web/edc/charter-on-education-for-democratic-citizenship-and-human-rights-education

Council of Europe. (2018). *Common European framework of reference for languages: learning, teaching, assessment. Companion volume with new descriptors.* Strasbourg: Council of Europe Publishing.

Coyle, D., Hood, P., & Marsh, D. (2010). *CLIL - content and language integrated learning.* Cambridge, UK: Cambridge University Press.

Creese, A., & Blackledge, A. (2010). Translanguaging in the bilingual classroom: A pedagogy for learning and teaching? *The Modern Language Journal, 94*(1), 103-115. doi:10.1111/j.1540-4781.2009.00986.x

Cummins, J. (1976). The influence of bilingualism on cognitive growth: A synthesis of research findings and explanatory hypotheses. *Working Papers on Bilingualism, No. 9.*

Cummins, J. (1979). Cognitive academic language proficiency, linguistic interdependence, the optimum age question and some other matters *Working Papers on Bilingualism, No. 19.*

Cummins, J. (1981). Empirical and theoretical underpinnings of bilingual education. *The Journal of Education, 163*(1), 16-29.

Cummins, J. (2008). Teaching for transfer: Challenging the two solitudes assumption in bilingual education. In J. Cummins & N. H. Hornberger (Eds.), *Encyclopedia of language and education* (2nd ed., Vol. 5: Bilingual Education, pp. 65-75): Springer.

Dailey-O'Cain, J., & Liebscher, G. (2009). Teacher and student use of the first language in foreign language classroom interaction: Functions and applications. In M. Turnbull & J. Dailey-O'Cain (Eds.), *First language use in second and foreign language learning* (pp. 131-144). Bristol: Multilingual Matters.

Dallinger, S., Jonkmann, K., Hollm, J., & Fiege, C. (2016). The effect of content and language integrated learning on students' English and history competences — killing two birds with one stone? *Learning and Instruction, 41,* 23-31. doi:10.1016/j.learninstruc.2015.09.003

Dalton-Puffer, C. (2007). *Discourse in content and language integrated learning (CLIL) classrooms*. Amsterdam: John Benjamins Publishing Company.

Dalton-Puffer, C., & Smit, U. (2013). Content and language integrated learning: A research agenda. *Language Teaching*, 46(04), 545-559. doi:10.1017/s0261444813000256

Daniel, S. M., Jiménez, R. T., Pray, L., & Pacheco, M. B. (2019). Scaffolding to make translanguaging a classroom norm. *TESOL Journal*, 10(1). doi:10.1002/tesj.361

Davis, M. H. (2006). Empathy. In J. E. Stets & J. H. Turner (Eds.), *Handbook of the sociology of emotions* (pp. 443-474). New York, NY: Springer.

de Boer, H., & Reh, S. (2012). *Beobachtung in der Schule – Beobachten lernen*. Wiesbaden: Springer VS.

Degen, C., Barth, E., & Yüksel, T. (2014). *Kleine Anfrage der Abgeordneten Degen, Barth und Yüksel (SPD) vom 29.09.2014 betreffend bilingualer Unterricht an hessischen Schulen und Antwort des Kultusministers*. (Drucksache 19/936). Wiesbaden: Hessischer Landtag. Retrieved from https://arbeitsplattform.bildung.hessen.de/fach/bilingual/bildungspolitik/material_bipo/00936.pdf

DESI-Konsortium. (2006). Unterricht und Kompetenzerwerb in Deutsch und Englisch. Zentrale Befunde der Studie Deutsch Englisch Schülerleistungen International (DESI). Retrieved from http://www.dipf.de/de/projekte/pdf/biqua/desi-zentrale-befunde

Detienne, M., & Vernant, J. P. (1978). *Cunning intelligence in Greek culture and society* (J. Lloyd, Trans.). Chicago: University of Chicago Press.

Detjen, J. (2017). Rationalität und politische Bildung. In D. Lange & V. Reinhardt (Eds.), *Konzeptionen, Strategien und Inhaltsfelder politischer Bildung* (Vol. 1, pp. 159-165). Baltmannsweiler: Schneider Verlag Hohengehren GmbH.

Deutsch, B. (2013). Mehrsprachigkeit und ‚CLIL' – zwei unverbundene Konzepte in der europäischen Sprachen- und Bildungspolitik? In S. Breidbach & B. Viebrock (Eds.), *Content and language integrated learning (CLIL) in Europe: Reseach perspectives on policy and practice* (Vol. 14, pp. 51-63). Frankfurt am Main: Peter Lang.

Deutsch, B. (2016). *Mehrsprachigkeit durch bilingualen Unterricht? Analysen der Sichtweisen aus europäischer Bildungspolitik, Fremdsprachendidaktik und Unterrichtspraxis*. Frankfurt am Main: Peter Lang.

Dewaele, J.-M. (2013). *Emotions in multiple languages*. New York: Palgrave Macmillan.

Dewaele, J.-M. (2017). Why the dichotomy 'L1 versus LX user' is better than 'native versus non-native speaker. *Applied Linguistics*. doi:10.1093/applin/amw055

BIBLIOGRAPHY

Dewey, J. (1938). *Experience and education*. New York: The Macmillan Company.

Diehr, B. (2012). What's in a name? Terminologische, typologische und programmatische Überlegungen zum Verhältnis der Sprachen im bilingualen Unterricht. In B. Diehr (Ed.), *Bilingualen Unterricht weiterdenken. Programme, Positionen, Perspektiven* (pp. 17-36). Frankfurt am Main: Peter Lang.

Diehr, B. (2016). Doppelte Fachliteralität im bilingualen Unterricht. Theoretische Modelle für Forschung und Praxis. In B. Diehr, A. Preisfeld, & L. Schmelter (Eds.), *Bilingualen Unterricht weiterentwickeln und erforschen* (pp. 57-84). Frankfurt am Main: Peter Lang.

Diehr, B., & Rumlich, D. (2021). Zur Einführung in den Themenschwerpunkt: Bilingualer Unterricht - aktuelle Herausforderungen und neue Chancen. *FLuL, 50*(1), 3-14. doi:10.2357/FLuL-2021-0001

Ditze, S.-A. (2007). Dissecting the body politic: Empowering CLIL-students with the classics of political philosophy. In P. Bosenius, J. Donnerstag, & A. Rohde (Eds.), *Der bilinguale Unterricht. Englisch aus der Sicht der Fachdidaktiken* (pp. 159-169). Trier: WVT Wissenschaftlicher Verlag.

Doff, S. (Ed.) (2010). *Bilingualer Sachfachunterricht in der Sekundarstufe. Eine Einführung*. Tübingen: Narr Francke Attempto.

Doyé, P. (2005). *Intercomprehension. Guide for the development of language policies in Europe: From linguistic diversity to plurilingual education*. Brussles: Council of Europe.

Dzik, D. (2020). Intercomprehension—a mere dream or a new way of learning in globalised world? *Politeja, 16*(3(60)), 155-166. doi:10.12797/Politeja.16.2019.60.10

Eberhard, D. M., Simons, G. F., & Fennig, C. D. (Eds.). (2020). *Ethnologue: Languages of the world*. (23 ed.). Dallas, Texas: SIL International.

Elsner, D., & Bündgens-Kosten, J. (2018). Awareness of multilingual resources: EFL primary students' receptive code-switching during collaborative reading. In J. Bündgens-Kosten & D. Elsner (Eds.), *Multilingual computer assisted language learning* (Vol. 114, pp. 59-77). Bristol: Multilingual Matters.

Elsner, D., Engartner, T., Nijhawan, S., & Rodmann, N. (2019). *Politik und Wirtschaft bilingual unterrichten*. Frankfurt am Main: Wochenschau Verlag.

Engartner, T., & Nijhawan, S. (2019). Emotionen in der sozioökonomischen Bildung als Lernanlässe und Lernvoraussetzungen. In A. Besand, B. Overwien, & P. Zorn (Eds.), *Politik mit Gefühl* (pp. 366-379). Bonn: bpb - Bundeszentrale für politische Bildung.

Erdin, Y., & Sali, P. (2020). Translanguaging: Insights into its theoretical underpinnings and classroom implications. *Journal of Language Research, 1*(2), 1-11.

European Commission. (1995). White paper: Teaching and learning towards the learning society. Retrieved from https://op.eur opa.eu/en/publication-detail/-/publication/d0a8aa7a-5311-4eee-904c-98fa541108d8/language-en

European Commission. (2006). *Content and language integrated learning (CLIL) at school in Europe*. Brussels: Eurydice.

Eurydice. (2006). *Content and language integrated learning (CLIL) at school in Europe*. Brussels: Eurydice.

Evans, P. (2003). Counterhegemonic globalization. In T. Janoski, R. Alford, A. Hicks, & M. Schwartz (Eds.), *The handbook of political sociology: States, civil societies, and globalization* (pp. 655-670). Cambridge: Cambridge University Press.

Fehling, S. (2008). *Language Awareness und bilingualer Unterricht - eine komparative Studie*. Frankfurt am Main: Peter Lang.

Feyerabend, P. (1993). *Against method* (3. ed.). London: Verso.

Fichten, W. (2005). Selbstbeobachtung von Forschung — Reflexions- und Erkenntnispotenziale der Oldenburger Teamforschung. In E. Eckert & W. Fichten (Eds.), *Schulbegleitforschung* (pp. 105-126). Münster: Waxmann.

Fischer, F., Waibel, M., & Wecker, C. (2005). Nutzenorientierte Grundlagenforschung im Bildungsbereich. *Zeitschrift für Erziehungswissenschaft, 8*(3), 427-442. doi:10.1007/s11618-005-0149-7

Flam, H. (2005). Emotion's map. A research agenda. In H. Flam & D. King (Eds.), *Emotions and social movements* (pp. 19-40). London: Routledge.

Flam, H., & King, D. (2005). *Emotions and social movements*. London: Routledge.

Fleckenstein, J., Preusler, S., & Möller, J. (2021). Sprachliches Selbstkonzept dual-immersiv unterrichteter Schülerinnen und Schüler. *FLuL, 50*(1), 50-68. doi:10.2357/FLuL-2021-0004

Frisch, S. (2016). Sprachwechsel als integraler Bestandteil bilingualen Unterrichts. In B. Diehr, A. Preisfeld, & L. Schmelter (Eds.), *Bilingualen Unterricht weiterentwickeln und erforschen* (pp. 85-102). Frankfurt am Main: Peter Lang.

Fukuyama, F. (1992). *The end of history and the last man*. Toronto: Maxwell Macmillan Canada.

BIBLIOGRAPHY

Fuller, J. (2015). Language choices and ideologies in the bilingual classroom. In J. Cenoz & D. Gorter (Eds.), *Multilingual education: Between language learning and translanguaging* (pp. 137-158). Cambridge: Cambridge University Press.

Gantefort, C. (2020). Nutzung von Mehrsprachigkeit in jedem Unterricht: Das Beispiel „Translanguaging". In I. Gogolin, A. Hansen, S. McMonagle, & D. Rauch (Eds.), *Handbuch Mehrsprachigkeit und Bildung* (pp. 201-206). Wiesbaden: Springer VS.

García, O. (2009). Education, multilingualism and translanguaging in the 21st century. In A. K. Mohanty & UNICEF. (Eds.), *Multilingual education for social justice: Globalising the local* (pp. 140-158). New Delhi: Orient BlackSwan.

García, O., & Li, W. (2014). *Translanguaging language, bilingualism and education*. Basingstoke, Hampshire: Palgrave Macmillan.

García, O., & Sylvan, C. E. (2011). Pedagogies and practices in multilingual classrooms: Singularities in pluralities. *The Modern Language Journal, 95*(3), 385-400.

Gaster, B. (1990). Assimilation of scientific change: The introduction of molecular genetics into biology textbooks. *Social studies of science, 20*(3), 431-454.

Geertz, C. (1973). *The interpretation of cultures: Selected essays* (Vol. 5019). New York: Basic Books.

Geertz, C. (2000). *Local knowledge: Further essays in interpretive anthropology* (3rd ed.). New York: Basic Books.

Genesee, F. (1987). *Learning through two languages: Studies of immersion and bilingual education*. Cambridge: Newbury House.

Gibbons, P. (2015). *Scaffolding language, scaffolding learning: Teaching English language learners in the mainstream classroom* (2nd ed.). Portsmouth: Heinemann.

Giddens, A. (2000). *Runaway world: How globalization is reshaping our lives*. New York: Routledge.

Gierlinger, E. (2015). 'You can speak German, sir': On the complexity of teachers' L1 use in CLIL. *Language and Education, 29*(4), 347-368. doi:10.1080/09500782.2015.1023733

Gilbert, M. A. (1995). *What is an emotional argument? Or why do argument theorists quarrel with their mates?* Paper presented at the Analysis and evaluation: Proceedings of the Third ISSA Conference on Argumentation.

Glaser, B. G., & Strauss, A. L. (1967). *The discovery of grounded theory; strategies for qualitative research*. Chicago,: Aldine Pub. Co.

Gogolin, I., Hansen, A., McMonagle, S., & Rauch, D. (Eds.). (2020). *Handbuch Mehrsprachigkeit und Bildung.* Wiesbaden: Springer VS.

Goodwin, C. (1994). Professional vision. *American Anthropologist, 96*(3), 606-633. doi:10.1525/aa.1994.96.3.02a00100

Grek, S. (2009). Governing by numbers: The PISA 'effect' in Europe. *Journal of Education Policy, 24*(1), 23-37. doi:10.1080/02680930802412669

Grosjean, F. (1989). Neurolinguists, beware! The bilingual is not two monolinguals in one person. *Brain and language, 36*(1), 3-15.

Hall, J. (2005). Homer economicus: Using The Simpsons to teach economics. *Journal of Private Enterprise, 30*(2), 165–176.

Hallet, W. (1998). The bilingual triangle. Überlegungen zu einer Didaktik des bilingualen Sachfachunterrichts. *Praxis des neusprachlichen Unterrichts, 45*(2), 115-125.

Hallet, W. (2007). Scientific literacy und bilingualer Sachfachunterricht. *Fremdspsrachen Lehren und Lernen, 36*, 95-110.

Hanesová, D. (2015). *History of CLIL.* In S. Pokrivčáková & et al. (Eds.), *CLIL in foreign language education: e-textbook for foreign language teachers* (pp. 7-16). doi:10.17846/clil.2015.7-16

Hawkins, M. R. (2018). Transmodalities and transnational encounters: Fostering critical cosmopolitan relations. *Applied Linguistics, 39*(1), 55-77. doi:10.1093/applin/amx048

Hayakawa, S., Tannenbaum, D., Costa, A., Corey, J. D., & Keysar, B. (2017). Thinking more or feeling less? Explaining the foreign-language effect on moral judgment. *Psychological Science, 28*(10), 1387-1397. doi:10.1177/0956797617720944

Heine, L. (2010). Fremdsprache und konzeptionelle Repräsentation: Bilingualer Unterricht aus kognitiver Perspektive. In S. Doff (Ed.), *Bilingualer Sachfachunterricht in der Sekundarstufe. Eine Einführung* (pp. 199-212). Tübingen: Narr.

Heine, L. (2013). Empirische Erforschung des bilingualen Unterrichts. In W. Hallet (Ed.), *Handbuch bilingualer Unterricht - Content and Language Integrated Learning* (1st ed., pp. 216-221). Seelze: Kallmeyer.

Heise, D. R. (1979). *Understanding events: Affect and the construction of social action.* Cambridge: Cambridge University Press.

Held, D. (2010). *Cosmopolitanism: Ideals and realities.* Malden: Polity Press.

Held, D. (2016). Climate change, migration and the cosmopolitan dilemma. *Global Policy, 7*(2), 237-246. doi:10.1111/1758-5899.12309

Hessisches Kultusministerium. (2016). Kerncurriculum gymnasiale Oberstufe - Politik & Wirtschaft. Retrieved from https://kultusmini sterium.hessen.de/sites/default/files/media/kcgo-pw.pdf

Hessisches Statistisches Landesamt. (2020). *Gymnasien in Hessen*. Wiesbaden: Hessisches Statistisches Landesamt. Retrieved from https://statistik.hessen.de/sites/statistik.hessen.de/files/Gymnasien_2019_2020_03022020.xlsx

Homans, G. C. (1958). Social behavior as exchange. *American Journal of Sociology, 63*(6), 597-606.

Hornberger, N. H., & Link, H. (2012). Translanguaging and transnational literacies in multilingual classrooms: A biliteracy lens. *International Journal of Bilingual Education and Bilingualism, 15*(3), 261-278. doi:10.1080/13670050.2012.658016

Hurajová, A. (2015). Content and language integrated learning as a bilingual educational approach in the European context. *European Journal of Science and Theology, 11*(6), 5-14.

Informationszentrum für Fremdsprachenforschung der Philipps-Universität Marburg. (2019). Bibliographie moderner Fremdsprachenunterricht: Sonderdruck zum Kongress der DGFF 2019 in Würzburg, Digitalisierung 2015-2019. Retrieved from https://www.uni-giessen.de/faculties/f05/engl/tefl/teflhybrid/linksanddocuments/ifsbibliographiedigitalisierung

Ingram, J. D. (2016). Cosmopolitanism from below: Universalism as contestation. *Critical Horizons, 17*(1), 66-78. doi:10.1080/14409917.2016.1117815

Jackson, T. (2009). *Prosperity without growth: Economics for a finite planet*. London: Earthscan.

Javorčíková, J., & Zelenková, A. (2019). CLIL: Conceptual differences in teaching "realia" to philological and non-philological students. *Journal of Language and Cultural Education, 7*(3), 18-34. doi:10.2478/jolace-2019-0019

Kachru, B. B. (1992). *The other tongue: English across cultures* (2nd ed.). Urbana: University of Illinois Press.

Karliner, J. (1997a). *The corporate planet: Ecology and politics in the age of globalization*. San Francisco, CA: Sierra Club Books.

Karliner, J. (1997b). Grassroots globalization: Reclaiming the blue planet. In J. Karliner (Ed.), *The corporate planet: Ecology and Politics in the age of globalization* (pp. 197-223). San Francisco: Sierra Club.

Keysar, B., Hayakawa, S. L., & An, S. G. (2012). The foreign-language effect: Thinking in a foreign tongue reduces decision biases. *Psychological Science, 23*(6), 661-668. doi:10.1177/0956797611432178

Klewitz, B. (2019). *Bilingualer Sachfachunterricht Politik und Wirtschaft: Unterrichtseinheiten in der Arbeitssprache Englisch*. Tübingen: Narr Francke Attempto.

Klewitz, B. (2021). *Content and language integrated learning (CLIL): A methodology of bilingual teaching*. Stuttgart: ibidem Press.

Klieme, E., Eichler, W., Helmke, A., Lehmann, R. H., Nold, G., Rolff, H.-G., . . . Willenberg, H. (2006). Unterricht und Kompetenzerwerb in Deutsch und Englisch. Zentrale Befunde der Studie Deutsch Englisch Schülerleistungen International (DESI). *Deutsches Institut für Internationale Forschung*. Retrieved from https://www.dipf.de/de/forschung/aktuelle-projekte/pdf/biqua/desi-zentrale-befunde

KMK (Sekretariat der Ständigen Konferenz der Kultusminister der Länder in der Bundesrepublik Deutschland). (2006). Konzepte für den bilingualen Unterricht – Erfahrungsbericht und Vorschläge zur Weiterentwicklung. Retrieved from http://www.kmk.org/fileadmin/Dateien/veroeffentlichungen_beschluesse/2006/2006_04_10-Konzepte-bilingualer-Unterricht.pdf

KMK (Sekretariat der Ständigen Konferenz der Kultusminister der Länder in der Bundesrepublik Deutschland). (2013). Konzepte für den bilingualen Unterricht – Erfahrungsbericht und Vorschläge zur Weiterentwicklung. Retrieved from https://www.kmk.org/fileadm in/Dateien/veroeffentlichungen_beschluesse/2013/201_10_17-Kon zepte-bilingualer-Unterricht.pdf

Köller, O., Leucht, M., & Pant, H. A. (2012). Effekte bilingualen Unterrichts auf die Englischleistungen in der Sekundarstufe I. *Unterrichtswissenschaft*(4), 334-530. doi:10.3262/UW1204334

Königs, F. G. (2015). Keine Angst vor der Muttersprache - vor den (anderen) Fremdsprachen aber auch nicht! Überlegungen zum Verhältnis von Einsprachigkeit und Zweisprachigkeit im Fremdsprachenunterricht. *Zeitschrift für interkulturellen Fremdsprachenunterricht, 20*(2), 5-14. Retrieved from http://tujourn als.ulb.tu-darmstadt.de/index.php/zif/article/view/756/758

Korstjens, I., & Moser, A. (2018). Series: Practical guidance to qualitative research. Part 4: Trustworthiness and publishing. *Eur J Gen Pract, 24*(1), 120-124. doi:10.1080/13814788.2017.1375092

Korte, K.-R. (2015). Einleitung. In K.-R. Korte (Ed.), *Emotionen und Politik: Begründungen, Konzeptionen und Praxisfelder einer politikwissenschaftlichen Emotionsforschung* (1 ed., pp. 9-24). Baden-Baden: Nomos Verlagsgesellschaft mbH & Co. KG.

Kramsch, C. J. (1993). *Context and culture in language teaching*. Oxford: Oxford University Press.

Kramsch, C. J. (1998). *Language and culture*. Oxford: Oxford University Press.

Krechel, H.-L. (2013). Organisationsformen und Modelle in weiterführenden Schulen. In W. Hallet (Ed.), *Handbuch bilingualer Unterricht - Content and Language Integrated Learning* (1st ed., pp. 74-80). Seelze: Kallmeyer.

Kristiansen, A. (2001). Animation and teaching - enhancing subjects from the curriculum by using "The Simpsons" in High School English teaching. Retrieved from https://www.simpsonsarchive.com/other/papers/ak.paper.html

Kuckartz, U. (2016). *Qualitative Inhaltsanalyse. Methoden, Praxis, Computerunterstützung* (3 ed.). Weinheim: Beltz Juventa.

Küppers, A., & Trautmann, M. (2013). It's not CLIL that is a success — CLIL students are! Some critical remarks on the current CLIL boom. In S. Breidbach & B. Viebrock (Eds.), *Content and language integrated learning (CLIL) in Europe: Reseach perspectives on policy and practice* (Vol. 14, pp. 285-296). Frankfurt am Main: Peter Lang.

Kurasawa, F. (2004). A cosmopolitanism from below: Alternative globalization and the creation of a solidarity without bounds. *European Journal of Sociology/Archives européennes de sociologie, 45*(2), 233-255.

Lasagabaster, D. (2013). The use of the L1 in CLIL classes: The teachers' perspective. *Latin American Journal of Content & Language Integrated Learning, 6*(2), 1-21.

Lasagabaster, D., & Sierra, J. M. (2010). Immersion and CLIL in English: More differences than similarities. *ELT Journal, 64*(4), 367-375. doi:10.1093/elt/ccp082

Leisen, J. (2015). Zur Integration von Sachfach und Sprache im CLIL-Unterricht. In B. Rüschoff (Ed.), *CLIL revisited - eine kritische Analyse zum gegenwärtigen Stand des bilingualen Sachfachunterrichts* (pp. 225-244). Frankfurt am Main: Peter Lang.

Letiche, H., & Statler, M. (2005). Evoking mētis: Questioning the logics of change, responsiveness, meaning and action in organizations. *Culture and Organization, 11*(1), 1-16. doi:10.1080/14759550500062219

Lewin, K. (1946). Action research and minority problems. *Journal of Social Issues, 2*(4), 34-46. doi:10.1111/j.1540-4560.1946.tb02295.x

Lewis, G., Jones, B., & Baker, C. (2012). Translanguaging: Origins and development from school to street and beyond. *Educational Research and Evaluation, 18*(7), 641-654. doi:10.1080/13803611.2012.718488

Lewis, G., Jones, B., & Baker, C. (2013). 100 bilingual lessons: Distributing two languages in classrooms. In C. Abello-Contesse (Ed.), *Bilingual and multilingual education in the 21st century: Building on experience* (pp. 107-135). Bristol: Multilingual Matters.

Li, S., & Luo, W. (2017). Creating a translanguaging space for high school emergent bilinguals. *CATESOL Journal, 29*(2), 139-162.

Li, W. (2011). Moment analysis and translanguaging space: Discursive construction of identities by multilingual Chinese youth in Britain. *Journal of Pragmatics, 43*(5), 1222-1235. doi:10.1016/j.pragma.2010.07.035

Li, W. (2017). Translanguaging as a practical theory of language. *Applied Linguistics*. doi:10.1093/applin/amx039

Liebscher, G., & Dailey-O'Cain, J. (2005). Learner code-switching in the content-based foreign language classroom. *The Modern Language Journal, 89*(2), 234-247. doi:10.1111/j.1540-4781.2005.00277.x

Lin, A. M. Y. (2013). Classroom code-switching: Three decades of research. *Applied Linguistics Review, 4*(1), 195-218. doi:10.1515/applirev-2013-0009

Lin, A. M. Y., & He, P. (2017). Translanguaging as dynamic activity flows in CLIL classrooms. *Journal of Language, Identity & Education, 16*(4), 228-244. doi:10.1080/15348458.2017.1328283

Lincoln, Y. S., & Guba, E. G. (1985). *Naturalistic inquiry*. Beverly Hills, CA: Sage.

Lo, Y. Y. (2014). How much L1 is too much? Teachers' language use in response to students' abilities and classroom interaction in content and language integrated learning. *International Journal of Bilingual Education and Bilingualism, 18*(3), 270-288. doi:10.1080/13670050.2014.988112

Lohe, V. (2017). „Aber ich kann doch gar kein Türkisch!" – „na und?" – heterogene Lerngruppen und mehrsprachiges Unterrichtsmaterial. In C. Fäcke & B. Mehlmauer-Larcher (Eds.), *Fremdsprachliche Lehrmaterialien: Entwicklung, Analyse und Rezeption* (pp. 189-215). Frankfurt am Main: Peter Lang.

Lohe, V. (2018). *Die Entwicklung von Language Awareness bei Grundschulkindern durch mehrsprachige digitale Bilderbücher: Eine quasi-experimentelle Untersuchung zum Einsatz von MuViT in mehrsprachigen Lernumgebungen*. Tübingen: Narr Francke Attempto.

Mackay, D., Zundel, M., & Alkirwi, M. (2014). Exploring the practical wisdom of mētis for management learning. *Management Learning, 45*(4), 418-436. doi:10.1177/1350507614541197

MacSwan, J. (2017). A multilingual perspective on translanguaging. *American Educational Research Journal, 54*(1), 167-201. doi:10.3102/0002831216683935

BIBLIOGRAPHY

Malthus, T. R. (1806). *An essay on the principle of population, as it affects the future improvement of society. With remarks on the speculations of Mr. Godwin, M. Condorcet, and other writers.* London: printed for J. Johnson, in St. Paul's Churchyard by T. Bensley, Bolt Court, Flest Street.

Märsch, N. (2007). Historische Entwicklung des bilingualen Lehrens und Lernens: Bilingualer deutsch-französischer Bildungsgang an Gymnasien. In O. Mentz, S. Nix, & P. Palmen (Eds.), *Bilingualer Unterricht mit der Zielsprache Französisch. Entwicklung und Perspektiven.* (pp. 23-40). Tübingen: Narr Francke Attempto.

Marsh, D. (1994). Bilingual education & content and language integrated learning. In International Association for Cross-cultural Communication (Ed.), *Language teaching in the member states of the European Union (lingua).* Paris: University of Sorbonne.

Marsh, D. (2002). CLIL/EMILE: The European dimension: Actions, trends and foresight potential. Retrieved from https://jyx.jyu.fi/dspace/bitstream/handle/123456789/47616/david_marsh-report.pdf?sequence=1

Marsh, D. (2012). Content and language integrated learning (CLIL). A development trajectory. Retrieved from http://helvia.uco.es/xmlui/bitstream/handle/10396/8689/2013000000658.pdf?sequence=1&isAllowed=y

Marsh, D., Díaz-Pérez, W., Frigols Martín, M. J., Langé, G., & Pavón Vázquez, V. T., C. (2020). *The bilingual advantage: The impact of language learning on mind & brain.* Jyväskylä: EduCluster Finland, University of Jyväskylä Group.

Martinovic, I., & Altarriba, J. (2013). Bilingualism and emotion: Implications for mental health. In T. K. Bhatia (Ed.), *The handbook of bilingualism and multilingualism* (2nd ed., pp. 292-320). Chichester: Wiley-Blackwell.

Massing, P. (2003). Kategoriale politische Urteilsbildung. In H.-W. Kuhn (Ed.), *Urteilsbildung im Politikunterricht. Ein multimediales Projekt.* (pp. 91-108). Schwalbach/Ts: Wochenschau Verlag.

Mauss, I. B., & Robinson, M. D. (2009). Measures of emotion: A review. *Cognition and Emotion, 23*(2), 209-237. doi:10.1080/02699930802204677

May, S. (1997). School language policies. In *Encyclopedia of language and education* (pp. 229-240). Boston, MA: Springer.

May, S. (2014). *The multilingual turn. Implications for SLA, TESOL and bilingual education.* New York: Routledge.

Meier, G. S. (2017). The multilingual turn as a critical movement in education: Assumptions, challenges and a need for reflection. *Applied Linguistics Review, 8*(1), 131-161. doi:10.1515/applirev-2016-2010

Mendieta, E. (2017). From imperial to dialogical cosmopolitanism. *Ethics & Global Politics, 2*(3), 241-258. doi:10.3402/egp.v2i3.2044

Merino, J. A., & Lasagabaster, D. (2015). CLIL as a way to multilingualism. *International Journal of Bilingual Education and Bilingualism, 21*(1), 79-92. doi:10.1080/13670050.2015.1128386

Merkel, W. (2017). Kosmopolitismus versus Kommunitarismus: Ein neuer Konflikt in der Demokratie. In P. Harfst, I. Kubbe, & T. Poguntke (Eds.), *Parties, governments and elites. The comparative study of democracy* (pp. 9-23). Wiesbaden: Springer VS.

Meyer, H. D., & Zahedi, K. (2014). Open letter to Andreas Schleicher, OECD, Paris. *Policy Futures in Education, 12*(7), 872-877. doi:doi:10.2304/pfie.2014.12.7.872

Mohanty, A. K. (2019). *The multilingual reality: Living with languages*. Bristol: Multilingual Matters.

Moore, D. (2002). Code-switching and learning in the classroom. *International Journal of Bilingual Education and Bilingualism, 5*(5), 279-293. doi:10.1080/13670050208667762

Moore, P., & Nikula, T. (2016). Translanguaging in CLIL classrooms. In *Conceptualising integration in CLIL and multilingual education* (pp. 211-234). Blue Ridge Summit, PA: Multilingual Matters.

Nail, T. (2015). Migrant cosmopolitanism. *Public Affairs Quarterly, 29*(2), 187-199.

National Research Council. (2001). *Scientific research in education*. Washington, DC: National Academies Press.

National Research Council. (2002). *Scientific research in education*. Washington, DC: National Academies Press.

Nijhawan, S. (2013). *A visit by five yellow people from Springfield, USA, to a German 9th grade: What can The Simpsons contribute to bilingual teaching in Politics & Economics?* Studienseminar für Gymnasien. Frankfurt am Main.

Nijhawan, S. (2014). Vom Comic zum Zeichentrickfilm - Sachfachunterricht mit "The Simpsons". *Praxis Fremdsprachenunterricht (Englisch), 11*(3), 13-15 + Material.

Nijhawan, S. (2017). Bridging the gap between theory and practice with 'design-based action research'. *Studia Paedagogica: Special issue on Teacher Education and Educational Research, 22*(4), 9-29. doi:10.5817/SP2017-4-2

Nijhawan, S. (2019). CLIL and the functional use of the L1 in Politics, Economics & Culture. In A. Kreft & M. Hasenzahl (Eds.), *Aktuelle Tendenzen in der Fremdsprachendidaktik* (Vol. 64, pp. 147-163). Berlin: Peter Lang.

Nijhawan, S. (2020a). Bilingualer Politikunterricht. In S. Achour, M. Busch, P. Massing, & C. Meyer-Heidemann (Eds.), *Wörterbuch Politikunterricht* (pp. 39-42). Frankfurt am Main: Wochenschau Verlag.

Nijhawan, S. (2020b). Finding the 'perfect equilibrium of emotional and rational learning' in content and language integrated learning (CLIL) in the social sciences. In M. Simons & T. Smits (Eds.), *Language education and emotions: Research into emotions and language learners, language teachers and educational processes* (pp. 181-201). London: Routledge.

Nijhawan, S. (2020c). Mehrsprachige politische Bildung: Der bilinguale Unterricht als didaktischer Ansatz zur Legitimation emotionaler Argumente. In I. Juchler (Ed.), *Politik und Sprache: Handlungsfelder politischer Bildung* (pp. 79-93). Wiesbaden: Springer VS.

Nijhawan, S. (2022). Translanguaging... Or 'trans-foreign-languaging'? A comprehensive CLIL teaching model with judicious and principled L1 use. *Translation and Translanguaging in Multilingual Contexts (TTMC), 8*(2). doi:10.1075/ttmc.00087.nij

Nijhawan, S., Elsner, D., & Engartner, T. (2021a). *#climonomics - Europäische Klimakonferenz mit Schüler*innen*. Frankfurt am Main: Wochenschau Verlag.

Nijhawan, S., Elsner, D., & Engartner, T. (2021b). The construction of cosmopolitan glocalities in secondary classrooms through Content and Language Integrated Learning (CLIL) in the social sciences. *Global Education Review, 8*(2-3), 92-115. Retrieved from https://ger.mercy.edu/index.php/ger/article/view/607

Nijhawan, S., Schmerbach, L., Elsner, D., & Engartner, T. (2020). *Globalization - Aufgaben für den bilingualen Politikunterricht*. Frankfurt am Main: Wochenschau Verlag.

Nikula, T., & Dafouz, E. (2016). *Conceptualising integration in CLIL and multilingual education*. Bristol: Multilingual Matters.

Nikula, T., & Moore, P. (2019). Exploring translanguaging in CLIL. *International Journal of Bilingual Education and Bilingualism, 22*(2), 237-249. doi:10.1080/13670050.2016.1254151

Ohlberger, S., & Wegner, C. (2018). Bilingualer Sachfachunterricht in Deutschland und Europa: Darstellung des Forschungsstands. *Herausforderung Lehrer*innenbildung – Zeitschrift zur Konzeption, Gestaltung und Diskussion, 1*(1), 45-89.

Onwuegbuzie, A. J., & Johnson, R. B. (2006). The validity issue in mixed research. *Research in the Schools, 13*(1), 48-63.

Osler, A., & Starkey, H. (2005). *Changing citizenship: Democracy and inclusion in education*. Maidenhead, England: Open University Press.

Osler, A. H., & Starkey, H. W. (2015). Education for cosmopolitan citizenship: A framework for language learning. *Argentinian Journal of Applied Linguistics, 3*(2), 30-39.

Osterhage, S. (2009). Sachfachkönnen *(scientific literacy)* bilingual und monolingual unterrichteter Biologieschüler: Ein Kompetenzvergleich. In D. Caspari, W. Hallet, A. Wegner, & W. Zydatiß (Eds.), *Bilingualer Unterricht macht Schule: Beiträge aus der Praxisforschung* (pp. 41-50). Frankfurt am Main: Peter Lang.

Otheguy, R., García, O., & Reid, W. (2015). Clarifying translanguaging and deconstructing named languages: A perspective from linguistics. *Applied Linguistics Review, 6*(3), 281-307. doi:10.1515/applirev-2015-0014

Palshaugen, Ø. (2009). How to generate knowledge from single case research on innovation? *International Journal of Action Research, 5*(3), 231-254. doi:10.1688/1861-9916_IJAR_2009_03_Palshaugen

Park, M. S. (2013). Code-switching and translanguaging: Potential functions in multilingual classrooms. *Teachers College, Columbia University Working Papers in TESOL & Applied Linguistics, 13*(2), 50-52.

Pavón Vázquez, V., & Ramos Ordóñez, M. d. C. (2018). Describing the use of the L1 in CLIL: An analysis of L1 communication strategies in classroom interaction. *International Journal of Bilingual Education and Bilingualism*, 1-14. doi:10.1080/13670050.2018.1511681

Pérez-Cañado, M. L. (2012). CLIL research in Europe: Past, present, and future. *International Journal of Bilingual Education and Bilingualism, 15*(3), 315-341. doi:10.1080/13670050.2011.630064

Rabbidge, M. (2019). The effects of translanguaging on participation in EFL classrooms. *The Journal of AsiaTEFL, 16*(4), 1305-1322. doi:10.18823/asiatefl.2019.16.4.15.1305

Raufelder, D., Bukowski, W. M., & Mohr, S. (2013). Thick description of the teacher-student relationship in the educational context of school: Results of an ethnographic field study. *Journal of Education and Training Studies, 1*(2). doi:10.11114/jets.v1i2.108

Reinmann, G. (2005). Innovation ohne Forschung? Ein Plädoyer für den Design-Based Research-Ansatz in der Lehr-Lernforschung. *Unterrichtswissenschaft, 33*(1), 52-69.

Richards, K. (2003). *Qualitative inquiry in TESOL*. New York: Palgrave Macmillan.

Robertson, R. (1990). Mapping the global condition: Globalization as the central concept. *Theory, Culture & Society, 7*(2), 15-30. doi:10.1177/026327690007002002

Robertson, R. (1995). Glocalization: Time-space and homogeneity-heterogeneity. In M. Featherstone, S. Lash, & R. Robertson (Eds.), *Global modernities* (pp. 25-44). London: Sage Publications.

Roller, M. R., & Lavrakas, P. J. (2015). *Applied qualitative research design: A total quality framework approach.* New York: The Guilford Press.

Ronjat, J. (1913). *Le développement du langage observé chez un enfant bilingue.* Paris: H. Champion.

Rösler, D., & Schart, M. (2016). Die Perspektivenvielfalt der Lehrwerkanalyse—und ihr weißer Fleck. Einführung in zwei Themenhefte. *Informationen Deutsch als Fremdsprache, 43*(5), 483-493.

Rowe, L. W. (2018). Say it in your language: Supporting translanguaging in multilingual classes. *The Reading Teacher, 72*(1), 31-38.

Rumlich, D. (2016). *Evaluating bilingual education in Germany CLIL students' general English proficiency, EFL self-concept and interest.* Frankfurt am Main: Peter Lang.

Sahlberg, P. (2006). Education reform for raising economic competitiveness. *Journal of Educational Change, 7*(4), 259-287. doi:10.1007/s10833-005-4884-6

Sahlberg, P. (2011). The fourth way of Finland. *Journal of Educational Change, 12*(2), 173-185. doi:10.1007/s10833-011-9157-y

Sander, W. (2007). *Politik entdecken - Freiheit leben didaktische Grundlagen politischer Bildung (2 ed.).* Schwalbach/Ts.: Wochenschau Verlag.

Scanlan, S. J., & Feinberg, S. L. (2000). The cartoon society: Using "The Simpsons" to teach and learn sociology. *Teaching Sociology, 28*(2), 127-139.

Schaenen, I., Kohnen, A., Flinn, P., Saul, W., & Zeni, J. (2012). 'I' is for 'insider': Practitioner research in schools. *International Journal of Action Research, 8*(1), 68-101.

Schastak, M. (2020). *Bilinguale Interaktion beim Peer-Learning in der Grundschule. Eine Mixed-Methods Studie mit bilingual türkisch-deutschsprachig aufwachsenden Schüler*innen.* Opladen: Verlag Barbara Budrich.

Scherer, K. R. (2005). What are emotions? And how can they be measured? *Social Science Information, 44*(4), 695-729. doi:10.1177/0539018 405058216

Scholl, T., & Schmelter, L. (2021). Zur Integration von sprachlichem und konzeptuellem Lernen im bilingualen Unterricht. *FLuL, 50*(1), 15-30. doi:10.2357/FLuL-2021-0002

Schön, D. A. (1983). *The reflective practitioner: How professionals think in action.* New York: Basic Books.

Schulze-Engler, F., & Doff, S. (Eds.). (2011). *Beyond other cultures: Transcultural perspectives on teaching the new literatures in English*. Trier: WVT Wissenschaftlicher Verlag.

Schwab, G., Keßler, J.-U., & Hollm, J. (2014). CLIL goes Hauptschule - Chancen und Herausforderungen bilingualen Unterrichts an einer Hauptschule. Zentrale Ergebnisse einer Longitudinalstudie. *Zeitschrift für Fremdsprachenforschung, 25*(1), 3-37.

Scott, J. C. (1998). *Seeing like a state: How certain schemes to improve the human condition have failed*. New Haven, CT: Yale University Press.

Sein, M. K., Henfridsson, O., Purao, S., Rossi, M., & Lindgren, R. (2011). Action design research. *MIS Quarterly, 35*(1), 37-56. Retrieved from http://search.ebscohost.com/login.aspx?direct=true&db=buh&AN =59551157&lang=de&site=ehost-live

Sellar, S., & Lingard, B. (2013). The OECD and global governance in education. *Journal of Education Policy, 28*(5), 710-725. doi:10.1080/0268 0939.2013.779791

Siege, H., & Schreiber, J.-R. (2016). *Orientierungsrahmen für den Lernbereich globale Entwicklung im Rahmen einer Bildung für nachhaltige Entwicklung (2nd ed.)*. Berlin: Cornelsen.

Singer, P. (2015). *The most good you can do: How effective altruism is changing ideas about living ethically*. New Haven, CT: Yale University Press.

Skutnabb-Kangas, T., Phillipson, R., & Mohanty, A. K. (2009). *Social justice through multilingual education*. Bristol: Multilingual Matters.

Stark, J. L. (2014). The potential of Deweyan-inspired action research. *Education and Culture, 30*(2), 87-101. doi:10.1353/eac.2014.0013

Statista. (2021). *Statistiken zum Thema Schule*. Hamburg: Statista. Retrieved from https://de.statista.com/themen/250/schule

Stein-Smith, K. (2016). The role of multilingualism in effectively addressing global issues: The sustainable development goals and beyond. *Theory and Practice in Language Studies, 6*(12), 2254. doi:10.17507/tpls.0612.03

Steinlen, A. K., & Piske, T. (2016). Minority language students as at-risk learners: Myth or reality? Findings from an early German-English partial immersion program. In *Anglistentag Paderborn 2015: Proceedings (37)* (pp. 9-28). Trier: WVT Wissenschaftlicher Verlag.

Stets, J. E., & Turner, J. H. (2006). Introduction. In J. E. Stets & J. H. Turner (Eds.), *Handbook of the sociology of emotions* (pp. 1-7). New York, NY: Springer.

Swaffar, J., & Vlatten, A. (1997). A sequential model for video viewing in the foreign language curriculum. *The Modern Language Journal, 81*(2), 175-188.

Teixeira, P. (2018). Conquering or mapping? Textbooks and the dissemination of human capital theory in applied economics. *The European Journal of the History of Economic Thought, 25*(1), 106-133.

Thaler, E. (2008). Internet-Videos: Fremdsprachenlernen für die "You Tube"-Generation. *Praxis Fremdsprachenunterricht, 5*(1), 14-18.

Thamm, R. A. (2006). The classification of emotions. In J. E. Stets & J. H. Turner (Eds.), *Handbook of the sociology of emotions* (pp. 11-37). New York, NY: Springer.

The Design-Based Research Collective. (2003). Design-based research: An emerging paradigm for educational inquiry. *Educational Researcher, 32*(1), 5-8. doi:10.3102/0013189x032001005.

Thiollent, M. (2011). Action research and participatory research - an overview. *International Journal of Action Research, 7*(2), 160-174. doi:10.1688/1861-9916_IJAR_2011_02_Thiollent

Tholen, B. (2017). Bridging the gap between research traditions: On what we can really learn from Clifford Geertz. *Critical Policy Studies, 12*(3), 335-349. doi:10.1080/19460171.2017.1352528

Thürmann, E. (2010). Eine eigenständige Methodik für den bilingualen Sachfachunterricht? In G. Bach & S. Niemeier (Eds.), *Bilingualer Unterricht: Grundlagen, Methoden, Praxis, Perspektiven* (5th ed., pp. 71-89). Frankfurt am Main: Peter Lang.

Timperley, H. (2007). *Teacher professional learning and development: Best evidence synthesis iteration [BES]*. Wellington: Ministry of Education.

Trilling, B., & Fadel, C. (2009). *21st century skills: learning for life in our times*. San Francisco: Jossey-Bass.

Vertovec, S. (2007). Super-diversity and its implications. *Ethnic and Racial Studies, 30*(6), 1024-1054. doi:10.1080/01419870701599465

Vimont, M. P. (2015). Thick description in applied contexts: Using interpretative qualitative observations to form quantitative indicators in food security research. *Journal of the Anthropological Society of Oxford, 7*, 191-204.

Vollmer, H. J. (2006). Language across the curriculum. Expertise for the Council of Europe. *Language Policy Division*. Strasbourg: Council of Europe. Retrieved from https://rm.coe.int/16805c7464

Vollmer, H. J. (2010). Bilingualer Sachfachunterricht als Inhalts- und als Sprachlernen. In G. Bach & S. Niemeier (Eds.), *Bilingualer Unterricht: Grundlagen, Methoden, Praxis, Perspektiven* (5th ed., pp. 47-70). Frankfurt am Main: Peter Lang.

Vygotsky, L. S. (1978). *Mind in society* (M. Cole, v. John-Steiner, s. Scribner, & e. Souberman, eds.). Cambridge, MA: Harvard University Press.

Weber, F. (2016). Emotion und Kognition in der politischen Bildung. In C. Deichmann & M. May (Eds.), *Politikunterricht verstehen und gestalten* (pp. 165-183). Wiesbaden: Springer VS.

Weber, M. (1919). *Wissenschaft als Beruf.* München: Duncker & Humblot.

Wegner, A. (2011). *Weltgesellschaft und Subjekt bilingualer Sachfachunterricht an Real- und Gesamtschulen; Praxis und Perspektiven.* Wiesbaden: VS.

Welsch, W. (1999). Transculturality - the puzzling form of cultures today. In M. Featherstone & S. Lash (Eds.), *Spaces of culture: City, nation, world* (pp. 194-213). London: Sage.

Whorf, B. L. (1956). *Language, thought, and reality; selected writings.* Cambridge: Technology Press of Massachusetts Institute of Technology.

Wittgenstein, L. (1963). *Tractatus logico-philosophicus = logisch-philosophische Abhandlung.* Frankfurt am Main: Suhrkamp.

Wohnig, A. (2020). Elsner, Daniela, Tim Engartner, Subin Nijhawan, und Nina Rodmann (2019): Politik & Wirtschaft bilingual unterrichten. *Politische Vierteljahresschrift, 61*(2), 421-423. doi:10.1007/s11615-020-00237-3

Wolff, D. (2003). Content and language integrated learning: A framework for the development of learner autonomy. In D. Little, J. Ridley, & E. Ushioda (Eds.), *Learner autonomy in the foreign language classroom: Teacher, learner, curriculum and assessment* (pp. 198-210). Dublin: Authentik.

Wolff, D. (2009). Strategien im bilingualen Sachfachunterricht. *Fremdsprachen Lehren und Lernen, 38*(1), 137-157.

Wolff, D. (2011). Der bilinguale Sachfachunterricht (CLIL): Was dafür spricht, ihn als innovatives didaktisches Konzept zu bezeichnen. *Forum Sprache*(6), 75-83.

Wolff, D. (2017). Bilingualer Sachfachunterricht in Deutschland 2017. Retrieved from https://www.goethe.de/de/spr/unt/kum/clg/21074378.html

Wu, J. S., & Lee, J. J. (2015). Climate change games as tools for education and engagement. *Nature Climate Change, 5,* 413. doi:10.1038/nclimate2566

Zydatiß, W. (2007). *Deutsch-Englische Züge in Berlin (DEZIBEL). Eine Evaluation des bilingualen Sachfachunterrichts an Gymnasien.* Frankfurt am Main: Peter Lang.

ibidem.eu